Selling Your Graphic Design & Illustration

Other books by Tad Crawford and Arie Kopelman:

Selling Your Photography: The Complete Marketing, Business and Legal Guide

By Tad Crawford:

Legal Guide for the Visual Artist

The Writer's Legal Guide

Edited by Arie Kopelman:

ASMP Guide to Professional Business Practices in Photography

TAD CRAWFORD and ARIE KOPELMAN

Selling Your Graphic Design & Illustration

The Complete Marketing, Business and Legal Guide

ST. MARTIN'S PRESS • New York

All rights reserved. For information, write:
St. Martin's Press
175 Fifth Avenue
New York, N.Y. 10010

Library of Congress Cataloging in Publication Data

Crawford, Tad, 1946–
  Selling your graphic design and illustration.

  1. Graphic arts—Marketing. 2. Magazine
illustration—Marketing. 3. Illustration of books—
Marketing. I. Kopelman, Arie, joint author.
II. Title.
NC1001.6.C7   741.6′068   80-28354
ISBN 0-312-71252-9

Manufactured in the United States of America

To Evelyn, Jack, and Simon, with love.
T.C.

To David, Jonathon, and Jane, with love.
A.K.

To the Graphic Artists Guild, whose support of designers and illustrators and advocacy of professional standards has been of immeasurable value.
T.C. & A.K.

Summary Contents

Complete Contents

Introduction: How to Use This Book

THIS BOOK CONTAINS three separate guides in one volume: A *Marketing Guide*, a *Business Guide* and a *Legal Guide*. Selling and marketing are emphasized in the first section, with good reason. You must have a steady flow of jobs to succeed on any level—from full- or part-time professional to beginner or student just getting started. The business guidance and legal protection outlined in the last two sections are crucial to your continued achievement in the field as either experienced professional or accomplished amateur supplementing other income.

The marketing strategies and data in Part I are unique; they have never before been digested in book form. They include the widely respected approaches of some of today's most successful graphic designers, studios, and illustrators. The business and legal sections cover virtually everything you need to know about contracts, pricing, taxes, copyrights, starting a business, and invasion of privacy and other legal risks.

In addition, throughout the book you will find some of the most easily understood standard business forms ever published, to protect you in situations involving assignments, estimates, invoices, model releases, and copyrights.

The *Marketing Guide* confronts the most basic questions that you must deal with: Where are my markets? How can I reach them effectively? What techniques can I use to promote myself and my work effectively?

In reply, we start by evaluating *all* the major markets. For each market we provide the basic tool or market guide that will lead you to the clients in that field. Each market has its own guide—no single "artist's guide" published anywhere in the world contains more than a small fraction of the names and addresses in *each* of the nearly 30 guides discussed in our text.

We cover all kinds of assignments, with considerable emphasis on markets you (and many others) may not have previously considered.

Much attention is given to the use of direct-mail promotions of your work and how these can be executed efficiently and inexpensively.

The last chapter in the *Marketing Guide* describes the functions of agents and galleries for selling originals and securing assignments. We discuss where the agents and galleries can be found and how to handle your contracts with them.

The *Business Guide* starts with pricing and billing expenses. This data is critical, because you must charge enough to cover costs, but you can't price yourself out of the market. We show you an easy-to-use method for calculating the price you need to charge on each job to cover overhead expenses and assure your own required profit level. The range of going rates is then presented for virtually all types of professional work, depending on the use, the media in which it will appear, and the size of the market. Negotiation tactics are also covered.

In the contracts chapter we focus first on simple letters that you can write and use as agreements. We then move on to the more complex assignment, licensing, and royalty agreements, including book contracts. Most importantly, you are provided with simplified but highly protective standard forms to use in connection with your day-to-day jobs and studio work. Throughout the chapter, and in using the forms, you will learn how to protect yourself on all basic issues, including fees, use rates, travel time, cancellations, postponements, expense reimbursement, advances, client usage rights, ownership of originals, and credit lines.

The chapter on taxes explains the kinds of deductions you can take as a full-time or part-time professional, or as a beginner. We also review the steps you *must* take to secure a deduction for the expenses of your "office at home." For the beginner and part-timer especially, we explain the rules for taking deductions from your regular income as a result of "losses" you incur from your fledgling free-lance activities.

Other chapters in the *Business Guide* show you how to get your business started, what records and reports you need to keep or file with the IRS to stay out of difficulty, tax advantages of various forms of business (including incorporation), what to look for when signing a lease, and how to deal with sales taxes, and techniques for organizing your reference files.

In a separate chapter we take much of the mystery out of personal and business insurance. You will learn how to protect your property *and your income,* and the methods used to mimimize insurance cost while maximizing coverage.

In the *Legal Guide,* we deal with the major legal problems confronting graphic designers and illustrators. The foremost area is copyright, which, simply defined, is the exclusive right of reproduction. We explain how federal law works to protect your copyright ownership, when and exactly how to register your copyright (including a step-by-step explanation of government forms), and the techniques for registering works for a single $10 fee. Also covered is the operation of the notorious "work for hire" agreements, how to sell only a portion of your copyright, the proper form for copyright notices, and exactly where the notice must be placed.

The chapters *Invasion of Privacy and Releases* and *Beyond Privacy* deal with some of the gravest legal risks you will face. Lawsuits for tens of thousands of dollars (and more) have been brought when peoples' likenesses were improperly used without a release. Explained clearly, perhaps for the first time, are the specific situations in which use of a likeness may be invading someone's privacy in connection with either public figures or lesser-known individuals. Also covered are the legal dangers involved with representations of other peoples' property and animals, and the potential risks of libel and misappropriating a celebrity's right of publicity. Easy-to-use model-release forms complete the discussion in this field.

The final chapter explains what to look for and where to go for assistance when you are choosing a lawyer (including where you may find a volunteer lawyer). Tips on using small-claims courts and collection agencies are also included.

Following the main text is a handy guide to the many organizations of professionals in the graphic arts.

When you have absorbed most of the material, you may well conclude that selling graphic design or illustration at any level requires a serious understanding of the business. While it may seem to be a complex business at first, it is also a challenging field full of promise and considerable opportunity. For this reason we hope that the chapters that follow will serve to clarify and simplify for you matters that might otherwise remain bewildering and obscure, if not altogether impenetrable.

PART I

Marketing Guide

CHAPTER 1

Finding Assignment Markets and Clients

SELLING DESIGN OR ILLUSTRATION services is like selling anything else. It requires time, talent, energy, and a knowledge of where the markets are. Unless you are famous you cannot expect the market to come to you. You must seek it out. This chapter will guide you to the markets and will tell you what they expect.

Those markets are huge but largely hidden. The published material you see every day gracing newsstands, billboards, bookstores, and the like represents only a tiny fraction of your actual sales potential. That will become apparent as you review the makeup of the national and regional markets in the lists that follow.

This chapter is devoted entirely to finding clients and showing you how to identify specific buyers for markets in which you have an interest. Chapter 2, *Beyond Assignments,* covers the market for your original artwork and discusses teaching opportunities. Chapter 3, *Marketing Tools and Techniques,* describes the sales ammunition you will need and how to use it. Chapter 4 completes the Sales and Marketing section with a discussion of how agents and galleries can supplement your marketing efforts.

The approach that follows is necessarily organized market by market. You need not, however, be that mechanical in your own selling.

For example, several years ago a graphic artist graduated from school with no clients, no job, and very little money. He did, however, have a strong and very distinct visual style. He carefully went through all the trade publications and annual award books in the advertising and editorial fields (see pages 47–56), seeking samples relating to his style and, thereby, the names of art directors who might respond to his work.

He culled only 200 names and thereafter pooled his modest resources to print several hundred copies each of two nicely illustrated cards. These were sent to the people he had on his list. Within a few months he was working regularly. The story is unusual only in that recent graduates generally require a year or two (and often longer) to develop a clearly defined visual style in their work.

A parallel case may be closer to home for some readers. A part-time professional had developed great ease and facility in drawing and painting children and wished to expand commercially. She searched through an array of local and regional magazines, newspapers, retailing catalogs, and brochures, pulling out advertisements and samples that featured children. She called virtually all these advertisers, got the names of the various ad agencies and in-house corporate art directors involved, and arranged for appointments whenever possible or sent illustrated card samples in other cases.

She had reasoned, correctly, that children's themes struck a special note with these people. Her work with children was, in fact, excellent enough to secure several assignments from this initial marketing effort. As a result, she soon emerged as a full-time professional. Needless to say, this technique could be applied to any area of specialization that you have developed.

You should keep such creative uses of the information provided here in mind, as we proceed to describe the various markets and how you can reach the individual clients in each field.

National and Regional Markets

The names of clients or buyers in most markets are readily available if you know where to look. They are identified, at least by company name and often by individual contact, in specialized trade directories, each covering one particular industry (advertising, audiovisual, magazine publishing, book publishing, public relations, and so on).

No single reference can possibly provide the necessary information for all those industries together, since there are thousands of firms and potential clients in *each* field. The few so-called marketing or sales guides that claim to have all this information in one volume are frequently dated or strikingly incomplete.

The sections that follow show, market by market, the sources of information you need for your business, where to find them, and how to use them.

It will take some effort and perhaps expense on your part to secure this information, but it will definitely be worth it. If you are willing to spend many hundreds or thousands of dollars on your equipment and education, you must be prepared to allocate a small percentage of that money to securing material that will give you a head start in selling what the equipment and education produces. Many fine designers and artists who refuse to make a serious marketing effort fail in business. Others with less talent for visual work than for business have been known to succeed. For some these consequences may be dismaying; for others the lesson is clear.

ADVERTISING AGENCIES

In every market—national, regional, and local—the work of designing and illustrating print advertisements created primarily by ad agencies is one of the best-paid though most highly competitive fields. While most large agencies design a high percentage of their ads, virtually no agencies have staff illustrators for finished art. In addition, agencies are a crucial market for storyboard and comp artists, as well as retouchers and letterers.

While the advertising business is centered in New York City, there are over 2,700 ad agencies throughout the United States, including many hundreds in each region of the country.

Indeed, some of the largest agencies are headquartered in Chicago. Regional centers for the field are in Atlanta, Boston, Dallas, Houston, Los Angeles, Philadelphia, San Francisco, St. Louis, and other major cities.

Two-thirds of the 2,700 recognized agencies in the United States each have annual billings in excess of $1 million. That is, their clients paid the agency at least that amount in the past year for fees, advertising space purchased (in magazines, newspapers, and other publications), and/or television or radio time purchased as well as production and preparation costs for the ads involved.

Your Best Guide to This Market Is:

STANDARD DIRECTORY OF ADVERTISING AGENCIES ("The Advertising Red Book"). Published by the National Register

Publishing Company, 5201 Old Orchard Road, Skokie, Illinois 60077, telephone (312) 470-3100.

This book is available in most business and reference libraries. Single copies are $52 from the publisher. While the book is updated three times each year, you only need one copy to begin building your mailing and contact list. You will probably make most changes on the list from information you personally develop in phone calls and agency visits. Thus, if you buy the book for the convenience of using it in your own place of business, it will probably only result in the one-time charge of $52.

In this guide look for:
1. Alphabetical listing of over 3,000 agencies with addresses and telephone numbers (plus 1,000 foreign agencies).
2. Geographic cross-reference by state and city enabling you to pick up needed data about all agencies in your region and permitting you to cast the net as widely as you require.
3. Name of senior art director in many (but definitely not all) cases. The remainder of the art-buying staff is rarely named. The latter is a minor shortcoming, since you usually must call for an appointment anyway and you can check for the correct name or names at that time with a secretary or receptionist. Of course, in large agencies there may be a dozen or more art directors to see. In addition, sometimes a single "art buyer" in those agencies will be in charge of having portfolios reviewed by the rest of the art department.
4. Listing of agency clients and specific accounts. This is an important tip-off to direct you in what work to show the agency and whom to ask for when telephoning the agency for an appointment. For example, you may want to ask for the art director on an account that is likely to use work that you may specialize in, such as fashion, medical, or industrial, depending upon the listing of accounts provided in this book.
5. Gross billings. The size of the agency given by these dollar amounts may indicate financial stability; it may also indicate the value of your marketing effort. You will find that the larger agencies usually have the most work and, further, the greatest competition for that work. The gross-billings information frequently indicates the percentage of those billings devoted to print media (as opposed to television or radio). The larger agencies usually spend 60 to 80 percent or more on television,

but the gross dollar amount left over for print is still very substantial. Smaller agencies often spend higher percentages in the print media than in television, but the dollar amounts including graphic and other production costs may be modest.

6. Agencies in five specialized fields. Five specialties and the agencies in those fields are listed at the front of this book. The specialties are: catalogue and direct mail (85 names); financial (27 names); medical (48 names); minorities including black and Hispanic (31 names); resort and travel (41 names).

Madison Avenue Handbook, as a supplementary reference, lists by name a significant number of the art directors and buyers at over 200 agencies in New York City, 100 in Chicago, over 50 each in Atlanta, Boston, and Los Angeles, and several dozen more in Dallas, Detroit, and Houston. It is available in many business libraries or for $13.95 from the publisher, Peter Glenn Publications, 17 East 48 St., New York, New York 10017, telephone (212) 688-7940.

AUDIOVISUAL PRODUCERS

The rapid growth of the audiovisual field is immense but rarely appreciated. The 35mm audiovisual slide market increased from $168 million in 1968 to $1.9 billion in 1978; that is a 1600 percent increase in a decade.

Approximately one-half the work in this field is in graphics and text, with a portion of the balance including illustration. Further growth is projected because educational, governmental, and corporate users find the audiovisual medium an exceptionally economical format when compared to film or tape.

Your Best Guide to This Market Is:

AUDIO-VISUAL MARKET PLACE, published annually by R. R. Bowker, 1180 Avenue of the Americas, New York, New York 10036, telephone (212) 764-5100; available in many business, reference, and educational libraries or for $29.95 from the publisher.

In this guide look for:

1. Listing of 500 firms (alphabetically and by state) that produce for their own accounts (often hiring or buying services from others).
2. Listing of 400 production companies (alphabetically and by

state) that produce under contract to others (many production companies hire graphic artists for charts, graphs, illustrations, titles, and more).

3. For each of the listings just indicated, note the ratio of filmstrip and slide-show work to other production (such as motion picture or sound cassette). Most firms provide this directory with that data, thereby giving a clear indication of their potential for the designer or illustrator.

BOOK PUBLISHERS

Book publishers buy an immense amount of design and illustration for hardcover book jackets and paperback covers. There are nearly 50,000 new titles published every year, and the jackets and covers are seen as important tools in the struggle for "visibility" and book sales. In addition, free-lance book design in all areas and illustration of text, reference, and juvenile books are major sources of income for graphic artists.

Your Best Guide to This Market Is:

LITERARY MARKET PLACE, published annually by R. R. Bowker, 1180 Avenue of the Americas, New York, New York 10036, telephone (212) 764-5100; available in virtually all library reference sections or for $29.50 from the publisher.

In this guide look for:

1. Alphabetical listings of over 2,000 publishers and their primary publishing specialty categories.
2. Geographic breakdown (by state) indicating publishers in your area that would be accessible for a personal visit.
3. Art directors' names, which are frequently included in the alphabetical listings of publishers. Art directors are the people who are usually responsible for assigning book covers or jacket design and illustration.
4. The number of titles published in the prior year by each publisher. This is a key determinant of whether the time spent in visiting or otherwise contacting this company would be potentially productive.

CARDS, CALENDARS AND POSTERS (See Novelty, Decorative, and Paper Products)

CARTOON AND FEATURE SYNDICATES

The markets for individual cartoons and cartoon strips include magazines (see Magazines, on page 15–19), local newspapers in your area, and, most important, the syndicate organizations which sell a broad array of feature materials, including cartoons, to hundreds of newspapers around the country.

Your Best Guide to This Market Is:

WORKING PRESS OF THE NATION, VOLUME 4: FEATURE WRITER, PHOTOGRAPHER AND SYNDICATE DIRECTORY, published annually by the National Research Bureau, 424 North Third Street, Burlington, Iowa 52601, telephone (319) 752-5415; available in library reference sections, business libraries or for $80 from Automated Marketing Systems, 310 South Michigan, Suite 1150 Chicago, Illinois 60604, telephone (312) 663-5580.

In this guide look for:
1. Section 5, which is an alphabetical list of over 250 news and feature syndicates including addresses, telephone numbers, chief officers, and editors.
2. The names of the specific cartoons and other features carried by each syndicate, so you will have an idea of the type of material it uses and whether your own work is appropriate in a specific case. For example, while no single syndicate is likely to carry two features that are similar, a syndicate may be looking for material that is a variation of what its competitors have found success with.
3. The names, in alphabetical order, of virtually every syndicated feature and which syndicate it is sold through. Thus if you have an idea that is a variation of an existing feature, you can see who syndicates that work, knowing that you will probably have to go elsewhere to find your own market.

COLLEGES AND UNIVERSITIES

Work in this field usually involves design or illustration of catalogs, brochures, student recruitment or alumni bulletins, and the like.

The further off the beaten track you go, the less likely you are to face a hoard of competitors, especially in this field. In most cases the person to see at a college or university is the publications or public-relations director. Many campuses also have a development or funding office that could be interested in professional-quality work.

There are a number of standard directories covering the 2,000 American colleges and universities. They are invariably broken down by state, and this is critical because you will want to schedule trips so that you can visit at least two or three campuses in a single day. Obviously it makes sense to call in advance for an appointment, since scheduling is such a critical factor in making the most effective use of your marketing time.

Among the standard references are:

AMERICAN UNIVERSITIES AND COLLEGES, published by the American Council on Education, 1 Dupont Circle, Washington, D.C. 20036.

EDUCATION DIRECTORY; COLLEGES AND UNIVERSITIES, published by the National Center for Education Statistics, United States Department of Education, Superintendent of Documents, U.S. Government Printing Office, Publications Department, Washington, D.C. 20402 (Stock #017-080-02011-4, $6.25 per copy).

If these two standard references are not available in your local library, it is virtually certain that the reference room will have some other equally authoritative source for this information.

CORPORATIONS

Work directly for corporate clients may consist of material prepared for advertising, public relations, annual reports, and a vast array of other corporate communications. There are two primary and quite distinct markets involved in this area. Many companies handle a significant proportion of their advertising program directly, rather than through advertising agencies. The officer you want to reach for this is the advertising manager. Equally significant, many companies prepare a broad range of illustrated corporate material such as brochures, press releases, annual reports, and recruitment publications through its public-relations or corporate-communications office.

Your Best Guides to This Market Are:

O'DWYER'S DIRECTORY OF CORPORATE COMMUNI-
CATIONS, published annually by J. R. O'Dwyer Co., Inc., 271
Madison Avenue, New York, New York 10016, telephone (212)
679-2471; available in business and some reference libraries or for $60
per copy from the publisher.

In this guide look for:
1. A basic listing of public-relations executives at over 2,000
   companies and 300 major trade associations.
2. A geographic breakdown detailing companies in your area and
   whom to see within those companies.
3. A listing of investor-relations officers (who may have responsibility for producing annual reports) and employee-communica-
   tion officers (who may be responsible for producing house
   organs).
4. A breakdown into 37 industry groups of all the companies listed
   in the directory (for example, among the industries covered are
   drugs, transportation, leisure time, and of course many others
   that may relate to your own specialties).

STANDARD DIRECTORY OF ADVERTISERS, published
by the National Register Publishing Company, Inc., 5201 Old
Orchard Road, Skokie, Illinois 60077, telephone (312) 470-3100;
available in reference and business libraries, or for $109 per single
copy from the publisher. The separate "classified" edition is also
$109. The classified edition provides an industry-by-industry break-
down of the companies named.

In this guide look for:
1. An alphabetical and geographic breakdown of 7,000 companies
   that advertise, with the key advertising and public-relations
   personnel indicated.
2. A special classified version, which can be more valuable because
   it provides the same names broken down into 51 separate
   business categories such as transportation, sports, and the like,
   which may dovetail with whatever specialty you bring to the
   marketplace.

DECORATIVE ACCESSORIES (See Novelty, Decorative, and Paper Products)

ENTERTAINMENT INDUSTRY

The motion picture, recording, television, and theatrical companies generate some of the most important and prestigious work for both designers and illustrators of posters, album covers, advertising, and other promotional materials.

Your Best Guide to This Market Is:

CELEBRITY SERVICE INTERNATIONAL CONTACT BOOK, published annually by Celebrity Service, Inc., 171 West 57th Street, New York, New York 10019, telephone (212) 757-7979; available in some business libraries or from the publisher for $8.

In this guide look for:
1. Separate listings of the major motion picture, television, and legitimate theater producers and production companies in New York City and Los Angeles, including addresses and telephone numbers. You will have to call to find out the name of the person in charge of art direction.
2. A listing of over 100 of the major recording companies in New York City and Los Angeles.
3. Related listings of organizations which produce events requiring promotional materials, including legitimate theaters, auditoriums, arenas, and sports enterprises.
4. Advertising agencies associated with the entertainment industry—an important group since they frequently engage designers and illustrators to create and complete the artwork for their numerous print media advertising campaigns.

Other Guides to This Market Include:

Photography Market Place, second edition, by Fred W. McDarrah, editor, published in 1977 by R. R. Bowker, 1180 Avenue of the Americas, New York, New York 10036, telephone (212) 764-5100. It is available in some reference libraries or can be secured from the publisher for $15.50. The book lists some 100 of the largest recording companies, including art directors and public relations people. Owing to its publication in 1977, it will definitely require some updating, but remains useful.

The International Buyer's Guide of the Music-Tape Industry. This book is published annually by Billboard Publications, 1515 Broadway, New York, New York 10036 or 9000 Sunset Boulevard, Los Angeles, California 90069 ($35). It lists several thousand recording companies in the United States and abroad, providing names, addresses and telephone numbers. It does not list art buyers. You will have to call to secure those names.

GRAPHIC DESIGNERS

Graphic designers have recently become a key client group for illustrators and even other designers. They produce, under contract, the annual reports, brochures, and other publications of many corporations, large and small. As a result, they are constantly hiring illustrators who work in the corporate-industrial field and other designers when a need arises.

Your Best Guides to This Market Are:

MEMBERSHIP DIRECTORY OF THE AMERICAN IN-STITUTE OF GRAPHIC ARTS (AIGA), $15 from AIGA, 1059 Third Avenue, New York, New York 10021, telephone (212) PL2-0813. A large number of the leading graphic designers are members of AIGA, and this directory is designed to indicate which among the approximately 1,600 members of AIGA work in the graphic-design field (some 60 percent do).

THE DESIGN DIRECTORY, published annually by Wefler & Associates, Inc., P.O. Box 1591, Evanston, Illinois 60204, telephone (312) 454-1940. This is currently the best resource for finding designers and is available from the publisher for $41. It lists some 1100 design firms nationwide, by city and state, and includes the size, specialties, and names of principals of most firms.

THE BEST EVER. A catalog of the Mead Library of Ideas—International Annual Report Exhibit. This catalog lists 15 to 20 annual winners of one of the top shows in the graphic design field. It includes the designers' names and the addresses of their firms and shows samples of pages from the prize-winning reports. The catalog is available free of charge from Mead Library of Ideas, World Head-quarters, Courthouse Plaza Northeast, Dayton, Ohio 45463, tele-phone (513) 222-6323. Mead, of course, is one of the major manufacturers of quality papers in the country. If you can secure catalogs for the past few years, you will have an excellent list of several dozen or more top designers. If Mead is out of stock, you might try the libraries of major photography or art schools, or trade associations active in the design field.

AMERICAN SHOWCASE. This is a book that photographers, illustrators, and designers purchase space in for illustrated self-promotion. Each section includes a listing of professionals in the field. The section on designers lists approximately 1,000 designers and their telephone numbers. Unfortunately, it does not list addresses. Nonetheless, from the area codes you can spot the designers in your area and contact them by phone or look up the addresses yourself for a mailing.

American Showcase is sold in some bookstores (usually in the art sections) and by the publisher: American Showcase, 10th floor, 724 Fifth Avenue, New York, New York 10019, telephone (212) 245-0981 ($27.50 in soft cover).

L.A. WORKBOOK. This is a communications-industry handbook for California, listing the names, addresses, and telephone numbers of over 1,000 designers in the Los Angeles and San Francisco areas. It is available for $28 from Alexis Scott, publisher, 6140 Lindenhurst Ave., Los Angeles, California 90048, telephone (213) 657-8707.

HOUSE ORGANS (COMPANY PUBLICATIONS)

You never see most of these house-organ publications, but there are literally thousands of them. Many are slick and extremely professional, comparable to major consumer magazines. Others are rather modest affairs, to say the least. A great many of these publications hire designers and illustrators on a free-lance basis, and the ones with the highest circulations tend to pay on a level comparable to the sums paid by consumer magazines, and in a few cases even more than that.

Your Best Guide to This Market Is:

WORKING PRESS OF THE NATION, VOLUME 5: INTERNAL PUBLICATIONS DIRECTORY, published annually by the National Research Bureau, 424 North Third Street, Burlington, Iowa 52601, telephone (319) 752-5415; available in library reference sections, business libraries, or for $80 from Automated Marketing

Systems, 310 South Michigan, Suite 1150, Chicago, Illinois 60604, telephone (312) 663-5580.

In this guide look for:
1. Basic alphabetical list (with addresses but not telephone numbers or personnel) of the publications of several thousand companies, clubs, government agencies, and other groups.
2. The industrial categories' cross-reference, which pinpoints publications possibly related to your work specialty.
3. Circulation cross-reference, which pinpoints the publications with the largest circulations (usually the better-paying markets). Some 1,600 publications are below 10,000 circulation and would probably be less attractive markets than the 600 publications with circulations between 10,000 and 50,000 or, more significantly, the 100 with circulations from 50,000 to 100,000, and the additional 150 house organs that have circulations exceeding 100,000.

The significance of this market should not be underestimated. That latter group of 150 company publications with over 100,000 circulation is nearly as large in number as the entire group of well-known general-circulation publications currently published in the United States and sold on newsstands.

An indirect source for this market would also be the corporate communications officers named in *O'Dwyer's Directory of Corporate Communications,* listed under the Corporations section. In addition, some 100 of the more widely circulated house organs are mentioned in *Photography Market Place, Second Edition* (for publisher information and availability see the listing of this book in the Entertainment Industry section).

INDUSTRIAL COMPANIES (See Corporations)

MAGAZINES (CONSUMER AND TRADE)

For corporate in-house magazines, see House Organs. The remainder of the magazine field consists of three elements: (1) consumer magazines, including regional and Sunday supplements, (2) business (trade) magazines, and (3) foreign publications.

The consumer magazines represent the smallest element of the magazine market, though this may be the best-paying group for a modest number of well-established professionals. These, of course, are primarily the newsstand publications covering such subjects as fashion, news, shelter, sports, men's interests, women's service, and regionals. Business (trade) magazines are usually aimed at a single professional, trade, or industrial group and are most frequently distributed exclusively by mail to qualified professionals in that field, often free of charge (this is generally referred to as controlled circulation).

Foreign publications can be classified under both the consumer and the trade groups, but contacting them presents special problems. A number of the largest and better-paying foreign consumer magazines have New York City editorial offices through which they may be approached—in addition, naturally, to their home-base locations, for which a reference follows.

Your Best Guides to This Market Are:

GEBBIE PRESS ALL-IN-ONE DIRECTORY, published by Gebbie Press, Box 1000, New Paltz, New York 12561, telephone (914) 255-7560; available in reference and business libraries or for $45 from the publisher.

In this guide look for:
1. Names, addresses, circulation figures, and brief descriptions of target audience for over 7,500 American consumer and trade publications (no phone numbers).
2. Breakdown of all these magazines into 200 well-defined categories that should line up well with some specialties. Among the categories are: airline travel, architecture, auto, clothing and fashion, drugs and pharmaceutical, farming, financial, home furnishings, music, sports, tourism, and women.
3. Separate listings of newspaper-distributed magazines (19, of which nine are over 1 million in circulation), daily and weekly newspapers listed by state and city (with addresses and circulation figures), and the major news and feature syndicates.

While the information in *Gebbie's* is not as comprehensive as the information in the two directories published by the Standard Rate and Data Service, which follow, the format is much easier to use and the information should be adequate for most purposes. In addition *Gebbie's* breakdown of the domestic magazine market into 200 categories appears to be the most useful presentation available for matching specialized interests with existing magazine specialties. After finding the publications that relate to the work you do, you can contact them to determine what specific needs they may have. Bear in mind, however, that a major drawback of *Gebbie's* is that the book does not list phone numbers, thereby limiting you primarily to mail inquiries.

CONSUMER MAGAZINE AND FARM PUBLICATIONS: published by Standard Rate and Data Service; 5201 Old Orchard Road, Skokie, Illinois 60077, telephone (312) 470-3100; available in reference and business libraries or for $45 for the single annual volume (without updates) from the publisher.

In this guide look for:
1. Names, addresses, and telephone numbers for 1,400 consumer magazines, large and small, general circulation and specialized.
2. Circulation and advertising-space rates for all magazines listed in the book. Advertising agencies rely on the book for this information in order to establish their print-advertising budgets. You will find it tells you how successful the publication actually is in relation to others and where they should be in the scale of payments to graphic artists, based on those numbers.
3. General editorial policy—usually a simple publisher's statement.
4. Most important, 51 separate categories of magazines from "Airlines" to "Youth" so that you can key your marketing effort closely to some of your own specialties and interests.

This book does not list art directors or picture buyers and does not discuss picture-buying policy. You can secure that data easily once you have selected the magazines in the guide that tie in well with your specialties.

You should also notice that within each category of magazine there are two groups listed: "Audited" and "Unaudited." The audited magazines are those whose circulation claims are verified by independent checking services. This serves as an assurance to advertisers of the validity of the publisher's claims. For graphic artists it also indicates which magazines are likely to be the better-paying publications (obviously those in the audited group).

BUSINESS PUBLICATIONS, published by Standard Rate and Data Service, 5201 Old Orchard Road, Skokie, Illinois 60077, telephone (312) 470-3100; available in reference and business libraries or for $45 from the publisher for the main annual volume (without monthly updates).

In this guide look for:
1. Names, addresses, and telephone numbers for approximately 4,000 business and trade publications.
2. Separation of all listings into 159 categories that may match up with some of your special interests.
3. Circulation and advertising-rate figures that provide a reasonable clue to the capacity to pay for graphics contributions.
4. A modest-size international section covering some 200 foreign publications in approximately 40 categories.

This is the most complete and up-to-date listing in the industry. Once you have selected the magazines that relate to your special interests, the data you require regarding buying policy and people to deal with can easily be secured on the telephone. In selecting magazines to contact, bear in mind that audited publications, those that have their circulation figures independently verified, are more likely to be a better market than unaudited publications.

ULRICH'S INTERNATIONAL PERIODICALS DIRECTORY, published annually by R. R. Bowker, 1180 Avenue of the Americas, New York, New York 10036, telephone (212) 764-5100; available in some reference and business libraries or for $69.50 from the publisher.

This book is truly for the lionhearted. It covers some 60,000 periodicals worldwide in over 1,000 specific subject headings.

The value of the book is in its subject headings. They are so specific that if you have specialized material, you can easily determine whom to contact abroad. For most of the publications listed, circulation figures are provided. Many, of course, are extremely low circulation publications. You can be sure that if the circulation is only a few thousand, the likelihood of a significant payment is remote. Thus, start out by contacting only the large-circulation periodicals in the categories that specifically relate to your kind of work.

A number of the largest foreign consumer publications also have New York City offices and frequently deal directly with United States free-lancers. Indeed, some of these magazines pay as much for artwork as their counterparts in the United States. The publications themselves are usually available from newsstand dealers who specialize in out-of-town or foreign periodicals. The name of the publication, if listed in the Manhattan telephone directory, may be found under the magazine's own logo name or that of its corporate parent. Both names, of course, are usually indicated in the publication's masthead, which may also provide the address of the New York City office.

Two other publications are worth noting:

Magazine Industry Marketplace provides detailed listings of some 2,600 magazines, with the names of art directors specified for about 25 percent of them. Many of these magazines, however, are scholarly or technical; only about 500 are consumer publications and about 400 are trade publications. It is available in reference libraries or for $35 from the publisher, R. R. Bowker, 1180 Avenue of the Americas, New York, New York 10036, telephone (212) 764-5100.

New York Publicity Outlets may be more useful because it lists the names of the art directors of some 300 major consumer magazines nationwide, together with the usual telephone numbers and addresses, and a breakdown into 15 specialty categories. It may be found in some reference libraries or for $47.50 from the publisher, Public Relations Plus, Inc., P.O. Box 327, Washington Depot, Connecticut 06794, telephone (203) 868-0200. The $47.50 includes the annual volume plus an update in six months.

MOTION PICTURE COMPANIES; MUSIC AND RECORDING COMPANIES (See Entertainment Industry)

NOVELTY, DECORATIVE, AND PAPER PRODUCTS

Products relying heavily on graphic images for their merchandising include calendars, greeting cards, mugs, posters, T-shirts, and more. This is one of the few markets in which your work can generate substantial royalties once you become well established—royalty payments which can sometimes continue for years. In addition, many companies will pay you an "advance," an up-front cash payment against which first royalties are offset.

This is an easy market to dismiss. It is not particularly glamorous, but the revenue potential is probably greater here than in many other areas. It is truly mass merchandising. But securing royalties for images on, for example, wall decor sold in every city and town in North America has to be given most careful consideration.

One other unusual feature of this market is that it may serve as an outlet for some of the *existing images* you have built up in your files over the years. You might find, for example, that a number of the book or magazine illustrations you have done can also serve as graphics for greeting cards or calendars. This, of course, demonstrates why you must exercise great care to secure return of your originals and to set limits on an initial client's reproduction rights when you do assignments (see the discussion of this subject in the contracts chapter, pages 86–97).

The standard guide to the novelty and paper-products industry has not been cited in any existing art market guide that we have seen, perhaps indicating a wider-than-usual area here for your opportunity.

Your Best Guide to This Market Is:

GIFT AND DECORATIVE ACCESSORY BUYERS DIRECTORY, Published by Geyer McAllister Publications, 51 Madison Avenue, New York, New York 10010, telephone (212) 689-4411; available only from the publisher. The directory is usually offered in conjunction with a subscription to the magazine titled *Gift and Decorative Accessories Magazine.* This monthly magazine costs $20 per year, and that charge includes a free copy of the directory.

In this guide look for:
1. A classified index of companies that may be using art and design incorporated into the following products: calendars (75 companies); graphics, including etchings, lithographs, and serigraphs (100); greeting cards (200); pictures in frames (175); pictures without frames (100); posters (50); prints (100); and wall accessories (200).
2. An alphabetical index at the beginning of the book providing each company's name and address and an indication, in most cases, as to whether the company is a manufacturer, importer, jobber, or representative. You will be interested primarily in manufacturers of those products, unless you manufacture your own line (such as greeting cards), in which case you might be interested in finding a jobber or representative.
3. A listing of regional buying centers in the back of the book. This list provides the addresses and telephone numbers of the major merchandising marts in the gift field throughout the country and tells which companies are exhibiting at those centers. If you are interested in this market and one of the centers is in your area, it is advisable to pay a visit so that you can become familiar with

the uses made of visual work in the field. The book lists centers in Atlanta; Boston; Chicago; Cleveland; Columbus, Ohio; Dallas; Denver; Detroit; High Point, Michigan; Indianapolis; Kansas City; Los Angeles (four centers); Miami; Minneapolis; Montreal; New York City (four centers); Pittsburgh; San Francisco (three centers); and Seattle.

GIFT AND DECORATIVE ACCESSORIES MAGAZINE, previously referred to, lists the major buying trade shows that occur throughout the year. Information about them is published month by month and compiled twice a year in the special May and November calendar issues, which publish the locations of trade shows throughout the country for the following six months. By going to a few of these trade-buying shows, you will become familiar with the products and meet people in some of the companies you might wish to do business with. Indeed, you might even be able to make sales of your work at the shows. In addition, if you are producing a line of your own items (such as cards or posters), you might wish to take space at one of these shows for the purpose of making sales to the retail buyers who usually attend in very large numbers.

Another important guide to this market is *Decor,* a monthly magazine of fine and decorative arts. The special annual edition titled *Sources* is a directory of suppliers and manufacturers of wall art, posters, fine prints, and graphics, with breakdowns based on the subject matter of visual material and types of media used (illustration, photography, and so on). The *Sources* issue is $6 from Commerce Publishing Company, 408 Olive Street, St. Louis, Missouri 63102.

You might also want to try contacting some of the British wall decor publishers, since that foreign market presents no language-barrier problems and names are readily available. *Kelly's Manufacturers & Merchants Directory* (The Buyers' Guide) lists some of these publishers under such titles as Greeting Cards, Christmas Cards, Posters, and Fine Arts. In the 92nd edition (1978-1979), there were 14 listed in the London area and 36 listed for the rest of England, Scotland, Wales, and Northern Island. This huge volume is most readily available in reference and business libraries. (Published by Kelly's Directories Ltd., Neville House, Eden Street, Kingston upon Thames, Surrey KT1 1BY, England.)

The interior-design field, including both designers and their suppliers, is at the upper income end of the decorative markets. It can be of considerable importance if you are seeking to sell fine prints and decorative graphics. This is certainly not a mass market, but the prices involved may be higher than in other aspects of the decorative-accessories field.

Three important publications, each updated annually, provide the marketing information you will need to reach this market: *Interior Design Buyers Guide* ($5 per copy) is published as an extra January issue of *Interior Design* magazine, 850 Third Avenue, New York, New York 10022, telephone (212) 593-2100. Included in this directory are the names of several hundred publishers of paintings, prints, graphics, and scenics. Additional names in these fields can be found in *Contract—Directory of Sources,* the special January issue of *Contract—The Business Magazine of Commercial Furnishing and Interior Architecture.* The directory is available from Gralla Publications, 1515 Broadway, New York, New York 10036, telephone (212) 869-1300 ($3 per copy).

A different slant is provided by the *Membership Directory of the American Society of Interior Designers, N.Y. Metropolitan Chapter* (available from the society at 950 Third Avenue, New York, New York 10022, telephone (212) 421-8765, for $150 per copy). This directory lists some of the most respected designers in the country. They are often in a position to recommend to business and residential clients the purchase of selected art works for inclusion in decorative schemes. You might also find out whether a local chapter of the American Society of Interior Designers in your area publishes a membership directory, to guide you to local participants in the design field. They can also be reached by using mailing labels of the national office of *The American Society of Interior Designers,* Room 1207, 730 Fifth Avenue, New York, New York 10019, telephone (212) 586-7111. The membership is approximately 12,000 nation-wide. Labels can be secured for any state or region and the cost is $60 per thousand names.

PUBLIC-RELATIONS FIRMS

A significant portion of corporate assignments are commissioned by public-relations firms on behalf of their corporate clients.

Your Best Guide to This Market Is:

O'DWYER'S DIRECTORY OF PUBLIC RELATIONS FIRMS, published annually by J. R. O'Dwyer Co., Inc., 271 Madison Avenue,

New York, New York 10016, telephone (212) 679-2471; available in reference or business libraries or for $50 from the publisher.

In this guide look for:
1. An alphabetical list of 905 public-relations firms throughout the United States.
2. A geographic cross-reference to identify firms in your own area.
3. A breakdown of these firms into 14 industry groups (such as fashion, beauty, entertainment, finance, food and health, and travel), which may key into your particular special abilities and interests.
4. The list of accounts for each firm, as well as another cross-reference that lists 6,000 clients so that you can find the public-relations firm for a company that you believe will have a special interest in your work.
5. The size of each public-relations firm is indicated by the number of employees and fee income so that you can determine whether your marketing effort is likely to be worthwhile.

SPECIAL RANDOM RESOURCES

American Showcase is a promotional book discussed in the section concerning advertising and self-promotion. Graphic artists who advertise in this book are permitted to mail promotion pieces to the entire list of 13,000 art directors, buyers, and others who receive the book. In addition, the list can be used by nonadvertisers for a fee of $250 plus postage and handling (for up to 5,000 names).

The list is strongest in the advertising and corporate sectors, and you can limit your order to names from a specific geographic area and category (for example, advertising art buyers from the West Coast). The policies of the publisher are, of course, subject to change on the issue of list availability. The address is *American Showcase,* 10th Floor, 724 Fifth Avenue, New York, New York 10019, telephone (212) 245-0981.

The *L.A. Workbook* is an extremely well-researched listing of art directors in advertising agencies and magazines, graphic designers, and others associated with the media in California. It also lists illustrators, photographers, and reps. It is published by Alexis Scott, 6140 Lindenhurst Avenue, Los Angeles, California 90048, telephone (213) 657-8707 ($28).

The *Thomas Register* is the annually updated standard reference of American manufacturers. It should be available in virtually all reference and business libraries. The seven-volume set is probably too costly and cumbersome for individual studios.

The book lists manufacturers in thousands of different industrial classifications, breaking them down by state and providing an indication of the size of each company listed. Many of the industrial classifications are consistent with graphics specialties. For example, the listing contains 500 pharmaceutical companies and 200 sporting-goods companies. In addition, it also lists some firms in the novelty and decorative markets, including 78 poster companies and 87 greeting and postcard companies. The *Thomas Register* is strongest in listing manufacturing companies and somewhat weaker in areas relating to art and media services. Nonetheless, if you have an interest in a select few industries and want to reach the companies in those industries in a particular geographic area, these volumes can be most helpful.

The *World Travel Directory* provides an annually updated guide to certain segments of the travel industry. The main feature is a complete listing of travel agents and tour wholesalers. In addition, and most interesting for graphic artists, the back of the book contains a complete listing of the world's tourist bureaus, both for states within this country and for various foreign countries. These tourist bureaus are the ultimate clients for the illustration and design work on countless travel brochures. The directory is available from Ziff-Davis Publishing Co., 1 Park Avenue, New York, New York 10016, telephone (212) 725-3500 ($45) and is also found in many reference and business libraries.

The *Mail Order Business Directory* lists some 6,300 active mail-order and catalog houses by state. This is an important market because mail-order and catalog firms rely on the use of large amounts of design work and illustration in the compilation of their brochures and other mail pieces. The book also indicates which among these companies are the 500 largest firms. The book is available in many reference and business libraries or can be ordered for $45 from the publisher, B. Klein Publications, P.O. Box 8503, Coral Springs, Florida 33065, telephone (305) 752-1708. The publisher also makes this list available in the form of perforated Cheshire labels in zip-code order at $35 per 1,000 names, or the complete list on labels for $220. (That cost goes up by an additional $7 per thousand for single-state selections. The minimum order is 3,000 names.)

Local Markets

(Architects and Builders/Chambers of Commerce, Hospital and Other Nonprofit Groups, Small Businesses) Your local area, of course, has its own assortment of advertising agencies, designers, and publishers. The national and regional references already cited in connection with clients can be used for your local market as well. Those sources may indeed provide more information about such details as specific clients, size of billings, and circulation figures than you might know personally. You, however, will personally have unique access to the special sources of local information that rarely find their way into national reference books. For these media-oriented clients, the combination of your local information and the data available in the resource books should create a high degree of marketing capability.

Accordingly, this section will be limited to markets that are both preeminently local in character and less favored with media. We will be concerned here with such clients as local nonprofit groups engaged in fund-raising, builders or architects engaged in local building projects, and small businesses. It's likely that you will know personally the people and organizations involved in these connections. Thus, the function of this section is limited to pulling together available information about marketing approaches to such clients that have worked well for others.

ARCHITECTS AND BUILDERS/CHAMBERS OF COMMERCE

Every new building facility generates the potential for a substantial number of clients. The builders or renting agents need a brochure designed, which may include an illustration of the completed structure in order to attract tenants. The construction company may be interested in renderings of each stage of construction for similar promotional reasons. In addition, if the new facility has some element of prestige attached to it, then the ultimate users—incoming businesses, tenants, and the like—may desire renderings of their new offices or headquarters to establish a particular image. In like manner the local chamber of commerce may have an interest in renderings of the new structure as a means of promoting local business activity and civic accomplishment.

Obviously it is useful to keep track of local building activity, starting with the earliest possible moment. To do this you should check with the city or town office that issues building and related permits. In this way you will stay abreast of the news regarding each emerging project and be informed of whom the principals are in connection with that project.

Your objective will be to secure some type of client relationship with one or more of those principals. Thereafter, you can hope to contact the others to multiply your markets.

HOSPITALS AND THEATRICAL AND OTHER NONPROFIT GROUPS

Hospitals, local charities, private schools, religious organizations, and theatrical and other performing-arts groups are continually engaged in fund-raising and often require brochures designed as well as renderings of the results of their latest efforts, such as hospital wings, library acquisitions, community activities, theatrical performances, and the like.

SMALL BUSINESSES

For designers, especially those getting started, small businesses are an important part of the market. Obviously virtually every new industrial firm and retail store will require some company-identity work, such as a logo or letterhead and so forth. Other possibilities range from the usual—such as announcements, business forms, and brochures—to the unusual—such as signage and shopping bags.

It is extremely important to reach such businesses as early as possible, well before operations have begun and such items have already been ordered. If they are designed and printed before you contact the company, the likelihood is that they will exhaust their present stock before considering ordering additional items, however well you might be able to design them.

One way to find out early about new businesses is to check frequently at the office of the city or town clerk. This may, in your area, involve a county clerk rather than a city or town clerk. In many states new businesses are required to register with an official having that or a similar title. Another valuable ally could be a friend in the commercial real estate business who keeps track of new leasing activity. You may even find a local real estate newsletter or trade publication which lists activities such as recent commercial leases which have been signed. Many of the tenants involved are likely to be new businesses.

One word of warning, however. The failure rate of new businesses is legendary. You must limit your exposure and financial risk. Whenever possible, get an advance for your own services and make arrangements for the large suppliers such as type houses and printers to bill the client directly unless the expenses are provided up front. If your client is a new magazine organized by an individual entrepreneur, these risks may be even higher, and you may find yourself taking such added precautions as getting paid immediately upon delivery of any finished artwork.

SUMMARY

As is obvious, much of the work secured on a local level develops out of new projects which can be monitored through public records involving construction permits or business registration. Another common element is the interrelated quality of local work. The local businesspeople are also likely to be found serving on the boards and committees of nonprofit groups and chambers of commerce. The work that you yourself may perform for such groups, occasionally perhaps on a volunteer basis when the cause is important to you, may also have an impact on your overall exposure within the business community. That exposure may well be the cornerstone of a successful practice in the graphic-arts field.

CHAPTER 2

Beyond Assignments: Markets for Original Art; Teaching Opportunities

THE MARKETS FOR SELLING original art relate primarily to illustration rather than graphic design. Indeed, even for illustrators the development of this potential income source is quite new. For example, the vast majority of the nearly two dozen galleries emphasizing the sale of living illustrators' paintings, drawings, and limited-edition prints were founded only within the past three to five years.

At present most sales involve only several dozen of the top illustrators, together with the works of leading artists of the past. Since, however, the number of collectors and galleries is growing, the trend is definitely toward a gradual expansion of the number and types of illustrators whose original works will become marketable. This points out, once again, the tremendous importance for illustrators of securing the return of the original works once your clients have made initial use of the illustration in reproduction form.

It appears that minimum prices are $1600 for an 18-by-24-inch color painting for a well-established and reasonably well-known illustrator whose works are just beginning to enter collections. For larger paintings, say 4-by-4 feet, the price might well be $3500 to $4000. For the handful of "star" illustrators, that price range might begin at about $2500 for the smaller pieces and $5000 for the larger pieces, ranging up to $10,000 or even $15,000 for those few extraordinarily unique illustrations that major collectors feel they must have.

The range for drawings appears to be about $200 to $1200 depending upon the size, the artist's reputation, and the quality of the particular work. It appears that prices would be somewhat lower than those already quoted for illustrators who are not well known or whose work has not yet developed any market among collectors of originals. The range for cartoon art may be substantially different and must be checked out on an individual basis.

The listings that follow cover the galleries that either primarily show the works of *living* illustrators or that are important factors in developing a market for that work; the few museums noted for their collections of illustration art; archives of graphic design; a guide to America's growing corporate art collections, which might in time become a major factor in the market for original illustration; and finally, the auction houses that have recently broadened the public interest in this expanding field.

Galleries

NORTHEAST

CROSSROADS OF SPORT, 5 East 47th Street, New York, New York 10017, telephone (212) 755-6100; specializing in originals and prints of outdoor sporting and wildlife subjects, including the work of illustrators known in these fields.

FRED DORFMAN, 831 Broadway, New York, New York 10003, telephone (212) 473-2017; largely a limited-edition print gallery now broadening its scope to include illustration originals.

EARTHLIGHT, 249 Newberry Street, Boston, Massachusetts 02116, telephone (617) 266-8617; specializing exclusively in the work of American illustration originals by living illustrators, primarily in the fields of fantasy, science fiction, and childrens' book illustration.

GOOD COMPANY, 339 Columbus Avenue, New York, New York 10023, telephone (212) 724-7244; specializing generally in the work of living illustrators.

GRAHAM GALLERIES, 1014 Madison Avenue, New York, New York 10021, telephone (212) 535-5767; primarily American fine art painting with works of some living illustrators and cartoonists as well as historically important illustrators.

GRAND CENTRAL ART GALLERIES, Hotel Biltmore, 43rd Street and Madison Avenue, New York, New York 10017, telephone (212) 867-3344; representational school of American fine art painting with some overlap into illustration, primarily involving historically significant works.

HEADQUARTERS GALLERY, 75 Pratt Street, Hartford, Connecticut 06103, telephone (203) 278-9628; emphasizing contemporary art including American illustration primarily in limited-edition graphics, with some originals; interested in women artists and science fiction within these areas.

ILLUSTRATION HOUSE, 53 Water Street, South Norwalk, Connecticut 06854, telephone (203) 838-0486; showings by appointment only; carries some living illustrators with an emphasis, however, on historically important illustrators.

NEWMAN GALLERIES, 1625 Walnut Street, Philadelphia, Pennsylvania 19103, telephone (215) 563-1779; American and European art with some overlap into illustration works, almost all of which are in the historically significant illustrator category, together with a bit of work from living illustrators.

JUSTIN G. SCHILLER LTD., 36 East 61 Street, New York, New York 10021, telephone (212) 832-8231; original illustrations primarily of children's book art from the 18th century to the present.

SPECTRUM FINE ART, 30 West 57th Street, New York, New York 10019, telephone (212) 246-2525; specializing primarily in spectator sports original illustrations, with some limited-edition prints as well.

SPORTSMAN'S EDGE, 136 East 74th Street, New York, New York 10021, telephone (212) 249-5010; specializing in contemporary outdoor sporting and wildlife originals, prints and sculptures, including the work of illustrators working in these fields.

SUPER SNIPE COMIC BOOK ART EUPHORIUM, 1617 Second Avenue, New York, New York 10028, telephone (212) 879-9628; showings by appointment only; originals and in some cases prints of cartoons, comic strips, and comic-book art.

MIDWEST

JACK O'GRADY, 333 North Michigan Avenue, Chicago, Illinois 60601, telephone (312) 726-9833; American fine art and some living illustrators.

WESTPORT WEST, 4105 Pennsylvania, Kansas City, Missouri 64111, telephone (816) 753-8504; primarily living illustrators' paintings, drawings, and limited-edition prints.

SOUTH

AMERICAN ILLUSTRATORS GALLERY, Colony Square, Atlanta, Georgia 30309, telephone (404) 892-8549; American fine art; primarily living and historically important illustrators.

WEST

BRUSTLIN WORKSHOP, 1233 Sutter Street, San Francisco, California 94109, telephone (415) 928-1233; primarily living and historically important illustrators.

MIRAGE GALLERY, 1662 12th Street, Santa Monica, California 90404, telephone (213) 459-3017; originals and limited-edition prints of living illustrators, many associated with the airbrush medium.

Illustration Collections in Museums

BENJAMIN FRANKLIN SATURDAY EVENING POST MUSEUM, 1100 Waterway Boulevard, Indianapolis, Indiana 46202, telephone (317) 634-1100; approximately 100 original illustrations, with 83 on display, of various *Saturday Evening Post* illustrators of the twentieth century when the magazine was owned by Curtis Publishing, including 4 original Rockwells and works by Alajalov, Clymer, Falter, Dohonos, Fischer, Stahl, Utz, and others.

BRANDYWINE RIVER MUSEUM, Post Office Box 141, Chadds Ford, Pennsylvania 19317, telephone (215) 459-1900; specializing in works by Howard Pyle and his students, including N. C. Wyeth, Frank Schoonover, and Maxfield Parrish; approximately 250 works of illustration in the permanent collection; exhibits change 4 times a year, with one always on the subject of Pyle and his students and one on some other historical aspect of illustration.

COLUMBUS MUSEUM OF ART, 480 East Broad, Columbus, Ohio 43215, telephone (614) 221-6801; a collection of 30 original Norman Rockwell paintings, which can be seen by appointment; the nearby WAGNALLS MEMORIAL, 150 East Columbus Street, Lithopolis, Ohio 43136, telephone (614) 837-4765, has 4 original Rockwells on permanent display.

DELAWARE ART MUSEUM, 2301 Kentmere Parkway, Wilmington, Delaware 19806, telephone (302) 571-9590; specializes in American art generally from 1860 to the present, with approximately 500 pieces of American illustration covering the period from 1870 to 1940; there is usually one gallery showing works from the collection of Howard Pyle and his students plus one other exhibit relating to some historical aspect of illustration.

LIBRARY OF CONGRESS—PRINTS AND PHOTOGRA-PHY DIVISION, First Floor, 10 First Street, S.E., Washington, D.C. 20540, telephone (202) 287-5000; a collection of American illustration encompassing the originals of well over 100 illustrators; on arrival they can show any specific collection; however, showings of special collections are best arranged in advance.

MUSEUM OF AMERICAN ILLUSTRATION (See Society of Illustrators, below).

MUSEUM OF CARTOON ART, Comly Avenue, Port Chester, New York 10573, telephone (914) 939-0234; over 50,000 originals of cartoons, editorial cartoons and illustrations, comic-book art, comic strips, and animated film artwork; a broad survey from the Colonial period to the contemporary, with an emphasis on the twentieth century.

NEW BRITAIN MUSEUM OF AMERICAN ART, 56 Lex-ington Street, New Britain, Connecticut 06052, telephone (203) 229-0257; probably the largest overall collection of illustration in the country, encompassing the period from approximately 1850 to the present, including 300 works of living illustrators; there is always at least one exhibit at the museum relating to American illustration; total collection includes 1500 pieces of original illustration.

OLD CORNER HOUSE, Stockbridge, Massachusetts 01262, telephone (413) 298-3822; a collection of 200 original Norman

Rockwell paintings, of which 50 are usually on display at any one time.

SOCIETY OF ILLUSTRATORS MUSEUM OF AMERICAN ILLUSTRATION, 128 East 63rd Street, New York, New York 10021, telephone (212) 838-2560; a growing collection of living and historically important illustrators, frequently part of revolving exhibits encompassing some 610 works of illustration; exhibits also include competition winners in editorial, advertising, and student art each year.

Archives of Graphic Design

COLUMBIA UNIVERSITY, RARE BOOKS AND MANUSCRIPTS LIBRARY, 535 West 114th Street, New York, New York 10027, telephone (212) 280-2231 (Room 654 of the Butler Library); includes copies of all books which have been accepted into the annual book design show sponsored by the American Institute of Graphic Arts (AIGA) from the year 1922 to the present; may be seen by appointment only.

FASHION INSTITUTE OF TECHNOLOGY—ADVERTISING DEPARTMENT ARCHIVES, 227 West 27th Street, New York, New York 10001, telephone (212) 760-7810; includes a selection of pieces entered but not exhibited at recent American Institute of Graphic Arts (AIGA) shows covering such items as posters and covers; available by appointment only to scholars and other researchers.

LIBRARY OF CONGRESS—POPULAR AND APPLIED ARTS SECTION—PRINTS AND PHOTOGRAPHY DIVISION, Room 1051, Jefferson Annex, 10 First Street, S.E., Washington, D.C. 20540, telephone (202) 287-5000; collections of segments of shows sponsored by the American Institute of Graphic Arts (AIGA) from recent years, covering such media as books, posters, and covers, and other archival materials in the field of the graphic arts and graphic communications.

MUSEUM OF MODERN ART DEPARTMENT OF ARCHITECTURE AND DESIGN, 11 West 53rd Street, New York, New York 10019, telephone (212) 956-2682; an extensive collection of lithographic posters from the late nineteenth century to the present;

some are normally on display, and others may be seen by appointment.

Corporate Fine Arts Collections

Industrial and banking corporations have recently become among the largest and most active collectors in the fine-arts field. Some of these collections include select works of American illustration. You may find it useful to consider approaching the consultant or corporate officer responsible for making decisions regarding your work if it has achieved sufficient quality or recognition to warrant consideration for collection at this level.

Your Best Guide to This Market Is:

AMERICAN ART DIRECTORY, edited by Jacques Cattell Press, published annually by R. R. Bowker, 1180 Avenue of the Americas, New York, New York 10036, telephone (212) 764-5100; available in most library reference sections, or for $42.50 from the publisher.

In this guide look for:
1. Names, addresses, and telephone numbers of some three dozen or more major corporations with large art collections.
2. The name of the specific consultant or corporate officer responsible for the collection.
3. Details of the nature of the collection, including breakdowns into media and time periods covered.

Auction Houses

While all the auction houses listed here may include illustrations in their general auctions of American art, the Phillips Gallery appears to be the only one, at present, that organizes auction events devoted exclusively or primarily to illustration art.

CHRISTIE'S EAST, 219 East 67th Street, New York, New York 10021, telephone (212) 570-4141.

WILLIAM DOYLE GALLERIES, 175 East 87th Street, New York, New York 10028, telephone (212) 427-2730.

PHILLIPS GALLERY, 525 East 72nd Street or 867 Madison Avenue, New York, New York 10021, telephone (212) 570-4842 or 570-4830.

PLAZA FINE ART AUCTIONEERS, 406 East 79th Street, New York, New York 10021, telephone (212) 472-1000.

PB 84, A DIVISION OF SOTHEBY-PARK BERNET, 171 East 84th Street, New York, New York 10028, telephone (212) 472-3583.

Opportunities in Teaching

There are at least five levels of income-producing instructional activity available to graphic artists:

1. Full-time regular faculty at a university, college, or art school.
2. Part-time regular faculty at a university, college, or art school.
3. Part-time occasional faculty with an adult-education program.
4. Regular part-time or oneshot appearances at workshops, often offered as summer programs.
5. Operation of a course or workshop for aspiring professionals or amateurs out of your own studio.

In addition, some graphic artists simply contribute instructional services to community groups in need of their assistance.

For the first four categories, motivation for participation differs widely. For some, teaching is simply another mode of self-expression and is enjoyed on that level. For others, the motivation is the need for money.

Your Best guide to This Market Is:

AMERICAN ART DIRECTORY, cited in the previous section concerning corporate art collections.

In this guide look for:
1. State-by-state listing of virtually all college-level schools of art, including address, telephone, and names of faculty members and degrees granted.
2. Specific disciplines covered at each school, so you can determine whether its orientation matches your own.

3. Number of students enrolled in each discipline, so you can determine the degree of emphasis a particular subject is given.
4. Similar details for major art schools abroad, should you happen to have an interest in that direction.

Finally, you should check local newspapers and other media for adult-education classes, community centers, and other groups that may require instructors.

After locating the most convenient educational institutions or organizations, you should then secure their catalogs and become thoroughly familiar with the courses they provide.

You will find that some places will be interested in you only if you can develop a new course to attract additional students, while others with a fixed curriculum will expect you to teach only what is already in the course catalog.

In any event, you will have to document your attainment of some status in the profession by means of degrees, honors, awards, articles by you or about you, activities in the community, and the like. All this should be compiled into a short resumé with accompanying documents as necessary.

The last item in our list of possibilities concerns teaching out of your own studio. This can be fairly profitable if you have a knack for that kind of business.

One outstanding professional in Connecticut gives a week-long seminar for six to eight aspiring professionals, who pay $400 each to work by his side and receive personal guidance on technical, esthetic, and business matters. At the other end of the spectrum, some artists give classes once or twice a week for 10 to 12 advanced amateurs, who each pay anywhere from $10 to $20 per session (or $70 to $200 per seven- to 10-session course).

If you become an instructor you will need to set a price that reflects both a portion of your overhead and direct costs (such as advertising, materials, and so on) and a reasonable fee compensating you for your time.

Whatever your direction, you may well find that instructional work provides both personal satisfaction and a reasonably attractive income supplement. This may be especially true in the early years of your professional career. Some highly accomplished amateurs have also supplemented their incomes by providing instruction to beginners.

CHAPTER 3

Marketing Tools and Techniques

THE TWO SUBJECTS COVERED in this section are virtually insepara-ble. The first is portfolios and presentations. The impact and competitive qualities of your portfolio and presentations will deter-mine your sales prospects. But advertising and promotion, the second topic, is what generates calls to see your work and serves as a continual reminder to people after you have seen them.

Art directors, art buyers, editors, and other clients see hundreds upon hundreds of portfolios and samples every year. Their initial reaction to a portfolio may be positive, but sweet remembrance is the more ample reward. As one art director recently commented:

> I love to see portfolios but I hate to get callbacks every week. Please send something that reminds me of your style of work rather than your tone of voice.

That thought, however biting, is based on reality in any market—from national ads to local builders. The time that elapses from your first presentation to the client's need for an illustration or design may be considerable. A visual reminder about the quality of your work has to be considered part of your presentation.

Accordingly, even though we have separated the subject of portfolios and presentations from advertising and promotion, you must consider them together in your business approach.

Portfolios and Presentations

WHAT TO SHOW—QUALITY VERSUS QUANTITY

The essence of most professional advice on the subject of portfolios and presentations is easy enough to summarize: Impact counts; less is more; where excellence is required, pretty good is worthless.

If you fully understand those points, you have grasped the essentials of successful marketing.

Portfolios and presentations are the means by which most assigned work is secured, both in the media world and in local work. The samples you show have to be directed toward the client's specific needs. Great car ads and extraordinary scenics will be ignored by most fashion art directors.

In some way you have to provide something the client isn't getting at present. If you are very well established, it might just be the ability to deliver good work on time. More frequently, and invariably for the beginner, the "something else" is a fresh and valid visual approach, with absolutely flawless execution.

Impact often results from carefully conceived, uncluttered graphics—single bold statements—that are easier said than done but are the invariable hallmark of recognized professionals. Samples of such work abound in the following books: AIGA *Graphic Design USA Annual,* American Institute of Graphic Arts, 1059 Third Avenue, New York, New York 10021, telephone (212) 752-0813 ($40); *Art Directors' Index to Illustration, Graphics and Design; American Showcase; Illustrators' Annual,* Society of Illustrators, 128 East 63d Street, New York, New York 10021, telephone (212) 838-2560 ($35); *Print Case Books,* 355 Lexington Avenue, New York, New York 10017, telephone (212) 682-0830 ($89.95); *The Creative Black Book* and *Typography Annual,* Watson-Guptill (for the Type Directors Club), 1 Astor Plaza, New York, New York 10036, telephone (212) 764-7300 ($25); as well as in trade magazine publications such as *Art Direction, Communication Arts,* and *Print.* The addresses and telephone numbers for those publications not given above are provided in the next section covering advertising and promotion.

Review carefully the images you find in these publications. Ask yourself why some work and others don't. Then scrutinize your own portfolio with the same degree of detachment.

As one art director stated:

You are establishing *taste* in what you are showing, so I judge you by the *worst* piece you show in your portfolio.

Or as another art buyer put it:

I am looking for a consistent individual viewpoint that will apply to some of the work I produce, not a hodge-podge of styles. I'll get the best person for each different style I need.

In short, though it may seem contradictory, most clients want predictability even in a fresh viewpoint. One bad piece amid many good ones, or too broad a mixture of styles, causes confusion. Alternatively, a couple of well-delineated and professionally related styles would probably be acceptable and welcome.

How much should you show? An art director, editor, or buyer should be able to go through your portfolio comfortably in ten minutes *at most*. Attention spans wander beyond that point, often sooner.

The concensus on the optimal number of slides to be shown in a slide tray is about 25 to 35, and the same number seems to hold true for prints, tearsheets, and the like. How many great pieces do you have anyway?

One rule is invariable in all markets: Ten great pieces will be remembered; 20 fair ones will be forgotten. Ten terrific shots mixed with 10 fair ones will only cause confusion. Or, as a highly regarded art director states: "When in doubt, leave it out."

In addition, you must leave behind a visual reminder or mail one soon after your meeting with a potential client or customer in any market. It needn't be elaborate—anything from an illustrated postcard to a poster. (The economics, production, and effects of various mailers and promotion pieces are discussed in the next section.)

APPOINTMENTS

Obviously you have to call first for appointments. Persistence or, better yet, tenacity, is invariably required. When you are at an agency, corporation, design firm, or publisher, try to see some extra people. A receptionist may let you know who else buys artwork. Sometimes the person you are seeing will want you to show your work around the organization. If the situation is informal, discreetly ask for the names of other people who might buy there and see whether they are free. You can save a tremendous amount of time and energy that way, covering several potential clients on one trip.

Unfortunately, sometimes your first appointment won't be an appointment; that is, it won't be in person. It may consist simply of leaving your portfolio at a potential client's office and picking it up later.

This "drop-off" system presents a number of problems. It is not advisable to leave your portfolio all by itself in a strange place. It might get lost or copied. This will not happen often, but a lost portfolio is a disaster, even if lost only once, whether or not someone signed for it where you left it.

It's always best to get a personal appointment, but many art directors, buyers, and editors are busy people. You could wait months to see some of them in person, if at all. In addition, some honestly don't want to see you because, alone, they can go through a portfolio in a couple of minutes flat. They often do know exactly what they are looking for, and unless your work relates to their specific needs, many would prefer not to have to deal with a complete interview situation. Frequently, though not always, the established professional will be accorded more favorable treatment.

The result is this: There are some places where you will have to leave your work if you want it seen. As to procedure, be sure you pick it up the next day or at the end of the same day if possible. Don't leave it over a weekend, especially a long weekend. Have someone sign for its having been received, if at all possible. Keep a record of exactly what's in your portfolio and which items are originals if any.

As to contents: Keep them short and sweet. Don't assume you need to be there to explain how a piece was done. Most art directors and buyers will tell you, as one recently told a New York symposium, *"A good portfolio doesn't need explanation, it explains itself."*

Another art director, who sees about 1,000 portfolios a year (20 per week during the one evening he sets aside for that purpose), candidly stated:

> Of the one thousand portfolios I see each year, I find two or three with so much impact and fresh vision that I will call those people in and use them. *The portfolio must compel you to work with that person.*

Many will tell you that those standards are a bit on the tough side, but the idea of presenting only your most excellent and compelling work is basically correct in any market.

Finally, when you do have an appointment, consider the image you create. There are no uniforms, but sloppy jeans, T-shirts, and sneakers might spell doom if you aren't an established "star."

A certain degree of informality is acceptable in this field, but it is usually a rather studied informality. It might consist of slacks (or a skirt for the woman graphic artist) and a jacket, with variations on that theme. Showing a portfolio in an art director's or corporate executive's office is a different task from executing the work in the privacy of your studio. In addition, designers invariably dress *less* informally than illustrators.

Your portfolio and personal presence together must convey one feeling: that you can do an exceptional visual job reliably, on time, and within a preestablished budget.

As for return engagements, don't ask for a new appointment until you have plenty of new work to show. Art directors and other clients do not appreciate repetition. The best strategy is to hold some pieces in reserve the first time. Use the first meeting to find out more about your potential client's specific interests. Next time you can gear your portfolio more exactly to that person's requirements, adding the pieces you held back at first, while dropping the ones that are irrelevant. The results can be striking in terms of what will now be a well-targeted marketing effort.

WHAT FORMAT TO USE

Many people use a zippered leather or leatherlike case holding a ring binder of acetate protectors in which they slip original prints, tearsheets, and other samples. Preferred sizes for the acetate protectors are 11 by 14 and 14 by 17. If your samples are double-page widths, you may need to have a size 13 by 20 made to order.

Tearsheets are often irreplaceable. They also become discolored over time and are easily made unpresentable with even modest handling. Accordingly, they should be laminated. You may prefer lightweight laminates to keep the overall weight of the portfolio manageable.

Some graphic artists use a rigid or semi-rigid case containing original art, loose sample boards, and laminated tearsheets. The size of the samples is not the crucial issue—after all, problem solving comes in many different sizes. Nonetheless, most people restrict their presentations to a few fairly uniform sizes if possible. Some of the more established professionals rely on showing work exclusively in slide-carousel form.

A recent innovation is the use of a self-contained (briefcase type) rearview slide projector that can be viewed in daylight. The image, however, is often not as sharp as an original, a print, a tearsheet, or a carousel projection. Accordingly, while this technique may be convenient for some informal local markets, its use at an ad agency or publication may be less effective than the traditional methods already described.

As to security measures, be sure your name, address, and telephone number are attached to the portfolio case and stamped or written on the back of every individual piece. This can be done discreetly so as not to interfere with the presentation. The purpose here is to allow for identification in the event that a piece is inadvertently misplaced.

Neatness is essential. Sloppiness is always noticed and rarely tolerated. *You are selling taste.* Keep the case clean. Replace the acetate sheets when they are worn.

The visual context of each piece may well determine its impact. If your illustration appears on a large page of typeset material, trim out some of the copy; place several pictures of this type together to form a better-looking, simulated single page. You might want to trim out all the copy except the caption and run several images together under the publication's logo, which you should have saved. This will invariably have more impact than a one- or two-column cut lost in a page of type, regardless of how good the piece is.

Work carefully on the sequence of your presentation. Does it tell a story? Are there groups of related images, or just abrupt jumps from one unrelated subject to another? Obviously the latter will distract from the image you must create of fully comprehending the interrelated qualities of your visual images.

Advertising and Self-Promotion

When you budget for your own advertising and self-promotion, two factors should dominate: continuity and quality.

One solution that will satisfy those requirements, whether you are just starting out or are well established, is the effective use of mailing pieces. A good mailer sent to a select list is always helpful, especially when coupled with a well-organized follow-up program of telephone calls and the like.

You must plan such promotion over the period of an entire year, possibly making mailings every two or three months. Thus the basic problem becomes cost containment.

CONTROLLING PROMOTIONAL COSTS

An illustrator's agent, noted for exceptionally effective promotional techniques, recently explained his methodology at a New York business seminar. It is astonishingly simple. He regularly negotiates for 300 to 500 run-on copies (either free or at nominal run-on cost) as a part of *every* job his artist is doing that will produce an interesting sample. He sends out no more than 50 to 100 at a time and follows up each mailing piece with telephone requests for an appointment to show the portfolio. Those leads that show promise get sent second and third mailings from the next run-on samples, and so on. Usually, the only cost in the entire operation is postage (admittedly important) and envelopes. The agent claims that every mailing produces one or two jobs.

A designer then explained that she arranges with a typesetter, photographer, and printer to give each of them well-placed credit lines in exchange for drastically reduced charges for printing and producing mailers. Since they all have the same clients (magazines and ad agencies), the arrangement makes a lot of sense. Indeed, such arrangements are quite common in this field.

Other techniques abound. One successful illustration studio has two basic layouts for a postcard, professionally designed. Using those two formats, they annually produce 12 different cards using 12 different examples of their best work, six placed in one format and six in the other. All 12 are printed at one time, with a single set of separations whenever possible.

Each buyer and editor on this studio's mailing list is sent one card each month, alternating the formats to avoid repetition, while maintaining identity through the use of one distinct logo. The beauty of postcards, as used in this case, is that they require no separate envelope, provide a modest savings in first-class postage, and afford immediate visual impact. The continuity of a monthly (or, for that matter, bimonthly or quarterly) mailing has a number of important consequences. Among them:

- You are less likely to be forgotten amid the hundreds of other people a potential client sees in a relatively short time.
- You convey a personal image of stable presence in a field where many clients need to be assured that the graphic artist they work with today will be around tomorrow.

The studio in this case has plans for expanding its postcard lines, making them available to the public through novelty distributors.

They recently began visiting local merchandise marts and contacting card manufacturers through information provided in the *Gift and Decorative Accessory Buyer's Guide,* discussed on page 20.

Along with continuity, you should consider the possibility of creating a particularly powerful impact at the very outset of your promotional campaign. You might, for example, mail one card or other sample to 25 to 50 people, and then send another to the same individuals two weeks later. With immediate telephone follow-up, you can quickly gauge the value of your effort.

The cost of producing and distributing mailers has many variables, such as:

- The number of separations you group together.
- Whether you use black-and-white or color reproduction. Color is much more expensive unless you are grouping separations and putting many pieces together to bring your costs down. For example, 12 cards produced with one separation and one print run may sacrifice a bit of quality but can reduce costs approximately eight to tenfold.
- Whether or not you can get numerous reprints (at your client's nominal print run-on cost or possibly free).
- The number of pieces you get on one sheet for a single print run (some cards, for example, can be run 6 or 12 at one time, vastly reducing press time and stock wastage).
- Whether you use bulk mail or first class. Bulk mail can save as much as 25 cents per unit, but it requires a special permit, it is not delivered on a set schedule, and it therefore does not allow for a predetermined telephone follow-up. You're better off with first class, if you can afford it, while using the reduced first-class rate especially for postcards, if available. Nonetheless, if you are sending out several thousand pieces at one time, the bulk-rate saving would be extremely significant.

After you weigh all the variables, certain conclusions emerge:

- An aggressive monthly or bimonthly program for mailing several hundred pieces at a time can probably be handled for under $2,000 to $2,500 per year (including postage), providing you don't print expensive posters or fold-outs.
- A modest quarterly mailing program, which should be adequate for most beginners, can be organized for $750 to $1,000 per year.
- A concentrated effort, possibly two mailings within a week or two

to a limited number of key people, may be needed to create initial impact.

- You must think in terms of *annual* costs. If you print one piece at a time, every few months, your costs will be much higher than if you prepare an entire year's promotions at one time.

ELABORATE MAILERS AND PAID TRADE ADVERTISING

As you become established, you may feel the need for a more substantial effort in the arena of advertising and self-promotion. For example, a few studios produce elaborate annual color booklets, incorporating their best work of the year. They distribute these booklets in the hope that they will stay on an art director's or art buyer's desk as a reference tool. At the least such efforts convey a message of success, but the cost in time and money is likely to be in the thousands of dollars rather than the hundreds required for a simple mailer.

Other graphic artists exert a similar effort to produce an exquisite poster-size sheet that is then sent out as a kind of prestige mailer. While these major projects are indeed impressive, one must question their value in relationship to the effectiveness of a simple postcard or other mailers that can be distributed with far greater frequency.

Some graphic artists who are attempting to secure national and large regional clients may also consider paid advertising in trade media that reach such art buyers. Among the possibilities are the various industry directories, such as *American Showcase; Art Directors' Index to Illustration, Graphics and Design; The Creative Black Book,* and *The Graphic Artists Guild Directory.* As the publishing information and prices on pages 47–51 indicate, advertising in these directories may be quite expensive and requires caution. If your samples are anything less than exceptional, you will be wasting your money. In addition, the directories generally aren't designed for illustrators living far outside urban, major media areas.

On the positive side, these promotional books, and others, have worked effectively for a number of graphic artists. They often reach audiences that are unfamiliar with your work and stay on shelves and desks as more or less permanent reference tools, unlike mailers, which disappear far sooner.

The Creative Black Book is an industrywide telephone and address directory for people in all the visual creative media. Your name and address will be listed free of charge upon request (if they aren't already there), and the book has become a standard information reference for that reason. While the book is more expensive to advertise your samples in than any other publication in the field, it is generally ackowledged to be in wide use throughout the nation among art directors, art buyers, and others in the field.

American Showcase and *Art Directors' Index* are large-format, carefully reproduced art-reference sources for art buyers and others in the field. They are also widely distributed throughout the industry.

Art Directors' Index provides an interesting, all-inclusive marketing program for the cost of an ad, which includes mailings and out-of-town presentations of work samples. The much less costly *American Showcase* does, however, provide mailing list access and discounts to advertisers using the directory's promotional mail handling services.

In addition, there has been a veritable explosion of promotional directories recently on the national and local scene. The *Madison Avenue Handbook,* a traditional industry reference tool, has begun taking color advertising for the first time. On the local level, creative directories have sprung up or expanded in California, Chicago, New England, and the sun belt (Houston-centered), while a book titled *RSVP* serves the New York area as something of a new-talent directory, with an extremely attractive cost per page.

The California directory, the *L.A. Workbook,* recently extended coverage to include San Francisco and Orange County in addition to its original base in Los Angeles. It currently carries more advertising and general information about the business than any other local directory.

You should also note that the *Graphic Artists Guild Directory* carries the largest number of pages of artwork from designers and illustrators, while maintaining some of the lowest costs for those advertisers.

The best way to find out about the possible value of an ad in one of these books is to buy or borrow a copy and then call advertisers, preferably ones whose work might be similar to yours. Ask about the results of their ads. Are they going to advertise in the next edition? If not, why not? Also check with as many art directors and art buyers as possible about their views on the book you are considering. Do they receive it? Do they use it for reference when hiring someone for a job? Are there other books they consider more valuable?

In two tables that follow we cover, first, nationally distributed books and, second, regional and local books. We show the circulation, contact phone numbers, and current cost of advertising in these promotional books. In addition, and by way of contrast, the cost of advertising in some of the trade magazines that are seen by art directors, art buyers, and others in the field is provided in a third

NATIONAL PROMOTIONAL BOOKS

	American Showcase	Art Directors' Index to Illustration, Graphics and Design	Creative Black Book	Graphic Artists Guild Directory	Madison Avenue Handbook
Basic Rates ($) color page	1,600 before June 15	3,400	4,250	650 plus separation cost	2,500
b&w page	1,375 before June 15	2,800	2,750	325	1,600
Reprints (run-on mailers)	2,000 free	1,000 free	$325 for 2,000 (free before May 15)	$75 color and $50 b&w for 1,000 copies	500 free
Circulation U.S. Free U.S. Sales Foreign	28,000 13,000 10,000 5,000	38,000 12,500 5,000 21,500	40,000 13,000 17,000 10,000	5,000 5,000 — —	20,000 6,000 13,000 1,000
Size/Format	Large	Large	Deskbook	Large	Deskbook
Basic Price $	27.50	22.00	25.00	Not sold	13.95
Address and Telephone	10th floor, 724 Fifth Avenue, New York, New York 10019; (212) 245-0981	John S. Butsch Assoc., 415 West Superior St. Chicago, Illinois 60610 (312) 337-1901	Friendly Publications 401 Park Ave. South, New York, New York 10016 (212) 684-4255	Graphic Artists Guild, Rm. 405, 30 East 20th Street, New York, New York 10003 (212) 982-9298	17 East 48th St. New York, New York 10017 (212) 688-7940
Special Features	Will handle your promotional mailings at cost plus $125 to any specialized group of art buyers in any geog. area, for first 5,000 names.	Includes: (1) Design help for your page layout (2) Consultation on use of promo mailing (3) Out-of-town presentations of your work (4) Possible representation on selected basis (5) handling promo mail'g.	Standard reference for names, addresses & telephones of illustrators, photographers and others throughout the industry	Members only directory, published once every two years.	Offers discounts to members of some professional organizations.

REGIONAL PROMOTION & OTHER BOOKS

	Art Directors' Annual	Catalogue of Los Angeles Illustrators	Chicago Creative Directory (Midwest)	Chicago Talent
Basic Rates ($) color pg b&w page ½ b&w pg	1,800 1,200 —	1,500 1,200 —	1,400 725 375	550 450 —
Mailers	—	500 free	500 free	$100 for 1,000
Circulation	20,000	2,000	7,500	10,000
Format	Large	Large	Deskbook	Large
Price ($)	34.95	12.00	20.00	15.00
Address and Telephone	Supermart Graphics (producer for Art Directors' Club), 22 E. 31st St., New York, New York 10016; (212) 889-6728	C. Winston Taylor, 17008 Lisette St., Granada Hills, California 91344; (213) 363-5761	Suite 311, 333 North Michigan Ave., Chicago, Illinois 60603; (312) 236-7337	Chicago Talent, Inc., Suite 14, 310 Melvin Drive, Northbrook, Illinois 60062; (312) 272-4434
Comment	Primarily for the Award Winners & Annual Show, plus some ads		Must be Chicago based or have Chicago rep to advertise	Must be Chicago based. Covers design, illustration, and photography

REGIONAL PROMOTION & OTHER BOOKS

Creative Directory of the Sun Belt	Illustrators' Annual	L.A. Workbook (California)	RSVP (New York)	The Book (New England)
1,200 900 500	— 400 —	1,450 850 500	400 175 —	1,800 1,000 600
500 free	—	$50-$100 for 50	$75-$125 for 500	color pg: 1,000 free
10,000	30,000	7,500	6,000	12,000
Deskbook	Large	Large	Deskbook	Deskbook
17.95	35.00	28.00	12.00	18.00
Ampersand, 1103 South Shephard Drive, Houston, Texas 77019; (713) 523-0506	Society of Illustrators, 128 East 63rd Street, New York, New York; (212) 838-2560	6140 Lindenhurst Ave., Los Angeles, California 90048; (213) 939-9869 or 657-8707	P. O. Box 314 Brooklyn, New York 11205 (212) 857-9267	P.O. Box 749 431 Post Road East, Westport, Connecticut 06880; (203) 226-4207
	Primarily for the Award Winners & Annual Show, plus some ads	Most ads, talent, art director & other listings of regional books	Oriented toward selected newer talent	

table. Traditionally, graphic artists have not advertised in these media magazines. Nonetheless, it may be worth considering whether an advertisement in one of these magazines every three months might be as effective as a single ad in one of the promotional books, since the costs of those two situations would be roughly comparable. Bear in mind, in making such a comparison, that the directories may remain in use for a year or more while the magazines may not receive such sustained attention.

You should also talk to art directors and art buyers in your area. Find out what local trade publications they use and then contact the publishers to secure information about advertising rates and schedules.

Bear in mind that you may be able to get editorial coverage in the magazines listed in the preceding table and in local trade publications even though you don't advertise in them. As explained earlier, it is probably worthwhile to subscribe to some of them just to keep up with visual developments in the field. In addition, you may find in the course of reviewing them that you have work suitable for their type of editorial coverage. If you do, you should send it to them yourself. With all the competing material cascading off the presses, you cannot rely on their stumbling upon your material by chance, though of course that happens from time to time.

PROFESSIONAL AWARDS AND COMPETITIONS

The major national and local art directors and communications-awards shows can provide valuable exposure for a reasonable, and in some cases minimal, cost. The best of them publish winning entries in a single, widely distributed volume that usually becomes an important trade reference for art buyers, art directors, editors, and others throughout the country. This is also true for a few local and regional competitions that distribute a catalog of the accepted entries within their geographic areas. Inclusion in such publications, especially if you have won a major award, can act as an important supplement to your own direct-mail and other advertising efforts. Accordingly, before entering, check with the sponsoring organization and make sure it gives the graphic artist full credit in any publication. If it does not, the time and money you spend will be nearly worthless. In addition, be sure to contact each show that interests you for official forms before sending in any of your work.

COMMUNICATIONS INDUSTRY MAGAZINES (VISUAL)

	Art Direction	CA—Communication Arts	Graphics Design: USA	Print	U & lc
Page Rates* ($) color pg. b&w page ½ b&w pg.	1,190 590 354	1,400 1,000 Not available	1,590 1,100 620	1,670 995 655	— 2,250 1,310
Circulation	10,000 paid	41,000 paid	20,000 free (controlled)	16,000 paid	117,000 (controlled)
Frequency	Monthly	Bi-monthly	Monthly	Bi-monthly	Quarterly
Telephone	(212) 354-0450	(415) 326-6040	(212) 759-8813	(212) 682-0830	(212) 371-0699
Address	19 West 44th Street, New York, New York 10036	P.O. Box 1300 410 Sherman Ave., Palo Alto, California 94303	120 East 56th St., New York, New York 10022	355 Lexington Ave., New York, New York 10017	2 Hammarskjold Plaza, New York, New York 10017

*Primarily special rates for studios: designers, illustrators and photographers (not including *Graphics Design* USA/NY rates).

NATIONAL AWARDS IN THE COMMUNICATIONS FIELD

Name, Address and Telephone Number	Categories	Basic Entry Fee Per Item	Additional Hanging or Publication Fee, If Accepted	Entry Due Date	Publication of Accepted Entries
DESI American Institute of Graphic Arts (AIGA) 1059 Third Avenue New York, New York 10021 (212) 752-0813	All categories of advertising, corporate, editorial and promotional design.	$8	$50	Mid-January	In new volume, covering finalists, titled AIGA Graphic Design USA ($40 from Watson-Guptill, New York, New York).
ANDY Advertising Club of New York 3 West 51 Street New York, New York 10019 (212) 541-4350	Advertising, promotion and corporate—all media.	$10	$50	Mid-November	All exhibited work reproduced in black-and-white in The Andy Awards ($17.50 from the Advertising Club of New York or Crain Communications, Chicago). Paid ads are accepted for the book. (Approx. $500 per page; circulation 3,000 increasing to 5,000)
Art Directors Club of New York 488 Madison Avenue New York, New York 10022 (212) 838-8140	Advertising—all media; editorial—print media; promotion—print media. Separate awards in photography and illustration.	$12	$55	Late November	All exhibited work reproduced in the Art Directors Annual ($34.95). Circulation approximately 20,000.
CA— Communication Arts magazine P.O. Box 10300 Palo Alto, California 94303 (415) 326-6040	Art Annual: illustration and photography CA Annual: design and advertising	$6	None	Mid-March for Art Annual; July 1 for CA Annual	No exhibit; accepted work reproduced in Art Annual July issue of Communication Arts (41,000 circulation), or CA Annual, the November-December issue.

Name, Address and Telephone Number	Categories	Basic Entry Fee Per Item	Additional Hanging or Publication Fee, If Accepted	Entry Due Date	Publication of Accepted Entries
Chicago Communications Collaborative 54 East Erie Chicago, Illinois 60611 (312) 787-6118	All print media, editorial and advertising plus television and radio advertising.	$25	$50 to $75	Varies. Contact their office.	Accepted work reproduced in black-and-white in the show's catalog ($12 to $15 from the Chicago Communications Collaborative).
Cleo 30 East 60 St. New York, New York 10022 (212) 593-1900 or 5900 Wilshire Blvd. Suite 2200 Los Angeles, California 90036 (213) 937-7337	All advertising, some emphasis on radio and television; many print categories, broken down by product lines.	$45 increasing to $60	None	December 1 generally; February 1 for work published after December 1.	No reproduction of finalists' (accepted) work. Names and addresses of all prize winners and finalists listed in an issue of Cleo magazine.
Creativity Art Direction magazine Suite 802 19 West 44th Street New York, New York 10036 (212) 354-0450	Advertising and editorial—wide range of print media categories and separate categories for photography and illustration.	$4	$9	Mid-May	All exhibited work reproduced in the annual Creativity ($24.50 distributed by Art Direction Book Company, New York).
Mead Annual Report Competition Mead Library of Ideas, Marketing Communications Department, Mead Paper Corporation Courthouse Plaza—Northeast Dayton, Ohio 45463 (513) 222-6323	Awards to annual report designers, with photographers and illustrators credited.	None	None	Mid-June	Portions of top 20 annual reports reproduced in black-and-white in The Bestever, a catalog of the exhibit (available free of charge from Mead).

Name, Address and Telephone Number	Categories	Basic Entry Fee Per Item	Additional Hanging or Publication Fee, If Accepted	Entry Due Date	Publication of Accepted Entries
Publication Design Annual Society of Publication Designers 555 Fifth Avenue New York, New York 10017 (212) 697-1246	Design, photography and illustration awards for editorial contents of consumer, trade, and corporate magazines and newspapers.	$5 (members) and $7 (nonmembers)	$50 (members) and $60-65 (nonmembers)	Mid-January	All exhibited work reproduced in annual volume of *Publication Design* ($25 from Hastings House, New York). Paid ads are accepted for the book at approximately $500 per page. (Circulation is currently 3,000 copies.)
Society of Illustrators Annual 128 East 63 Street New York, New York 10021 (212) 838-2560	All categories of advertising, corporate and editorial illustration.	$7	$25	Early October	All exhibited work reproduced in the *Illustrators' Annual* ($35) Paid ads also accepted at approximately $400 per page. (Circulation is 30,000 copies.)
Type Directors Club 12 East 41 Street, Rm. 401 New York, New York 10017 (212) 683-6492	Type used in virtually any communications medium	$6	$50	Early February	All exhibited work reproduced in *Typography Annual* (new in 1980–81 from Watson-Guptill, New York, with 10,000 circulation).

Important shows and awards that tend to focus on local or regional submissions include the following:

Art Directors Club of Boston
120 Boylston Street, Room 806
Boston, Massachusetts 02116
(617) 426-8084

Art Directors Club of New Jersey
841 Mountain Avenue
Springfield, New Jersey 07081
(201) 232-6800; closing date December 1

Art Directors Club of Philadelphia
2017 Walnut Street
Philadelphia, Pennsylvania 19103
(215) 569-3650; closing date early February

Belding Awards
Advertising Club of Los Angeles
3105 Wilshire Boulevard
Los Angeles, California 90010
(213) 382-1228; closing date in March

Best in the West
American Advertising Federation
Suite 425
50 California Street
San Francisco, California 94111
(415) 421-6867; closing date in February

CASLA Awards
Communication Arts Society of Los Angeles
1258 North Highland Avenue
Suite 102
Hollywood, California 90038
(213) 469-8301; closing date mid-November

Connecticut Art Directors Club
P.O. Box 1974
New Haven, Connecticut 06521
Closing date varies; usually late April

Designers Round Table
Suite 519
320 Southwest Stark
Portland, Oregon 96204
(513) 227-7332

San Francisco Advertising Club
Cable Car Awards
681 Market Street
San Francisco, California 94105
(415) 986-2878; closing early March

Society of Typographic Arts
1 IBM Plaza
Chicago, Illinois
(312) 670-3614

An important aspect of these competitions frequently is their quasi-commercial character. Entry fees are usually modest, but hanging fees, if there is an exhibit, are usually high. The economics are designed, reasonably enough, to help support the sponsoring organization.

You, on the other hand, should try to get your client on the job submitted to pick up part of or all the costs of the entry (and hanging fee, if accepted). All parties are usually credited anyway, so it makes no sense for you to give someone else a free ride on your initiative in entering. Art directors, editors, and others in the field are usually in a position to secure such entry and other payments from their employers. The prestige of winning can be as important for your clients as it is for you. With three or four important shows per year, and perhaps two to three pieces in each show, if you are fortunate enough to be accepted in all of them, you could end up with a bill for $500 for entering and exhibiting. That is great exposure for the money, and even better if you are splitting the cost with clients or associates.

SUMMARY

- For under $2,000 per year, you can probably develop a modest monthly or bimonthly mailing program of cards, reprints, or run-on print orders that provides both high-quality visual impact and continuity.
- If your budget is tight, try a quarterly program, which might be as low as $750 to $1,000 per year.

- As the budget expands, some graphic artists move up to larger and somewhat less frequent poster mailings. The cost differential is, however, quite significant, and the reduced impact from infrequency makes this strategy questionable.
- Some graphic artists believe a big splash (such as an advertisement in *The Creative Black Book),* though it costs over $4,000, will establish them right away if the art work displayed is strong enough. Among those who have poured a high percentage of their savings into this approach, at least a few have succeeded, but the risk is substantial.
- Others may well be attracted to the broad marketing program offered by the *Art Director's Index* or the far more modest page rates of the well-established *American Showcase.* Several of the regional promotion books, such as the *L.A. Work Book* (which is relied upon in the entire California market), have also produced good results, perhaps because they have fewer advertisers at present, so that each individual ad draws more attention. For the New York market the low-cost *RSVP* remains an attractive alternative, as is the *Graphic Artist Guild Directory* on the national level (though it is only published every two years).
- The most expensive media approaches and sophisticated brochure samples are probably best reserved for the more established graphic artist. You can succeed in achieving visual impact in a format as simple as regular postcard mailings, with some consideration perhaps being given to a promotion-book ad that clearly reaches your target audience.
- Before buying any promotion-book ad, be sure to check with current advertisers about their results and with art directors about their reference use of the book.
- You can get good exposure from Art Directors Club, AIGA, the Society of Illustrators, and other annual shows. Given the expenses involved in making multiple submissions to a number of shows, try to get your clients to split the cost. Indeed, in some cases they may pick up all the cost.
- If you do an excellent piece or campaign, consider submitting it to the trade magazines in the field for editorial coverage. Include a short note on any interesting aspect of how the job or campaign was done. If you *continuously* expose your best work to those publications you greatly increase the prospects for getting free promotion.
- Some graphic artists don't advertise or engage in promotion at all. The "stars" don't need it, but the rest of the field probably can't live without it.

CHAPTER 4

Agents: Reps and Galleries

General Functions

THE *agent's* PRIMARY ROLE is to sell the graphic artist's work. Some agents (also referred to as representatives) go beyond that and provide occasional guidance on your overall professional progress, much like business managers in other fields.

Assignment representatives (often called "reps") generally work very closely with their graphic artists, often on an exclusive basis in the cities they cover. These reps continually show work to, and seek assignments from, prospective clients in advertising, corporate, publishing, and related fields. They rarely handle more than eight to ten artists at one time. The primary center for assignment reps is New York City, with a growing number in Chicago, Los Angeles, and a few other major metropolitan areas.

Gallery representatives exhibit and sell the original works and fine prints of their artists to collectors. This rarely requires frequent contact, although the relationship can become quite intense when planning and executing an exhibit that involves decisions about choices of works to hang, framing, matting, advertising, publicity, and the opening party.

Assignment Representatives (Reps)

LOCATING A REP

Most assignment representatives (reps or representatives) concentrate on securing advertising-agency, magazine, and book-publishing accounts and, to a lesser degree, record-album, annual-report, and other accounts. They usually represent only illustrators and photographers. A few represent designers, but that is not common.

The artist-rep relationship requires frequent contact and considerable rapport between the two. The rep is constantly showing the portfolio, developing estimates, discussing new jobs, and delivering finished jobs.

The number of jobs a rep can bring in will vary widely. Some reps try to keep their artists working every day and are capable of generating enough work to accomplish that. Some graphic artists, however, can't handle that level of intensity for an extended period. Accordingly, the rep and artist must determine an acceptable pace that will allow for work on personal projects as well as completion of job obligations arranged by the rep. Obviously there is no set rule here. Every relationship will be different on this score. Equally true, if the rep can't bring in whatever level of jobs both agree is necessary, the relationship will certainly deteriorate, probably ending within a period of 6 months or less.

Good reps are quite scarce, and the total number is probably under 300 in New York City, which is their major media market center. Due to this scarcity and to general economic pressures, few reps, if any, make a practice of handling new talent (artists without at least a few regular clients in advertising or corporate fields). In any event, most people believe it is preferable, when starting out, to gain as much selling and marketing experience as possible on your own, before even considering association with an assignment representative.

Interestingly, the reps in New York, Chicago, and Los Angeles often represent artists from cities other than their own who execute work in special styles not readily available locally. For example, many New York reps, in addition to their New York artists, show the work of Los Angeles and San Francisco artists. Similarly, a number of Chicago reps show the work of leading artists in New York City who have unique styles that may not be available among the Chicago artists.

A high percentage of New York representatives are members of the Society of Photographer and Artist Representatives (SPAR). A directory of their members can be obtained from SPAR at Post Office Box 845, F.D.R. Station, New York, New York 10150, telephone (212) 628-9148 (enclose $8.10 and a self-addressed stamped envelope with 30¢ postage). You will then be able to send each member a card or other sample of your work in the hope that it will generate sufficient interest to warrant an interview. If you are approaching West Coast reps, many are listed in the *L.A. Workbook* ($28 from the publisher, Alexis Scott, 6140 Lindenhurst Avenue, Los Angeles, California 90048, telephone (213) 657-8707).

ASSIGNMENT REPRESENTATIVE'S CONTRACT

Once you and a rep have decided to work together, you should enter into some kind of written agreement. Many arrangements are never documented in writing, and that is probably a mistake since a simple exchange of letters will usually cover the major points. Some reps use a standard contract form made available to members of SPAR. That is, of course, only one of a number of possible approaches, and the form should always be modified to reflect your particular circumstances. Whether you use an exchange of letters, the SPAR form, or a new agreement you have drafted, the arrangement should cover the following points:

- *Representative's exclusivity.* Normally, the representative is your exclusive assignment agent in the market or geographic area covered by the agreement. Accordingly, those areas of work and geographic territory should be carefully specified. Frequently, different agents are engaged for the different major markets (New York, Chicago, West Coast, Europe). Similarly, different reps may be engaged for advertising, editorial, and television.
- *Commissions.* The generally accepted commission is 25 percent of the fee. A few agreements provide for a 20 percent commission; some also provide an extra 5 percent on out-of-town accounts (due to higher sales costs on those jobs).
- *House accounts.* Accounts that you have been working on prior to forming a relationship with a new representative are referred to as house accounts. Commissions on these accounts are typically lower than 25 percent (frequently 12.5 percent). Some artists prefer to pay no commission at all on house accounts. The problem then is that the representative might well ignore the account, and it may diminish sharply. Therefore, it is usually preferable to pay some commission even on house accounts and to increase the percentage as overall billing is increased from the new rep's effort.
- *Expenses.* No commissions are paid on expenses, such as travel, which are normally charged to the client. When jobs are under-

taken on a flat-fee basis, the expenses normally billed must be subtracted from the total price before the commission is calculated.

- *Billing for jobs.* Since you invest considerable time and often advance expenses to complete the job, you should handle the billing and pay the rep as soon as money is received. In many cases if the artist is too inexperienced or just too busy to handle the necessary records, the representative should handle the billing. In any event the artist and rep should both agree on the wording and amount of all bills.
- *Advertising and promotion.* The costs of promotional expenses (such as mailers and paid advertising) are sometimes split equally, in other cases they are divided 75/25 in accordance with the typical fee/commission split. The ratio invariably depends on the total financial interrelationship between artist and representative.
- *Termination.* The termination provisions are the areas of greatest sensitivity in the contract situation. In most contracts either party can terminate on 30 days' notice or less. Generally the representative receives some commission after the termination based on work you do for those accounts secured by the representative in question. The theory here is that the rep is entitled (for a reasonable period) to compensation for efforts that in fact generate current income for the artist, even though they are no longer working together.

  The usual provision is that the representative receives full commissions for a *maximum* of approximately 6 months on accounts that he or she secured prior to the time of termination. These commissions are called "residuals." During the first year of association, residuals are sometimes limited to approximately a 3- to 4-month period. Thereafter they typically increase to a maximum of 6 months after no more than about 1½ to 2 years. In many cases the representative will seek to have the 6-month period apply immediately, and the point may require fairly intense negotiation.

  Residuals are generally not paid on any of the original house accounts unless the rep took over the responsibility for them. However, if the representational association has lasted for a considerable period of time (perhaps over 2 years), a reduced residual (perhaps 12.5 percent) might be paid for up to 6 months on such house accounts.
- *Following termination.* The contract should provide that all sums owed by either party to the other, on previously billed work or

work in process, will be paid promptly upon receipt from the client. In addition, the representative must agree to return your portfolio immediately upon termination.

- *Arbitration.* It would be wise to include a provision in the contract calling for arbitration of disputes between artist and representative, since that procedure is generally somewhat less costly and less time-consuming than court litigation.

Contracts with Galleries

Galleries known for selling original work and prints were provided on pages 29–31. The following points should be covered in writing whenever you become associated with a gallery, whether it is a commercial or cooperative organization.

- *Gallery's territory and exclusivity.* Some galleries may try to secure the exclusive right to represent you in the United States or worldwide. Unless it is an unusually powerful gallery with vast connections, that provision should not be accepted. More typically, your gallery will have a local market (its own metropolitan area) or possibly a regional market (such as New England or the Midwest). You should restrict exclusivity (if any) to the specific geographic area the gallery has handled in the past. Otherwise you may simply lose out on markets that the gallery cannot possibly reach.
- *Duration.* Keep the duration of the contract as short as possible, preferably for 1 or 2 years at most. Remember that the larger the geographic territory you give the gallery, the more important the duration of the contract. A long exclusive contract covering a wide territory can be disastrous if the gallery is unable to sell your work.
- *Type of work involved.* Limit the nature of the work you are providing the gallery. Some agreements include both originals, prints, and reproduction rights to those images in other media. That should not be accepted. In fact, most galleries have much less experience than you do in media other than originals and fine prints. There is rarely any reason for your gallery to get a commission on deals you make for reproduction on calendars, greeting cards, magazines, and the like. The one exception may be for posters, which are also sold in a retail gallery setting; although, even in that case most established artists do not split

independently distributed income from posters with their galleries.

- *Commissions.* Gallery commissions are usually 33⅓ percent to 50 percent. The range is a function of gallery overheads, promotional expenses, and the like. Remember that if the contract is an exclusive one, it will cover sales you make directly in the market specified to be exclusively the purview of your gallery. This means that you will probably owe a commission to the gallery on such sales. Sometimes the commissions on sales that you make directly are at a reduced rate.

- *Exhibits.* Try to secure agreement on the number of one-person and group shows that you will be in over a specified period of time. Establish who has artistic control over those shows, with reference to choice of works, frames, matting, and placement. Also determine who will be paying for the promotional expenses of these shows in areas such as advertising, opening party, and catalog.

- *Pricing.* Both you and the gallery may wish to control pricing, and the contract should specify who has the final say here. A good reason for your control is to prevent sales that are artificially low-priced to "insiders" who will help build the gallery's own inventory for later resale at a higher profit. While this is a most unlikely situation, the possibility of it can never be entirely discounted.

- *Accounting and payments.* You should receive statements of sales indicating the quantity of each print sold, the price, and, where possible, the buyer's name and address. These should be sent quarterly, semiannually, or, alternately, whenever a sale is made. The applicable payment should accompany each statement.

    As a parallel provision, you should be accorded the right to inspect the books and records of the gallery with reference to the sales or loans of your work, upon reasonable notice.

- *Copyright.* The contract should specify that the copyright on all work belongs to you and that any buyer will be put on notice that purchase of a work conveys no reproduction rights whatever.

- *Consignments.* If you are leaving work on consignment with a gallery, establish a procedure whereby each piece that you leave is signed for, with an acknowledgment that you are the owner of all rights and title to the print until it is sold. This may protect your right to get the work back in the event the gallery goes bankrupt. A few states, including New York and California, have statutes that provide for this safeguard.

As another protection in this area, provide that in the event of any bankruptcy or act that can be reasonably deemed to indicate insolvency or threatened bankruptcy, the contract is automatically terminated, and you have the immediate right to enter the premises and obtain your work.

- *Damage or loss.* Try to require the gallery to insure your work against damage, loss, or theft, at least up to the amount you would receive if they were sold (in effect, the wholesale rather than the retail value). It is especially important that the work be insured while it is in transit to a museum or buyer, when risks of loss or damage are greatest.

- *Change of ownership.* The gallery business is highly personal, and you should have the right to terminate the agreement if the business changes hands.

- *Arbitration.* You should include a provision in the contract calling for arbitration of disputes between yourself and the gallery, since that procedure is generally somewhat less costly and less time consuming than court litigation.

PART II

Business Guide

CHAPTER 5

Pricing Assignments and Billing Expenses

The Pricing Dilemma

PRICING IS THE end product of time, talent, costs, and competition. You will want your time to be adequately compensated. In addition, you must recover your costs and simultaneously remain competitive.

As to competition, the tables in this chapter on pages 74–85 provide a sampling of typical going rates for most of the existing markets. These prices, however, always vary somewhat from one community or region to another. The tables thus should be seen as useful starting points. They do show clearly the relationships between one type of work and another and the range of pricing for each specific market. With those tools you can refine the information as it applies to your geographic area and specialty.

Graphic artists frequently discuss these matters with one another, especially when they are just getting started. You should make it a point to be in touch with others at your level of experience. In addition, friends who are art directors, art buyers, or editors may also provide helpful guidance on pricing matters. Consult them from time to time, when their own interests are not affected.

If you are starting out you may not have all the studio facilities or equipment available to some of your competition, and your prices may reflect this, unless of course your talent and skill can overcome those drawbacks.

Few graphic artists, however, want to be known as the cheapest

67

in town. This reflects both ego and good business judgment. Most professionals believe that the majority of clients are looking for a reasonable combination of acceptable price and quality. Many clients undoubtedly fear that the absolutely lowest price necessarily means a large compromise in quality.

It is an equally perverse truth that some clients will seek out only the most expensive professionals in certain fields (certainly including illustration and design), provided those professionals have established a suitable image of outstanding reputation or quality.

However, for the bulk of professionals—full-time, part-time, or just beginning—pricing requires the good sense to charge approximately the "going rate" for similar services, taking account of the overall experience, talent, and reputation you bring to the situation.

The discussion and tables of going rates for assignments follow two sections covering cost recovery and the billing of expenses, and negotiation tactics.

Cost Recovery and Billing of Expenses

Your pricing for a job must result in a complete recovery of all direct costs of that job, plus additional revenue to offset a fair portion of your general overhead. If the competitive price structure does not permit this to occur, you will be out of business unless you can reduce your costs in some manner.

Graphic-design work is generally done on a fee-plus-expenses basis. Illustration usually involves quite modest specific job expenses which, until recently, were not billed to the client. Now, however, whenever expenses are substantial in illustration (for example, models, travel, toll telephones, and the like), and frequently even for small items, clients are billed for all expenses.

One difference in the two fields involves mark-ups. Designers generally apply a mark-up on expenses and add that to the bill. The usual range is from 15 percent to 25 percent. Some designers charge a higher percentage mark-up on lower cost items (for example, below $100). In sharp contrast, it is extremely unusual, if not unheard of, for an illustrator to charge any mark-up at all on expenses billed to clients.

Another important difference between illustrators and designers is that some designers who create print advertisements then act as advertising agencies by placing the ads in various magazines or newspapers. This service properly allows the designer to secure a commission or agency discount from the publication that may amount to 15 percent of the cost of the space. If enough space is purchased, the applicable commissions may well exceed the basic design fee.

For work done on a fee-plus-expenses basis, it is, of course, crucial to bill *all* expenses. A complete list can be found in Chapter 6, *Contracts,* on the graphic-design assignment agreement form (p. 93).

You must, however, avoid surprises for your client. Make sure the client understands, in advance, what charges are going to be made. You should provide a detailed estimate of expenses wherever possible. It will protect both you and your client. Thereafter, scrupulously document all items of expenditure for each job.

When you work on a flat-fee basis, the situation actually does not change much. In almost all cases today you have to know what your expenses are going to be in advance. On the fee-plus-expenses basis, you will probably supply the client with a written estimate in advance. You need that same information to set a flat fee on any job.

In addition to recovering all your direct expenses, you must recover a fair portion of general overhead on each job. Those are the items that are never billed to clients and include such expenses as commissions, equipment amortization, fixtures, legal and accounting services, office salaries, rent, sales and promotional expense, telephone charges, insurance, and utilities.

You or your accountant should approximate as closely as possible the number of jobs you are likely to complete over a given period and divide that number into the total of your overhead expenses. The result is the amount of money you must build into every fee before there is a net profit (salary) left over for you. That is merely the point at which all costs are covered.

Consider the following modest operation (beginners may well have even lower expenses, and studios with several employees could be much higher).

Overhead Charge	*Annual Cost ($)*	
Rent	$ 4,800	($400 per month)
Equipment	1,000	(7,000 to last 7 years)
Utilities and phone	1,800	(150 per month)
Promotion	1,000	
Insurance	500	
Accounting and legal	1,000	
Salary	3,900	(part-time bookkeeper/ secretary @ 75 per week)
Miscellaneous	1,000	
Total	$15,000	

At 50 jobs per year, the pro rata portion of this overhead total is $300 per job. Thus, even at this relatively modest level, you need to charge over $300 per job, plus all direct job expenses, in order to break even. In addition, you must charge a total of $600 per job to net $15,000 per year ($300 profit for 50 jobs).

Alternatively, if the number of jobs goes up to 75 without significant additional overhead, the break-even point drops to about $200 per job. However, if the number of jobs drops to 25, the break-even point rapidly escalates to $600 per job. (Again, the break-even does not include any allowance for net profit. That is merely the point at which all costs are covered.)

The following table summarizes the situation for a variety of different activity levels, assuming constant overhead (usually, however, overhead increases with a substantial increase in the number of jobs).

Break-Even Points and Profitability

Total Number of Jobs per Year		25	50	75
Annual Overhead ($)		15,000	15,000	15,000
Break-even per Job ($) Overhead divided by number of jobs; assumes all direct costs billed or included in fee		600	300	200
	Annual Inc.	*Charge Per Job*		
Total Charge per Job* Needed to net annual income from $10,000 to $30,000	10,000	1000	500	333
	15,000	1200	600	400
	20,000	1400	700	466
	25,000	1600	800	533
	30,000	1800	900	600

*Break-even, plus net income divided by total number of jobs per year. Thus, if you do 50 jobs per year, your break-even is $300 per job and you need to charge an average of $700 per job to net $20,000 for the year.

It is no surprise that the table shows that the higher your fees, the fewer the jobs you need for a specified level of net income. For example, to net $20,000 per year you can do 50 jobs for $700 each or

75 jobs for $466 each. Of course, the higher-paying jobs may also be the most complex, so the trade-off in work effort is never clear-cut.

The main point is that you should see where you fit in the above pattern. Are you charging enough above your break-even to ensure a reasonable income level, given the number of jobs you do? Are you better off modifying your fee structure or securing more work? With the above analytical tools you can begin to develop answers to some of these questions.

Negotiation Tactics

Many highly skilled graphic artists pale at the thought of negotiating their fees and expenses on each job. This is unfortunate, because mastery of a few basic principles of negotiation would drastically alter those attitudes. While we cannot cover all aspects of the subtle interaction involved in active negotiation, the guidelines that follow may help you see the situation in a less threatening light.

- If you want something, ask for it. Virtually no one makes concessions that aren't requested.
- The more information you have about the concessions someone usually gives, and the less you reveal about that, the better off you are.
- Often, the greater your demands, the better your treatment. If you do not demand professional treatment, you will not receive it.
- Add something sensible to your demands that you know in advance you're willing to surrender. The other side also needs to feel it has won concessions.
- If you can't afford to say no, you can't afford to negotiate. In other words, you'll never know what your going rate could be unless you're willing to risk losing a few deals.
- If a client can't afford an advance or a deposit now, you're going to be in trouble later.
- The key to negotiating clout in this field is the quality of the samples you show and your sense of security (or insecurity) about them.

The Going Rates

The rates that follow provide a fairly wide range of prices within various job categories. This reflects the fact that each individual's overhead, cost structure, and income requirement is unique. In addition, the desire to do a particular job, to get a particular tearsheet or sample can be a factor, especially for beginners.

The tables do not, however, tell the whole story. You must understand both the need for flexibility and the intricate relationship between usage and pricing.

A graphic artist charged a mass-market paperback publisher $1,000 for the complex hand-lettered book title logo that appeared on the book's front cover. *The artist carefully retained all other rights.* A major motion picture company bought the rights to the book and purchased, from the artist, the rights to use the logo in all ads for the film and in the on-screen title sequence. For that additional use the artist received $5,500 plus screen credit plus a royalty on all merchandise such as T-shirts, games, posters for sale, and the like that carried that logo. Before negotiating with the film company, the artist had the good sense to research the amount that company would likely have paid to commission a new logo design, and that effort was well rewarded.

In a similar vein, it is not unusual when devising corporate-identity programs to consider the relationship between the potential growth of the client and subsequent utilization. One designer charges a basic minimum of $2,000 for logo-letterhead design in four applications to moderate-size corporate clients, provided, however, that the fee is doubled if the design appears in national consumer advertising or is used beyond a 4-year period. The theory here is that the reasonableness of the original fee will not cause substantial inconvenience up front to the client, and the magnitude of the subsequent use makes even the additional fee at a later date appear to be something of a bargain.

We have also seen gifted illustrators and designers team up to provide clients with package designs, and even product concepts, on a royalty basis, securing in the neighborhood of 5 percent, and sometimes more, of net receipts, with a substantial advance payment against that royalty.

More obvious examples of careful dealing include making sure you reserve all film, record album, book cover, and related rights when doing illustrations for theater and film posters or specifying that "billboard requires an additional fee" when completing either an illustration or a design for a magazine advertisement.

In short, the prices provided here are in accordance with certain specified uses. If greater uses are made, you should invariably seek additional compensaion whenever possible. Your agreements with clients should reflect that, as discussed in the Usage sections of Chapter 6, *Contracts* (see pages 89, 94, 96, 98, and 105).

In illustration the basic transaction is that the client acquires rights to the image *for the specified usage.* Any other uses require additional compensation. In a magazine advertisement, for example, that generally means usage in a single advertising layout wherever that may be run (usually involving multiple insertions, unless a single insertion rate has been bargained for). Similarly, usage limited to the hardcover edition of a certain book does not include foreign editions or the soft-cover edition unless specifically authorized. These points will be developed in greater detail in the contracts chapter; nonetheless, you should keep them in mind when referring to the going rates that follow.

In graphic design the situation is more complex, and reuse fees have only recently started to become commonplace. Accordingly, you will find that some clients have already become accustomed to paying for reuse, as they do in illustration and photography, while other clients will resist and claim that they must secure "all rights." In each case this will be a matter for individual negotiation. In addition, as previously discussed on page 68, advertising designers sometimes place their ads in the print media and properly receive "agency" discounts for that service. These discounts or commissions may well exceed the applicable design fee.

Finally, for additional information there is another source that you will find extremely useful. The standard reference for pricing graphic design and illustration assignments is *Pricing and Ethical Guidelines,* published by the Graphic Artists Guild, Room 405, 30 East 20th Street, New York, New York 10003, telephone (212) 982-9298 ($12). This book is generally considered to be indispensable for all people working in the field.

The Going Rates: Illustration
Advertising, Promotion & Corporate

	Minor Uses (smaller companies, limited application, distribution or print run)	Average Uses	Major Uses (larger companies, widest application, distribution or print run)
MAGAZINE & NEWSPAPER ADVERTISEMENTS (full page; 4 color)*			
National Consumer Magazines & National Newspaper* Campaigns	$1,200–2,500	$2,000–2,500	$3,000–4,000
Regional Consumer Magazines; Major City Newspaper; Trade & Professional Magazines	$600–800	$1,000–1,500	$2,000–2,500

*National newspaper campaigns may be approximately 25% less. Black & white or ½ pages: approximately 25% to 50% less. 4 color spots (national): average 500; range 300–750.

BILLBOARDS, &
POSTERS FOR
PROMOTION, FILM,
THEATRE*

Major studio's film	$2,500–3,000	$5,000–7,500	$8,000–10,000 +
National billboards	$2,000–2,500	$3,000–4,000	$5,000 +
Regional billboards; Independent film; Corporate promotion poster	$1,200–1,500	$1,500–2,500	$2,500–3,500 +
Billboards in 1 major city; Broadway theatre poster	$1,200–1,400	$1,500–2,000	$2,500–3,000 +
Billboards in 1 small city; Off Broadway & non-N.Y. theatre poster	$1,000	$1,500	$2,000–2,500

*Additional fees are customary for additional media uses (e.g. on album cover, book jacket etc.).

The Going Rates: Illustration
Advertising, Promotion & Corporate

	Minor Uses	Average Uses	Major Uses
BROCHURE, CATALOGUE & ANNUAL REPORT (full page; 4 color)*			
Fortune 500 company	$800–1,000	$1,000–1,800	$2,000–3,000 +
Other major company	$700–800	$1,000–1,200	$2,000 +
Smaller company	$600–700	$750–1,000	$1,200–1,500

*Black & white & ½ pages: 20%–30% less;
4 Color covers: 25%–35% more;
4 Color spots: average $350–500; range is $300 (minor uses)–$750 (major uses);
Black & white spots: approximately 25% less tha the 4 color spots.

	Minor Uses	Average Uses	Major Uses
OTHER PROMOTIONAL MEDIA (4 color)*			
Album Cover or Promotional Calendar for Major Label or Corporation*	$1,000–1,500	$1,500–2,000	$2,500–4,000 +
Smaller Label Album Cover; Counter Card or Packaging (National)**	$1,000	$1,200–1,500	$2,000–3,000 +

* Black & white & smaller corporation: approximately 15%–25% less;
** Regional: 20%–25% less.

The Going Rates: Illustration
Editorial: Magazines, Books & Special Markets

	Minor Uses (smaller companies, limited circulation & print runs)	Average Uses	Major Uses (larger companies, widest circulation & print runs)
MAGAZINES (full page; 4 color)*			
National consumer & Fortune 500 company (house organ) magazines	$500–800	$850–1,000	$1,000–1,500 +
Regional consumer, Other major house organ & Trade/professional magazines	$350–450	$500–650	$700–850

*Black & white & ½ pages: 25%–35% less.
Covers & 2 page spreads: 50%–100% more.
Spots: average $125–250; range $75–400.

The Going Rates: Illustration
Editorial: Magazines, Books & Special Markets

	Minor Uses	Average Uses	Major Uses
BOOKS-INSIDE PAGES (full page; 4 color)*			
Trade books & college/adult text books	$250–300	$350–450	$500–800
Work books	$200–250	$250–300	$350–400

*Black & white & ½ pages: 25% less.
Black & white spots: $100–150 average; range from $50–200

	Minor Uses	Average Uses	Major Uses
BOOK JACKETS & COVERS (front only; 4 color)*			
Hardcover original	$350–500	$800–1,000	$2,000
Trade paperback	$750–900	$1,000	$1,500–2,000
Mass market	$800–1,000	$1,000–1,500	$1,500–$2,250
Text book (college)	$500–600	$600–800	$1,000
Work book	$250–300	$350–400	$500
Juvenile	$350–400	$500	$600

*Wraparound: Add 25%–35%.

The Going Rates: Illustration
Editorial: Magazines, Books & Special Markets

	Minor Uses (smaller companies; limited distribution and print runs)	Average Uses	Major Uses (larger companies; limited distribution and print runs)
CARD, CALENDAR, POSTER & JUVENILE BOOK MARKETS (advances against royalties)*			
Greeting & note cards;			
4 Color:	$175	$350	$500+
Black & white:	$100	$250	$400
Calendars & posters for sale;	$1,500	$2,000–2,500	$5,000
Juvenile books (4 color; 32 pages)	$2,500	$3,000	$5,000–8,000+

*Royalties: usually 5%–10%; sometimes higher after 1st or 2nd printing; based on list price for books (& publisher's receipts for other items); for books, 5% is for illustration only & 10% is for writing and illustration together.

The Going Rates: Graphic Design
Advertising, Promotion & Corporate

	Minor Uses (smallest companies, limited applications or distribution)	Average Uses	Major Uses (largest companies, widest applications or distribution)
LOGOS & IDENTITY PROGRAMS (research + 1st presentation)*			
Fortune 500 Companies	$1,500–2,000	$2,000–5,000	$5,000–10,000
Other Major Corporations	$1,000–1,500	$1,500–2,000	$2,500–6,000
Smaller Corporations & Non-profit Organizations	$300–400	$750	$1,000–2,000
Individuals	$300	$500–750	$1,000

*Additional presentation: Add 50%.

MAGAZINE &
NEWSPAPER
ADVERTISEMENTS
(1 page; 4 color)*

National Consumer Magazine & National Newspaper Campaign	$650–700	$750–1,000	1,500+
Regional Consumer Magazine; Trade & Professional Magazine; Major City Newspaper	$400–500	$500–800	$850–1,250

*Newspaper is 2 color or black and white at above rates.
Magazine black & white or ½ pages: approximately 25% less.
Spreads and covers: approximately 25% more.

The Going Rates: Graphic Design
Advertising, Promotion & Corporate

PRODUCT SHEETS & BOOKLETS (4 color, 1 layout, 8½ × 11)*	Minor Uses	Average Uses	Major Uses
One Side Only			
Fortune 500 Company	$300	$500	$1,000
Other Major Corporation	$275	$400	$750
Smaller Industrial Co.	$250	$350	$650
Department Store	$200	$325	$500
Non-profit Organizaton	$200	$300	$450
12 Pages (6 Sides)			
Fortune 500 Company	$1,800	$2,500	$5,000
Other Major Corporaion	$1,500	$2,000	$4,500
Smaller Industrial Co.	$1,200	$1,800	$3,500
Department Store	$1,200	$1,800	$3,500
Non-profit Organization	$800	$1,500	$2,500

*Additional Layouts: approximately 25%–50% more (each); Black & white: approximately 20%–25% less.

The Going Rates: Graphic Design
Book Design

	Minor Uses (smaller company, lowest print runs)	*Average Uses*	*Major Uses* (large company, highest print runs)
BOOK JACKETS + COVERS (1 concept; front + spine)*			
Hardcover Original or Trade Paperback	$350–400	$400–500	$500–700
Mass Market	$400–450	$500–600	$750–1,000
Text Book (Adult/College & Juvenile)	$300	$350–400	$450–500

*Additional concepts (per sketch): Average $100–150; range is $75–250.

The Going Rates: Graphic Design
Book Design

	Simple Design (title page, chapter opener & double page spread only)	Average Design (3 more subhead levels, bibliography, contents & part opener)	Complex Design (e.g. workbooks, catalogues, art & picture books, cookbooks)
COMPLETE BOOKS*			
Trade Book	$250–350	$300–450	$400–1,500+
Text Book	$300–400	$400–800	$500–1,000

*Highly stylized = upper end of range;
Unique design = range of 25% to 50% beyond above ranges.

	Type Layout Only	Format + Type Design	Format + Type Design + Art Direction
Juvenile	$300–650	$400–1,000	$700–1,500

Miscellaneous Hourly Fees & Markups

	Typical Charges	Range
MAGAZINE DESIGN	$35–40/hour	$25–75/hour
CORPORATE DESIGN/CONSULTATION	$40–50/hour	$25–75/hour
EDITORIAL PASTE UP/MECHANICAL	$12–15/hour	$10–30/hour
ADVERTISING PASTE UP/MECHANICAL	$15–20/hour	$12–35/hour
CHARTS & GRAPHS	$20–30/hour	$12–40/hour
EXPENSE MARKUPS (DESIGNERS)	18–20%	15–25%

The Going Rates: Textile Design

	Sketch	Design in Repeat
Wallpaper, drapery, upholstery, sheets, table cloths, shower curtains	$400–650	$600–850+
Smaller domestics (hand towels, pillow cases, etc.)	$300–450	$400–650+
Women's wear	$200–400	$400–850+
Men's & children's wear	$200–350	$350–600+

CHAPTER 6

Contracts

A CONTRACT describes the working relationship between two or more parties. The best time to get a contract in writing is when everybody is getting along fine and you don't need it. It's easy to work out the details then, and you're protected if something goes wrong later. Some agreements are oral and therefore difficult (but not impossible) to enforce. Others are wisely set down in writing.

If you get a contract from a client, read it with great care. Remember, it's not drafted for your benefit. If you don't understand it, get expert help. There's usually a good reason for your confusion. Also, remember that just because something is printed on a form, that doesn't mean it can't be changed by crossing out some words or adding others.

A written agreement can be incredibly short—even a few words. For example, suppose in a note to a client you say,

"I look forward to starting work on the illustration (or design) due November 1, for $500, to be used solely for your brochure."

If it is accepted, that's an agreement, a contract. It sets forth the fee, time of performance, and usage limitations (brochure only). It doesn't cover everything, but it's far better than nothing.

It would be preferable if the client countersigned your letter (*especially* if a big job is involved) but such action is not the only proof that agreement was reached. Any action the client takes that is consistent with the letter could constitute acceptance, such as sending you some written instructions, attending a joint meeting, or initialing a sketch.

Contracts come in many forms. Letter agreements are one. Standard purchase orders from clients and standard assignment agreement forms from designers and illustrators, if they are accepted, are other forms of contracts. A simple statement on an invoice may also form a contractual relationship. For example, suppose you state the following on your bill: "For record-album use only," and you previously had an oral understanding with the client accepting that limitation. Assuming the bill was paid without argument, the client would clearly be limited to record-album use only.

For more complex situations such as long-term assignments, with vast expenses and sophisticated multiple uses, specialized documents drafted by an attorney may be required. That is the exception. *Simple forms and short letters will cover most situations.*

The following discussion describes the points you should cover in most common agreements for assignment work. For these situations sample contract forms are also provided. The discussion concludes with checklists of items to consider when you are contracting to do a book or selling original art or textile designs. The specialized topic of contracts with agents (assignment reps and gallery representatives) is covered in Chapter 4, *Agents.*

Commercial and Publishing Assignments

The following points can be covered in a letter or in some cases with a simple note on an invoice. Also consider using the assignment-agreement forms at the end of the discussion on this (pages 93–95).

CONTRACT TERMS AND AGREEMENTS

1. *BASIC FEE AND SERVICES:* Specify the exact amount that is being paid to cover the precise service you will render. Describe the project completely and accurately (for example, 2-color brochure, or 4-color illustration for a specific article, and so forth). Also indicate the number of preliminary and final sketches or dummies included in the basic fee. If the situation calls for it, establish a price for additional sketches. That can eliminate surprises and avoid hard feelings between the graphic artist and client. If you sense that many client meetings will be called for, indicate the number that are included in the basic fee. Finally, designers should indicate whether they have agreed to oversee reproduction.
2. *MISCELLANEOUS FEES:* Try to cover as many of the following items as possible:

- *Cancellation and kill fees.* If the project has stages, indicate the percentage of your fee that is fair compensation for time expended at each point. For example, 50 percent after preliminary sketches are submitted, 75 percent after final sketches are submitted, and so forth. In any event, kill fees are, by trade practice, not less than 50 percent and they are often more.

    Under the laws of most states, if you have completed a job *in a professional manner* and according to specifications, you are entitled to a *full fee* even if the client doesn't like the finished work at all. Because of the problem of collection and the arguments that may ensue over what constitutes a "professional manner," you may decide to settle for less than a full fee in such circumstances simply as a matter of business strategy and to avoid wasting your valuable hours bogged down in a legal hassle. Those aspects of the situation also indicate the primary reason for specifying precise cancellation or kill fees whenever possible.

- *Travel time.* If extensive travel is required, as sometimes occurs with design projects, you should be compensated for the time involved. While there is no clear standard here, in many related fields compensation is half the usual fee for that amount of time expended. If the overall deal is large enough, however, you might decide to accept somewhat less.

- *Space or use rate.* Magazines have established space rates for illustrators, but these are frequently negotiable depending on the special aspects of your style. In the advertising field you may also find that the client will pay a certain fee for use of an advertisement in magazines plus an additional fee for use on billboards or in television commercials. These additional fees should be specified wherever possible (see also section 5, below, concerning usage).

    For designers in particular, the notion of additional fees for extended uses is relatively new, but it is rapidly gaining ground as a result of efforts made by the Graphic Artists Guild and others. For example, in the design of logo types and letterheads, it is not unusual to see an additional fee of 50 percent to 100 percent for use beyond 3 to 4 years or for appearances in national print advertising. Similarly, additional design fees for second and third books in a series that follow the first book design are becoming commonplace, as are additional fees for soft-cover books that follow the design in the hardcover edition.

    The main point to remember is that if a fee is agreed on for specific services or uses, it should be set forth in writing.

3. *EXPENSES:* If you are working for a fee plus expenses, it is safest for everyone if you provide a written estimate if expenses are at all substantial. Indicate that, per normal industry practice, expenses on approved items may if necessary exceed the budget by 10 percent without requiring further approval. Be sure to include all categories of applicable expenses on your estimate as shown on the form on page 93. If you mark up your expenses, as many designers do, that should be reflected in the initial estimate.

4. *ADVANCES AND PAYMENTS:* Many clients will at least advance out-of-pocket expenses if they are going to be quite large on a given job. On any job that will extend over a considerable period of time, some clients will accept a schedule of partial payments (for example, one-third up front, one-third upon partial completion, and one-third on final billing). You should indicate that all bills rendered must be paid within 30 days, with a service charge (often stated at 1.5 percent per month) for late payment. Service charges are in fact rarely, if ever, collected. Stating them on an invoice may, however, lead to quicker payment.

5. *USAGE:* You *must* be specific about usage. Whenever possible, indicate the general *category* of usage, the *media* it is slated for, the *title* if it is a publication or the name if it is a product. For example, "Advertising in trade magazines for product X only." That would entitle you to additional compensation for uses such as on television, in consumer magazines, in brochures, or in any connection associated with product Y. The more specific you are, the better. You should also become totally familiar with the different *categories* of uses provided in the pricing charts on pages 74–85. These are primarily advertising, corporate, promotional, and editorial. Those same pricing charts will also familiarize you with virtually all the relevant *media,* such as books, magazines (trade, consumer, and corporate), television, posters, billboards, and so on. If you then insert the publication *name* or product name, you will have a complete description of the usage.

The word "only" can also be very important. It establishes with certainty that no other use is permitted. If you think the word "only" will frighten your client, try an expression like "other rights reserved."

For designers, the same principles apply. If you want an additional fee for a logo used beyond 3 or 4 years or in a different medium than you anticipated, you should say so with precision, in writing. Either state exactly what the additional fee will be or establish that the fee will be no less than the going rate for original work that would be used for that new or extended purpose. The same applies to book designs used in second or third books in a series. In like manner some reasonable additional fee schedule could be worked out for pamphlets, brochures, and similar material where a basic format is likely to be followed for years to come and the designer of the first piece is reasonably entitled to some additional compensation.

There is, by the way, nothing unacceptable about selling multiple rights or even all rights, provided you are properly compensated for such extensive usage. Some of the highest-paid work indicated in the pricing tables on pages 74–85 has traditionally involved grants of rather extensive use for clients. Many clients who pay the going rate for advertising that will run in consumer magazines try to specify that they are acquiring all advertising rights. The issue is negotiable, but that is their starting point in some cases. Similarly, some clients who pay the top rate for annual-report usage take the position that this may include some minor brochure usage. A certain amount of give-and-take is bound to be involved in these situations. It is not unreasonable to suppose that a client paying $2,000 to $4,000 for annual-report covers or consumer-magazine advertising rights might seek more leeway than the client paying $350 for corporate recruitment–brochure work.

6. *RETURN OF ORIGINAL ART:* For illustrators, securing return of your originals is critical. The reason is simple enough. Those originals can often be resold as paintings and drawings for hundreds or even thousands of dollars (see Chapter 2 regarding markets for original art). Returning originals is a rapidly growing practice in the industry. A few years ago they were hardly ever returned. Now they are returned in the overwhelming majority of cases involving illustrations and in over half the situations involving designers. This is due in large measure to the pioneering work of the Graphic Artists Guild in educating both clients and illustrators. Accordingly, you should specifically state that all originals are to be returned.

Some clients purchasing all rights try to keep originals, and the point can be difficult to negotiate with them. Actually, they're usually concerned that you might permit uses conflicting with their use (especially use by a competitor). If you specifically agree not to do that, you may be able to resolve the difficulty and get your originals back without further disagreement.

In either commercial or editorial assignments, set a time limit for those originals that are to be returned (typically 30 to 60 days after first use) and try to specify that they should be returned in person, by messenger or by registered mail only, and undamaged as well.

In the event, however, of actual loss or damage, it is likely that you will have to establish some measure of expected sales value for your original work. This can be done most readily through a showing of the record of prior sales of related work. In some cases value may also be measured by the cost, including the artist's time, required to replace the lost or damaged work. It is useful to set forth an agreed value for any lost or damaged artwork. Nonetheless, you may still have to show that such value is reasonable if loss or damage should occur.

Finally, in the case of designers, the return of originals is most important for securing control over reuse. This arises, for example, in situations where it is understood that the designer is entitled to an administration fee for overseeing additional printings or other services.

7. *CREDIT LINE:* Credit lines are customary for illustrators in all editorial uses. In commercial work the artist's signature often remains legible in the reproduction, but a separate credit line is quite uncommon. For designers credits must be negotiated in virtually every instance. In any event, if you have any doubts, specify your requirements in your letter or assignment-agreement form.

Some publications do not place the credit adjacent to the image. You should not accept that practice. Specify that the credit *must* be adjacent to the artwork in question. If you want the credit in the form of a copyright notice, you must specify that as well.

Of course, there is great value in getting a credit line on a commercial job, especially if the result is excellent. It is certainly worth negotiating for. Some clients occasionally seek a reduced fee in exchange for a credit line, and that may be acceptable in a few special cases.

Finally, some individuals seek to enforce the credit-line requirement by stipulating that the fee will be doubled if the credit is missing or misplaced. Alternatively you might agree to a normal fee that includes a credit line, or an abnormally high fee if the credit is omitted.

8. *RELEASES:* You should not risk being responsible for the way your client uses your visual work, since you have no control over that usage. For that reason you should state that the client must notify you when releases are required and must absorb all liability for uses that exceed the authority of the releases, if any.

The graphic designer's form that follows can be used in three ways: (1) as an estimate, (2) to accept an assignment, and (3) as an invoice. The illustrator's form is to be used for accepting assignments or as an invoice. They are not, however, chiseled in stone. Use as much of them as you feel comfortable with. The more the better, of course, from the standpoint of your own protection.

You might consider getting these forms made up on a pad with your letterhead printed on it so that, with carbon paper, you can make up one copy for yourself and one for your client at the same time, or, alternatively, have the sheets made up in what is referred to as carbonless or NCR paper which serves the same purpose.

BILLING AND INVOICING

As indicated, the preceding forms can be used either to accept an assignment or to invoice (bill) your client after the job is finished.

If you use the forms for invoicing, be sure that the invoice reflects *exactly* the limits on usage and other items you have agreed to. If you use the form both to accept a job and to bill it, the language should be the same in both cases. If you are then paid for the job and the work is used, the client can't complain about not knowing exactly what the terms of the deal were.

However, if you don't use the forms, at least be sure your typed invoice or bill to the client states both what you are owed and what key terms were agreed to. For example, if you just say the bare minimum on your bill, such as "for hardcover trade book only, original art to be returned to artist," and you are subsequently paid and the job is used, it is clear your client must (1) pay you for any additional uses beyond the use on the hardcover trade edition and (2) return your artwork within a reasonable time.

However, if you don't use the forms and you don't state the key terms on your invoice, then you and you alone will be the cause of the problems that may arise thereafter because of ambiguity and misunderstanding about what was agreed to.

GRAPHIC DESIGNER'S ASSIGNMENT AGREEMENT FORM

(Your letterhead)

ESTIMATE ☐
CONFIRMATION ☐
INVOICE ☐

Client's name
Client's address

Date:
P.O./Job #

Completion Date _____ Client Materials to Designer By _____

Usage: Category _____ Media _____ Title _____
☐ Designer
Credit required: ☐ Illus./Photog., Placement _____

BASIC FEE & JOB DESCRIPTION (include pre-
liminary presentations and meetings) $ _____

OTHER FEES AS APPLICABLE $ _____

EXPENSES BILLED TO CLIENT
   Illustration/Photography $ _____
   Materials and supplies   _____
   Mechanicals   _____
   Messengers   _____
   Photographic reproduction   _____
   Printing   _____
   Toll telephones   _____
   Transportation and travel   _____
   Models and props   _____
   Shipping and insurance   _____
   Type   _____
   Stats   _____
   Dies   _____
   Other (specify)   _____

   EXPENSE TOTALS $ _____

Subtotal
(fees & expenses)   _____

ADVANCES DUE

Sales tax (if
applicable)   _____

$ _____ At _____
$ _____ At _____
$ _____ At _____

TOTAL   _____
Advances   −   _____
AMOUNT
DUE $ _____ *

(*Due within 30 days or subject to 1.5 percent per month service charge.)
SUBJECT TO ALL TERMS AND CONDITIONS ABOVE AND ON REVERSE SIDE
UNLESS OBJECTED TO IN WRITING BEFORE WORK BEGINS.

(Designer's Assignment Agreement Form—reverse side)

Terms and Conditions

1. *USAGE.* Rights granted depend upon payment and are limited solely to those stated under "usage." Editorial reproduction is limited to one-time North American use unless stated otherwise. All other rights reserved to designer. "Category" of use means advertising, corporate, editorial, identity/logo, etc.; "media" means album, brochure, billboard, book (hard or soft cover), magazine (consumer, corporate, or trade), point of purchase, poster, slide show etc.; "title" means name of product or publication.

2. *RETURN OF ORIGINAL ARTWORK.* Client agrees to return all original artwork safely and undamaged within 30 days of first printing or publication, by bonded messenger, air freight, or registered mail. Agreed value of original finished artwork is $ _____ .

3. *CREDIT LINE AND COPYRIGHT.* Adjacent credit line for designer and other creators must accompany any use if so specified on reverse side.

4. *RELEASES.* Client will indemnify designer against all claims and expenses, including reasonable attorney fees, due to uses for which no release was requested in writing or for uses that exceed authority granted by a release.

5. *EXPENSES.* Expense estimate is subject to normal trade variance of 10 percent and client's oral authorizations for additional items.

6. *CHANGES.* Client shall be responsible for all costs and additional fees arising out of client-specified changes, and designer shall have the first option to effect such changes.

7. *CANCELLATION.* Designer shall be paid in full, on a pro-rata basis, for all services supplied up to the date of any cancellation, plus all out-of-pocket expenses incurred to such date. Following any cancellation or breach by client, designer shall remain the owner of all the original art and copyrights attributable to work created by designer.

8. *ARBITRATION.* Client and designer agree to submit any disputes hereunder involving more than ($_____*) to arbitration in *(your city and state)* under rules of the American Arbitration Association. An award therefrom may be entered for judgment in any Court having jurisdiction thereof.

---

*Maximum amount you can sue for in small claims court (usually your quickest remedy).

ILLUSTRATOR'S ASSIGNMENT AGREEMENT FORM

(Your letterhead)	ESTIMATE ☐
	CONFIRMATION ☐
	INVOICE ☐
Client's name	Date:
Client's address	P.O./Job #

Delivery Schedule:

Usage: Category _____ Media _____ Title _____

Adjacent credit required: yes _____ no _____ ; specify if in
  copyright notice form: © (illustrator's name) 19_____

BASIC FEE & JOB DESCRIPTION

$ _____

CANCELLATION FEE
Before sketches: _____% of Fee
After sketches: _____% of Fee
After finish: _____% of Fee

OTHER FEES AS APPLICABLE $ _____

EXPENSES BILLED TO CLIENT $ _____
  (Itemize here)

ADVANCES DUE	Subtotal (fees & expenses) _____
	Sales tax (if applicable) _____
$ _____ At _____	TOTAL _____
$ _____ At _____	Advances − _____
$ _____ At _____	AMOUNT DUE $ _____

(*Due within 30 days or subject to 1.5 percent per month service charge.)
SUBJECT TO ALL TERMS AND CONDITIONS ABOVE AND ON REVERSE SIDE
UNLESS OBJECTED TO IN WRITING BEFORE WORK BEGINS.

Terms and Conditions

1. *USAGE.* Rights granted depend upon payment and are limited solely to those stated under Usage. Editorial reproduction is limited to one-time North American use unless stated otherwise. All other rights reserved to illustrator. "Category" of use means advertising, corporate, or editorial, etc; "media" means album, brochure, billboard, book (hard or soft cover), magazine (consumer, corporate, or trade), point of purchase, poster, slide show, etc; "title" means name of product or publication.
2. *RETURN OF ORIGINAL ARTWORK.* Client agrees to return all original artwork safely and undamaged within 30 days of first publication, by bonded messenger, air freight, or registered mail. Agreed value of original finished artwork is $_____.
3. *CREDIT LINE AND COPYRIGHT.* Adjacent credit line must accompany any use if so specified on reverse side.
4. *RELEASE.* Client will indemnify illustrator against all claims and expenses, including reasonable attorney fees, due to uses for which no release was requested in writing or for uses that exceed authority granted by a release.
5. *CANCELLATION.* In the event of cancellation or breach by client, illustrator shall remain owner of all original artwork and copyrights therein, and be paid cancellation fee no less than the amount specified on reverse side.
6. *REVISIONS.* Revisions not due to fault of illustrator shall be billed as an additional fee. Illustrator shall have first option to effect such revisions.
7. *ARBITRATION.* Client and illustrator agree to submit any disputes hereunder involving more than ($_____*) to arbitration in *(your city and state)* under rules of the American Arbitration Association. An award therefrom may be entered for judgment in any Court having jurisdiction thereof.

*Maximum amount you can sue for in small claims court (usually your quickest remedy).

CONTRACTING WITH NEW BUSINESSES

A significant portion of the work early in your career may come from businesses and individuals who, like yourself, are just getting started.

Those, unfortunately, are also the situations in which the greatest number of nonpayment cases arise due to business failure, especially in the case of new magazines being started by individual entrepreneurs.

In these situations the rules to follow are clear:

- Never pay out substantial sums in advance for your client's expenses without securing an immediate cash advance to cover all or nearly all of those items.
- Never accept a job without getting an agreement on a payment schedule based on partial payments at various stages of the project, with at least a modest payment right at the beginning.
- Stop work immediately if the client defaults at any point in the agreed payment schedule; the great probability is you're not going to collect another dime.
- If the new business is separately incorporated, the individual or individuals who run it will not be personally liable to you if that business cannot meet its financial obligations, unless they provide you with a personal written guarantee.
- Make sure you get paid in full, and immediately, for any final delivery of completed work.
- The failure rate for new magazines is astronomically high; you may be asked to do work on the logos, dummies, or illustrations for a new magazine, with payment to come from investors once your work is completed; that amounts to sheer speculation, and you should only do that if you recognize that you will probably never get paid. Accordingly, in such circumstances you should be treated like anyone else taking a capital risk and have a written agreement guaranteeing you a specific ownership in the publication should it succeed, in the event you care to work under such circumstances.

In short, working with new businesses and publications, and struggling to help them succeed, is challenging and exciting, but fraught with financial risk, unless you take reasonable precautions and recognize that, in any event, you can never secure complete protection.

Royalty Agreements for Novelty and Paper Products and Limited-Edition Prints

Uses of your illustrations or designs on greeting cards, calendars, posters, T-shirts, limited-edition prints, and the like often do (and usually *should)* involve royalty payments to you, based on sales of the products. In these novelty or paper-products fields, the royalties are usually a payment in the range of 5 percent to 10 percent (and sometimes more) of the manufacturer's or publisher's receipts. For limited-edition graphics, especially for signed fine prints, the royalty may be substantially higher (and the deal frequently includes retention by the artist of a small percentage of the edition printed, as artist's proofs). Advance payments against future expected royalties are also common in the field (see the chart of going rates on page 79).

The contractual terms associated with royalty transactions are most important. The following checklist should help guide you in handling such transactions.

1. *GENERAL PROVISIONS.* All the protections indicated in the designer's or illustrator's assignment-agreement forms (see pp. 93–96) covering limited reproduction, return of originals, releases, and arbitration should be included in the royalty agreement, in addition to the special provisions applicable to this field that follow.
2. *CREDIT AND COPYRIGHT.* The credit-line requirement should, and usually does, read as follows: "Copyright credit for artist required as follows: Copyright or ©, artist's name, year date."
3. *USAGE.* The client's usage should be limited to one specific product (such as cards). Many clients publish in several of the paper-products fields simultaneously and may want calendar, poster, and card rights as part of a single deal. If you cannot segregate the rights into separate transactions, you should at least try to insist on a separate advance for each such usage. In addition, try to prevent the client from having the payment of a royalty owed to you on one product count as an advance that may be due to you on a second product.
4. *ADVANCES.* Try to provide that any advance will be nonreturnable even if the client eventually changes his or her mind about publishing your work.

5. *ROYALTIES.* Often royalties are increased as the volume of sales increases, except in the case of limited editions, where the volume is usually quite modest. This is reasonable because at the higher volumes a publisher's fixed cost (for example, for plates) have been entirely absorbed, leaving a greater profit margin. A reasonable scale for greeting cards might, for example, be 5 percent on the first 10,000 units, 7.5 percent on the next 20,000, and 10 percent thereafter. Some card deals may be lower, of course, and others higher, possibly going to 12½% or even 15%, in a few cases.

6. *ACCOUNTING.* You should be assured of receiving regular statements of sales and royalties (for each item separately). Statements and payments are usually made quarterly in this industry, though some contracts call for monthly reporting and others for semiannual reporting. You should also have the right to inspect the books and records of the publisher relating to sales of your work, upon reasonable notice.

7. *EXCLUSIVITY.* Many publishers in this field try to tie up talent under an exclusive contract on the theory that they need a long period of time in which to promote the talent, and they want to be assured of a reasonable return on that effort. You, on the other hand, will have an interest in keeping the period of exclusivity as short as possible. The publisher may not do well with your work, and you would then want to be able to sell to others. If you cannot keep the period quite short (1 to 2 years, for example), at least get a financial guarantee allowing you to terminate in the event that certain sales or royalty goals are not met.

   In addition, you might try to limit the client's exclusivity to a specific product. From your point of view, the best solution is to limit the client's exclusivity to the single image or images being published, while those images are in print (that is, offered for sale). Many publishers will accept this limited exclusivity if they are pushed hard enough.

8. *RETURN OF RIGHTS.* If the publisher takes the product with your image off the market, you should be able to secure a return of the rights granted so that you can offer them to someone else.

9. *LIMITED EDITIONS.* In addition to the foregoing, you should also cover the following areas:
   • *Quality Control*—if possible specify the grade of paper, the name of the atelier, and your right to approve the individual prints as they are being produced;

- *Artist's Proofs*—specify the number you will receive (usually 10% of the edition);
- *Size of Edition*—specify the exact number.

Other aspects of fine-print sales are covered in *Legal Guide for the Visual Artist,* by Tad Crawford, Hawthorn Books, New York, New York ($9.95).

Books

Book contracts affect many illustrators and designers doing their own books and collaborating with others on books. Book designers usually work for a flat fee, as with any ordinary assignment (see the designer's agreement form on page 93). Sometimes, however, the designer may develop or collaborate on the project, or become so important to its success that a royalty arrangement and standard book contract (as follows) will be required. Illustrators, on the other hand, especially with juvenile books, are treated like co-authors and therefore often deal with specialized book contracts, also discussed here. Book contracts and collaboration agreements are treated separately in the discussion that follows.

BOOK CONTRACTS

Book contracts usually appear as publisher's form agreements. You should *never* sign one without consulting an expert. These form agreements are simply offers. Publishers expect a certain amount of bargaining on many points, provided your demands are within the realm of normal industry practice. With a reasonable amount of guidance, you should be able to handle much of the negotiating yourself.

The checklist that follows is for general reference only. The subject is treated in much greater depth in *The Writer's Legal Guide,* by Tad Crawford (New York, New York: Hawthorn Books, 1977; hardcover $10.95, paperback $5.95). See pages 98–123.

1. *BASIC GRANT OF RIGHTS.* The publisher should be restricted to publishing the work in *book* form in the English language.
2. *SUBSIDIARY RIGHTS.* Subsidiary rights are often critical to you. They involve secondary markets such as magazines, audiovisuals, retail calendars, posters, and more. The original book publisher rarely develops these markets but may, through

lack of careful bargaining on your part, retain a major financial interest in such uses. Many subsidiary-rights clauses provide for an equal split between author and publisher. You should restrict such splits to subsidiary rights in the book field (for example, a soft-cover edition) and reduce the publisher's share to a maximum of 10 to 25 percent outside the book field.

When the publisher acts as agent and secures foreign or magazine sales of subsidiary rights, the proceeds are typically divided as follows: on foreign rights—75 percent to the author and 25 percent to the publisher (though some leading authors have won $\%_{10}$ deals); on magazine rights—90 percent to the author and 10 percent to the publisher on the first serialization and an equal split on subsequent serializations. Nonetheless, on incidental "rights" sales of individual images by you, where a serialization of the book is not involved, you should retain 100 percent of the proceeds.

3. *RESERVATION OF RIGHTS.* To protect new markets and evolving media, you should be sure a contract says that all rights not otherwise granted to the publisher are reserved to you.

4. *ROYALTIES.* Royalties on bookstore sales (for trade books) are generally based on the retail selling price of the book. Basing royalties for those sales on the publisher's receipts (usually referred to as the "net price") will reduce your royalty by almost 50 percent.

The normal discount given by publishers to bookstores on trade books is 40 percent to 48 percent. Publishers who need to give a higher discount, will want you to share that burden with a reduced royalty. Some publishers try to reduce the royalty by the same percentage that the discount exceeds a normal discount. They are, however, usually willing to accept a royalty reduction of half that amount if you're willing to press the point hard. In any event, never accept a royalty of less than half your normal royalty. Other sales that may involve a reduced royalty include direct-mail and coupon-ad sales.

A commonly cited hardcover royalty deal is 10 percent of the book's retail price on the first 5,000 copies, 12.5 percent on the next 5,000 copies, and 15 percent thereafter. These amounts are, of course, subject to negotiation and may not be in the publisher's first offer. For quality (trade) paperbacks a common scale is 6.5 percent to 7 percent on the first 50,000 copies, increasing in steps to 10 percent after 100,000 to 150,000 copies. You should note carefully which sales are counted (and which are not) in determining these escalations.

Royalties on juvenile books are often thought to be lower, but that is not the case. Authors Guild surveys indicate that juvenile-book royalties are approximately the same as those just mentioned, except that the highest levels of 15 percent on hardcover and 10 percent on soft cover are very rare. If the book is about equal as to text and illustration, the writer and illustrator usually share on a 50-50 basis. If the book is primarily writing (as for preteens and older), the illustrator's share drops to one-third or sometimes less.

5. *ADVANCES.* An advance is a payment from the publisher made before any royalty is earned. It is intended to make it possible for you to produce the work and is subtracted later from actual royalty payments. Publishers' advances tend to equal about 75 percent to 100 percent of the first year's projected royalty, although that percentage may be lower in the case of juvenile books. Ask your editor what the sales projections are for the first year and what the likely selling price will be. Assuming a normal royalty, you will have a pretty good idea of how hard you can push in negotiating for your advance. For the typical 32-page children's book, illustrators' advances appear to range from $2500 to $5000, with a few award-winning illustrators able to command $7000 to $8000 and possibly more.

6. *STATEMENTS AND PAYMENTS.* Most book contracts call for semiannual accounting and payments and give authors the right to inspect the publisher's books upon reasonable notice.

7. *COPYRIGHT.* The standard practice is to copyright artwork in the artist's name, not the publisher's name.

8. *RETURN OF RIGHTS.* Book contracts should require the publisher to have the work in print within a reasonable period (typically 18 months). Most contracts provide for a reversion of all publishing rights to the author in the event that the publisher fails to keep the book in print.

9. *ARTISTIC CONTROL.* Book contracts usually place artistic control solely in the hands of the publisher. Even if you want consultation rights, you must negotiate for them. Obviously, then, if you want control or veto power over who designs the book or what the quality of the paper will be, you must negotiate for that separately.

10. *CREDIT.* If you have any special credit requirements, get them

in the agreement. This is particularly important in the case of collaborations (see collaboration agreements in the section immediately following).

11. *OPTIONS.* Most publishing contracts give the publisher an option on the author's next book. This provision is almost always deleted if the author insists.
12. *RETURN OF ORIGINALS.* The contract should specify that you will get all your original artwork returned to you, undamaged, within 30 days of the first printing.
13. *CANCELLATIONS.* You should provide for a reasonable fee for yourself if the sketches are not accepted, and still more if the sketches are accepted and the finished art is rejected.

There are also provisions covering noncompetition and various warranties. Noncompetition requires you not to do work that directly competes with sales of the book in question. In the warranties you promise that the work is original, not obscene, and not libelous. Publishers are loath to modify these provisions. You should make sure they are not overly broad.

COLLABORATION AGREEMENTS

Collaboration involved in book publishing is usually between an artist or a designer and a writer. In some cases the two simply sign separate agreements with the publisher, stipulate what work they will provide to that publisher, and have no relationship with each other. In other cases they work closely together, and an agreement between them is essential. Such an agreement should cover the following:

1. *MONEY.* Is it 50-50? Or is the book principally the work of one or the other? It's rare for anyone to get less than one-third in a collaboration. This refers to both royalties and advances. However, even in a 50-50 deal, if the graphic artist's expenses are higher than the writer's, these may be reimbursed before the 50-50 split takes effect.
2. *CREDIT.* Whose name goes first? Are both considered authors? Does the credit say "by J. Writer, illustrations by L. Illustrator," or are the two to be treated equally, with the credit simply stating that the book is by both of them? Obviously, it is better for the graphic artist if the credit reads "by L. Graphic Artist, text by J. Writer." Sometimes the issue is determined by looking at who came up with the original idea for the project or book.
3. *COPYRIGHT.* Usually a contract calls for the artwork to be

copyrighted in the artist's name and the text to be copyrighted in the writer's name. This protects both with respect to the work that they originate.

4. *SUBSIDIARY RIGHTS*. Often subsidiary income derived exclusively from the artwork remains solely the artist's property, although in some deals it's just a 50-50 split on everything.

Other issues to be considered are: whose agent handles the book? What happens if one party dies during the course of the project? Who exercises artistic control (if any)? Should disputes be resolved through arbitration? Who owns the book concept if you find you can't work together after you get started?

Sales of Originals

These transactions involve the sale of originals or limited-edition prints. Sales are usually made pursuant to a "bill of sale," which should provide the following:

- Names and addresses of the parties.
- Date.
- Price of the painting, print, or portfolio and terms for payment.
- A description of the item(s) transferred, including size, subjects, medium (black-and-white or color), whether framed or matted, and whether signed or unsigned.
- A statement that all reproduction rights and copyright are reserved and owned solely by the artist.
- A statement, if applicable, by the artist warranting that a print is "one of a limited edition of _____ copies, numbered as follows: _____."

In very special cases the artist might consider trying to secure additional rights, such as these:

- A royalty on any profits derived from retransfer of the artwork.
- A share of rental income or a limitation on exhibiting the artwork generally.
- Permission to reacquire possession of the work for brief periods for exhibition purposes.
- A prohibition against destroying or modifying the work.

Such additional provisions, often loosely referred to as moral rights, have only infrequently been imposed, although the State of California has recently enacted a law providing for the artist to secure a percentage of the profit on resales of artwork in certain cases.

Textile Designs

SALES

The field of textile design is changing radically and rapidly. Royalties and return of originals, unheard of only a few years ago, are no longer uncommon, thanks in part to the excellent work of the Graphic Artists Guild in disseminating information and encouraging higher professional standards. Limits on clients' or customers' uses, never asked for before, have now become almost commonplace. Accordingly, your order form or other bill of sale should specify the following:

1. *PATTERN NUMBER.* Specify the exact pattern being sold.
2. *SKETCH.* Indicate whether the client is buying the sketch only (the original pattern).
3. *REPEATS.* If repeats (additional versions of the original sketch) are ordered, indicate precisely what size, color, and price are involved with each one.
4. *USAGE LIMITS.* Common limits on usage are for fabric only, or even more specifically for bedding, toweling, or curtains only, or the like. This, of course, permits the designer to resell in related but noncompetitive markets.
5. *ROYALTY.* If a royalty deal is made the protections you will need regarding regular statements, accounting, right to inspect the books, and advances are set forth on pages 98–100 regarding royalty agreements in the novelty-product area. Royalties in the textile area are often in the range of 3 percent to 5 percent of manufacturer's receipts on the fabric based on your design, or the equivalent stated in cents per yard.
6. *RETURN OF ORIGINALS.* If you want your originals back, be sure to specify that and make the client aware of your requirement. It also helps to mount the design firmly on rigid board that won't bend when the design is sent to the mill for the print run. In any event, you would be wise to photograph each important design you do so that reproductions can be made in the event of loss or damage.
7. *SALES TAX.* You will probably be liable for, and therefore must collect, sales tax on many sales of textile designs, unless

you are limiting your client's right of usage *and* getting your originals returned. You should specify that the client is liable for sales tax on your bill of sale.

8. *ARBITRATION.* You may want to insert a requirement to arbitrate disputes as provided for in the designer's and illustrator's assignment agreement forms referred to on pages 93–96.

RECEIPT FOR DESIGNS SUBMITTED

In some cases you may have to leave designs for review and then pick them up later. You should get a receipt acknowledging exactly what you have left, and that receipt should specify the following:

- The identifying number and price of each sketch submitted.
- The customer's agreement not to copy your work or instruct anyone else to copy it.
- An agreement to pay you the price indicated for each sketch damaged or lost.
- A specific number of working days after which the design must be returned or the full purchase price will be considered due.
- An agreement to arbitrate disputes, as discussed under sales of designs.

SIMILARS AND "KNOCKOFFS"

You may be called upon to produce a design that is similar to an existing design. To protect yourself you should have a short form on which your client agrees that:

- The design is similar to but does not infringe upon the design in question (and describe that similar design);
- The client will indemnify you against all claims, costs, expenses, and attorney fees due to any suit for violation of copyright or other personal or property rights.

AGENTS

Many textile designers sell through commission agents. Often a considerable amount of work will be in the hands of one, or at most a limited number, of such agents, possibly for an extended period of time. Textile designers should take some reasonable steps to protect themselves in those situations. An agreement with the agent should specify the following:

- *The agent's commission*—in this connection there may be one "regular" commission for normal sales and another for sales to your own prior regular customers, often referred to as house accounts; the commissions on house accounts may well be lower than the commission on regular sales.
- *The scope of the agent's market*—which is usually expressed as a geographical limitation on the area in which the agent can represent you.
- *The agent's responsibility to take reasonable care of your work*—and possibly also a statement that the agent is liable for the work if it is handled negligently.
- *A time limit*—the period of time during which the contract shall be in force.
- *A provision for when you should be paid*—normally within 14 days after the agent is paid; also state when you should receive an accounting (quarterly statements are thought to be sensible), and include a provision for you to inspect the agent's books upon reasonable notice with respect to your own sales and proceeds.
- *Termination clause*—usually permitting discontinuance of the contract by either party on 30 days' notice and limiting the agent's commissions to sales as of the end of that 30-day period, and requiring return to you of all remaining originals in the agent's hands.
- *An arbitration clause*—as discussed under the subject of sales of textile designs.

Most important—and this is a subject which really cannot be covered by the contract—you should get the agent to sign for each piece received, including therein an estimate of its selling price, so that there is no confusion about which items the agent must account for either as sales or as returns of originals. At the very least, you should make up a form, a copy of which you deliver to the agent with every piece or group of pieces you present for sale. That form should indicate the pattern number and have a brief description of each piece. On the copy you retain you can note the sales price of each piece sold, leaving you with an accurate record of what remains with your agent.

CHAPTER 7

The Going Concern

MOST PEOPLE don't leap into a profession. They test and explore it first and gradually intensify their commitment. This is as true of illustration and graphic design as it is of any other entrepreneurial activity. Many illustrators and designers start part-time while going to school or working at another job. But once you begin to market your work effectively, questions inevitably arise as to the basics of operating a business. Should it be incorporated? Where should it be located? What kind of records do you need? What taxes will you have to pay?

Making decisions about these kinds of questions requires knowledge. Your knowledge can be gleaned from experience or from advisers with expertise in accounting, law, and business. The most important skill that you must have is that of problem recognition. Once you're aware that you face a problem, you can solve it—by yourself or with expert help.

Form of Doing Business

You will probably start out in the world of business as a *sole proprietor*. That means that you own your business, are responsible for all its debts, and reap the rewards of all its profits. You file Schedule C, "Profit or (Loss) From Business or Profession," with your Federal Tax Form 1040 each year and keep the records described in the next chapter. The advantages of being a sole proprietor are simplicity and a lack of expense in starting out.

However, you have to consider other possible forms in which your business can be conducted. Your expert advisers may decide that being a corporation or partnership will be better for you than being a sole proprietor. Naturally you want to understand what each of these different choices would mean. One of the most important considerations in choosing between a sole proprietorship, a partnership, and a corporation is taxation. Another significant consideration is personal liability—whether you will personally have to pay for the debts of the business if it goes bankrupt.

As sole proprietor, *you* are the business. Its income and expenses are your income and expenses. Its assets and liabilities are your assets and liabilities. The business is you, because you have not created any other legal entity.

Why consider a *partnership?* Perhaps because it would be advantageous for you to join with other professionals so you can share certain expenses, facilities, and possibly clients. Sometimes two or more heads really are wiser than one. If you join a partnership, you'll want to protect yourself by having a partnership agreement drawn up before starting the business. As a partner, you are liable for the debts of the partnership, even if one of the other partners incurs the debts. And creditors of the partnership can recover from you personally if the partnership doesn't have enough assets to pay the debts that it owes. So you want to make sure that none of your partners is going to run up big debts that you end up paying for from your own pocket. The profits and losses going to each partner are worked out in the partnership agreement. Your share of the profits and losses is taxed directly to you as an individual. In other words, the partnership files a tax return but does not pay a tax. Only the partners pay taxes, based on their share of profit or loss.

A variation of the partnership is the *limited partnership.* If you have a lot of talent and no money, you may want to team up with someone who can bankroll the business. This investor would not take an active role in the business, so he or she could be a limited partner who would not have personal liability for the debts of the partnership. You, as the creative party, would take an active role and be the general partner. You would have personal liability for the partnership's debts. You and the investor could agree to allocate the profits equally but to give a disproportionate share of any tax losses to the investor (such as 90 percent). This hedges the investor's risk, since the investor is presumably in a much higher tax bracket than you are and will benefit by having losses (although profits are naturally better than losses, no matter how much income the investor has).

The next avenue to consider is that of a *Subchapter S corporation.* This is a special type of corporation. It does provide limited liability for its shareholders, which is what you would be. However, there is basically no tax on corporate income. Instead, the profit or loss received by the corporation is divided among the shareholders, who are taxed individually as partners would be. An advantage of incorporation is the business deductions the Subchapter S corporation can take that would be denied to a sole proprietor. The corporation is able to deduct premiums for medical insurance and, in certain cases, for life insurance. It can also make the same tax-deductible contributions to a retirement plan for you that you would be able to make as a sole proprietor. The disadvantage of incorporating is the added expense and extra paperwork.

What you normally think of as a corporation is not the Subchapter S corporation but what we'll call the *regular corporation*. The regular corporation provides limited liability for its shareholders. Only the corporation is liable for its debts, not the shareholders. You should keep in mind, however, that many lenders will require shareholders to sign personally on a loan to the corporation. In such cases you do have personal liability, but it's probably the only way the corporation will be able to get a loan.

The key difference in creating a regular corporation is that it is taxed on its own taxable income. There is a federal corporate income tax with increasing rates as follows:

- 16 percent on taxable income up to $25,000 (15% starting 1982)
- 19 percent on taxable income from $25,000 to $50,000 (18% starting 1982)
- 30 percent on taxable income from $50,000 to $75,000
- 40 percent on taxable income from $75,000 to $100,000
- 46 percent on all taxable income over $100,000

In addition, there may be state and local corporate income tax to pay. By paying yourself a salary, of course, you create a deduction for the corporation that lowers its taxable income. You would then pay tax on your salary as would any other employee. If, however, the corporation were to pay you dividends as a shareholder, two taxes would be paid on the same income. First, the corporation would pay tax on its taxable income, then it would distribute dividends and you would have to pay tax on the dividends.

The advantages of the regular corporation include the ability to deduct as a business expense the cost of premiums for medical insurance and, in certain cases, for life insurance. Also, the corporation can make greater tax-deductible contributions to your retirement plan than you would be able to make as an individual. The disadvantages include, again, extra paperwork and the need for meetings, as well as the expenses of creating and, if necessary, dissolving the corporation.

From this brief discussion you can see why expert advice is a necessity if you're considering forming a partnership or a corporation. Such advice may seem costly in the short run, but in the long run it may not only save you money but also give you peace of mind.

Business Location

The location of your business is extremely significant. You must be able to reach the buyers with whom you'll be transacting business, whether they come to your studio or you go to their offices. You must consider the location not only from the marketing viewpoint but also with respect to rent, amounts of available space (compared to your needs), competition, accessibility of facilities that you need (such as stat houses or typesetters), and terms under which you can obtain the space. Speak to other illustrators and designers operating similar businesses in the area to find out all you can.

Since many illustrators and designers have their studios in their homes, it's worth considering this as the first option. You'll save on rent and gain in convenience. However, you may not be near your market, and you may also have trouble taking the fullest possible tax deductions for space that you use. The deduction of a studio at home is discussed on pages 132–134.

Another potential problem with having a studio at home is zoning. In many localities the zoning regulations will not permit commercial activity in districts zoned for residential use. If you didn't realize this you could invest a great deal of money setting up a studio, only to find you could not legally use it. But even when the zoning law says a home may not be used for commercial purposes, problems usually only arise when your business requires a flow of people to and from the premises, whether they are clients or people making deliveries. The more visibly you do business, the more likely you are to face zoning difficulties. If you are considering setting up your studio in a residentially zoned area, you should definitely consult a local attorney for advice.

What happens if you rent a commercial space for your studio and decide to live there? This has become more and more common in urban centers where rents are high. You run the risk of eviction, since living in the studio will probably violate your lease as well as the zoning law. Some localities don't enforce commercial zoning regulations, but you must be wary if you are planning to sink a great deal of your resources and time into fixing a commercial space with the plan of living there. Especially in this situation you should ask advice from an attorney, who can then also advise you how to negotiate your lease.

Negotiating Your Lease

It's worth saying a few words of warning here about the risks involved in fixing your studio. You can lay out thousands of dollars to put up walls; to put in wiring and plumbing; and to redecorate and refurbish your space in every way so that it's suitable for your special needs. What protects you when you do this?

If you're renting, your protection is your lease. The more you plan to invest in your space, the more protection you need under your lease. There are several crucial points to consider:

- length of the lease
- option to renew
- right to sublet
- ownership of fixtures
- right to terminate
- hidden lease costs

You have to know that you are going to be able to use your fixed-up space long enough to justify having spent so much money on it. A long lease term guarantees this for you. But what if you want to keep your options open? A more flexible device is an option to renew. For example, instead of taking a 10-year lease, you could take a 5-year lease with a 5-year option to renew. But you want to guarantee not only that you'll be able to stay in the space, but also that you can sell your fixtures when you leave. In most leases, the landlord owns all the fixtures when you leave, regardless of who put them in the space. If you want to own your fixtures and be able to resell them, a specific clause in the lease would be helpful.

The right to sublet your space—that is, to rent to someone else who pays rent to you—is also important. Most leases forbid this, but if you are selling fixtures, it can be important who the new tenant is. Your power to sublet means you can choose the new tenant (who can then stay there for as much of your lease term as you want to allow). On the other hand, you may not be able to find a subtenant. If your business and the rental market are bad, you may simply want to get out of your lease regardless of the value of the fixtures you've put into the space. In this situation the right to terminate your lease will enable you to end your obligations under the lease and leave whenever you want to. Remember that without a right of termination, your obligation to pay rent to the landlord will continue to the end of the lease term, even if you vacate the premises (unless the landlord is able to find a new tenant).

In every lease you should look for hidden lease costs. These are likely to be *escalators*—automatic increases in your rent based on various increasing costs. Many leases provide for increased rent if fuel prices increase. Others require you to pay a higher rent each year based on increases in the consumer price index. Of course you want to know about all these hidden costs—whether to include them in your budget or to try to negotiate them out of the lease.

This is a very brief discussion of the negotiation of your lease. Your attorney can aid you with the ins and outs of negotiating a lease.

Business Names

Registering the name of your business is usually done with the county clerk in the county in which you have your studio. The purpose of this registration is to ensure that the public knows who is transacting business. Thus, partnerships must file and disclose the names of the partners. Individuals doing business under an assumed name must disclose their true identity. But an individual doing business under his or her own name is usually not obligated to file with the county clerk. In any case, you should call the county clerk to find out whether you must comply with such requirements. The fee is usually not high.

Your Budget

Starting a business requires planning. You have to estimate your expenses and your income, not just for the first year but for as many years into the future as you can reasonably project. Some expenses happen only once, while others recur each year. You have to take both kinds into account and should refer to the example given on pages 69–71.

For starting costs you may have to pay only once; consider the following list:

- fixtures and equipment
- installation of fixtures and equipment

- decorating and remodeling
- legal and other professional fees
- advertising and promotion for opening

Of course you must realistically think through the outlays you are going to have to make. Daydreaming can be pleasant, but in business it can easily become a nightmare.

What about the outlays that you'll have to make every month? Here's a partial list:

- your own salary
- any other salaries
- rent
- advertising
- materials and supplies
- insurance premiums
- maintenance
- legal and other professional fees
- taxes (usually paid in four installments during the year)
- miscellaneous

Maybe the last category is the most important, because it's the unexpected need for cash that leads to trouble for most businesses. If you can plan properly you will ensure that you can meet all your needed outlays. And don't leave out your own salary. Martyrs don't make the most successful business owners. If you worked for someone else, you'd get a salary. To see realistically whether your business is making a profit, you must compute a salary for yourself. If you can't pay yourself a salary, you have to consider whether you'd be doing better working for someone else.

Your income is the next consideration. What sort of track record do you have? Are you easing from one field of illustration or graphic design into another field in which you're likely to have success? Or are you striking out toward an unknown horizon, a brave new world? You have to assess, in a fairly conservative way, how much income you're likely to have. If you just don't know, an assessment of zero is certainly safe.

What we're talking about is *cash flow. Cash flow* is the relationship between the influx of cash into your business and the outflow of cash from your business. If you don't plan to invest enough money in your business initially, you are likely to be *undercapitalized.* This simply means that you don't have enough money. Each month you find yourself falling a little further behind in paying your bills.

Maybe this means your business is going to fail. But it may mean that you just didn't plan very well. You have to realize that almost all businesses go through an initial start-up period during which they lose money. Even the Internal Revenue Service recognizes this. So after you plan for your start-up expenses and your monthly expenses (with an extra amount added in to cover contingencies you can't think of at the moment), you can see how much cash you're going to need to carry the business until it becomes profitable. Your investment should be enough to carry the business through at least one year without cash-flow problems. If possible, you should plan to make a cash investment that will carry the business even beyond one year. Be realistic. If you know that you're going to have a profit in the first year, that's wonderful. But if it may take you a year or two before you have a profit, plan for it. It's easy to work out the numbers so you'll be a millionaire overnight, but it's not realistic. In fact, it's a direct path to bankruptcy. But once you realize you need money to avoid being undercapitalized when you start or expand your business, where are you going to be able to find the amount you need?

Sources of Funds

The most obvious source of funds is your own savings. You don't have to pay interest on it, and there's no due date when you'll have to give it back. But don't think it isn't costing you anything, because it is. Just calculate the current interest rate—for example, the rate on short-term United States Treasury notes—on what you've invested in your business. That's the amount you could have by sitting back and sipping iced tea—without spending all those hours in the studio.

What if you don't have any savings and your spouse isn't keen on donating half of his or her salary to support your studio? Of course you can look for investors among family, friends, or people who simply believe you're going to create a profitable business. One problem with investors is that they're hard to find. Another problem is that they share in your profits if you succeed. And after all, isn't it your talent that's making the business a success? But if you're going to have cash-flow problems and are fortunate enough to find a willing investor, you'll be wise to take advantage of this source of funds.

The next source is your friendly banker. Banks are in the business of making money by lending money, so you'd think they'd be happy to have you as a client. You may be the lucky graphic designer or illustrator who finds such a bank, but most loan officers know that the commercial-art business carries high risks and is unpredictable. So if you're going to have any chance of convincing the bank to make a loan, you must take the right approach. You should dress in a way that a banker can understand. You should know exactly how much money you want, because simply saying "I need a loan" or asking for too much or too little money is going to create a bad impression. It will show that you haven't done the planning necessary to succeed. You should be able to detail precisely how the money will be used. You should provide a history of your business from a financial standpoint and also give a forecast.

One prediction you must make when you gaze into your crystal ball is that your business is going to generate the funds necessary to repay the loan. And you must have good business records, as discussed in the next chapter, in order to make an effective presentation to the bank. The loan officer must believe in the quality of management that you offer to your business. One other point to keep in mind is the importance of building a relationship with your banker. If he or she comes to know and trust you, you're going to have a much better chance of getting a loan.

But, frankly, bank loans are going to be very difficult for many illustrators and designers to obtain. Where can you turn next? The most likely source is borrowing from family and friends at a reasonable interest rate. Of course you have to pay back these loans whether or not your business succeeds (if you didn't have to pay back the money, you'd be dealing with investors rather than lenders). Another possibility is borrowing against your whole life insurance policy, if you have one. You can borrow up to the cash value, and the interest rate is usually far below the current rate at which you would be borrowing from a bank. And, if you have been able to obtain credit cards that have a line of credit (that is, that permit you to borrow up to $250, $500, or more on each card), you can exercise your right to borrow. Depending on the number of cards you have and the amounts of the credit lines, you may be able to borrow several thousand dollars in this way. You should plan to repay credit-card cash advances promptly to avoid the high interest rates imposed on money borrowed in this way.

Trade credit will undoubtedly be an important source of funds for you. It's invisible, but it greatly improves your cash flow. Trade credit is simply your right to be billed by your suppliers. The best way to build up trade credit is to be absolutely reliable. In this way your suppliers come to trust you and are willing to let you owe greater and greater amounts. Of course you must pay promptly, but you are paying roughly 30 days later than you would pay on a cash transaction.

The other side of the coin is your own extension of credit to your clients. This creates *accounts receivable*. Now, accounts receivable are an asset of your business, but how can you convert accounts receivable into cash when you desperately need it? You can *factor* your accounts receivable. This means that you sell your accounts receivable to another company—the factor—that collects the accounts receivable for you. What does the factor pay for the accounts receivable? The factor gives you the full amount of the accounts receivable, less a service charge. The effect of the service charge can be an annual interest rate of 30 to 50 percent for a small business. Incredible? Yes, and take warning. Using factors isn't the magic trick it appears at first. In fact, it's inviting disaster. If your cash flow is bad, factoring is likely to make it much worse in the long run. And the reason you would have to factor is poor planning in the first place. You were undercapitalized.

Another possible source of funds is the Small Business Administration (SBA). It's mentioned in passing here because it has not looked too favorably on loans to illustrators and graphic designers over the years. But it's certainly worth an exploratory telephone call to see whether your local SBA office might be atypical.

The true message is *not* to borrow unless you know you're going to be able to repay the money from your business. There's no point in borrowing from one source after another as your business slides closer toward bankruptcy. Not only should you *not* factor your accounts receivable, but you should not borrow against your life insurance cash value or draw on your credit lines unless you know definitely that you will be doing the business necessary to pay back that money. Being adequately capitalized is a necessity if you are to have that wonderful feeling of confidence that comes from knowing that your business has the stamina to survive early losses and succeed.

Expansion

Expanding is much like starting a business. You must be adequately capitalized for the expansion to be successful. This means reviewing your expenses and your income so you can calculate exactly how the expansion will affect your overall business. Then you have to decide whether you have the cash flow to finance the expansion from the income of the business. If you don't, once again you must consider sources of financing. If you're buying equipment, keep equipment-financing companies in mind as a potential credit source.

One of the most important reasons to expand is an economic one—the economies derived from larger-scale operations. These benefits may appear especially attractive to designers, although illustrators also can gain by expansion. For example, pooling with a number of other professionals may enable you to purchase equipment you couldn't otherwise afford, hire a receptionist that your business alone couldn't fully utilize, or purchase supplies in quantities sufficient to justify a discount. If you can hire an assistant who earns you enough money or saves you enough time to make more than the assistant's salary (and related overhead expenses), the hiring of the assistant may very well be justified.

On the other hand, expansion is hardly a panacea. In the first place, you'll probably have difficulty financing any major expansion from the cash flow of the business. Beyond this, expansion ties you into certain expenses. Suddenly you have an assistant, a secretary, a bookkeeper. You need more space, and your rent goes higher. You're taking more work so your expenses increase for all your materials. You find that you must take more and more work in order to meet your overhead. You may even consider a rep, if you can get one, because you need to do a greater volume of business. But the rep will take 25 percent in commissions, so that's hardly going to solve your need for more productive jobs.

Suddenly you realize that you've reached a very dangerous plateau and that you're faced with a choice that will have lasting consequences for your career. You expanded because you wanted to earn more. But the more resources that you brought under your control—whether equipment, personnel, or studio space—the more time you had to spend managing these resources to make them productive. Now, you must decide whether you are going to become a manager of a successful business or cut back and return to being primarily a designer or an illustrator. If you choose to be a manager, you had better be a very good one. If you go the expansion route, it's very painful to have to cut back if the business temporarily hits hard times—firing employees, giving up space you've labored to fix up, and so on. The alternative to being a manager is to aim for building a small business with highly productive accounts. You can be an artist again without worrying so much about the overhead and the volume you're going to have to generate in order to meet it. Of course, you'll make your own decisions, but be certain that you're keeping the business headed in the direction that *you* want it to take.

Extending Credit

It's worth discussing your credit policies, since cash flow is at the core of so many business problems. It may seem that you're locked into industry practice with respect to billing and being paid after completion of an assignment. But many professionals are now requesting advances, especially against expenses, so that they don't have to finance clients for months at a time.

But if you're forced to extend credit, what will this mean for your business? The longer an amount owed to you is overdue, the less likely you are to collect it. The following approximations are a good guide:

- If a debt is overdue 60 to 90 days, you have a 90 percent chance of collecting it.
- If a debt is overdue 3 to 6 months, you have a 70 percent chance of collecting it.
- If a debt is overdue 6 months to 1 year, you have a 60 percent chance of collecting it.
- If a debt is overdue 1 to 2 years, you have a 40 percent chance of collecting it.
- If the debt is overdue more than 2 years, the percentage you're likely to recover drops until the fifth year, when it becomes unlikely you'll ever collect.

What does all this mean? That you must have a firm policy about extending credit and pursuing collections. You should grant credit only to clients who have a good reputation (based on occupation, address and length of residence, bank references, professional credit-rating agencies, and personal references), a sound financial position, and measurable success in their own business (especially if the client is an agency or a corporate client that will expect to be billed as a matter of course), and who are willing to accept conditions that you may place on the extension of credit (such as maximum amounts of credit you extend, maximum amounts of time for payment, and similar provisions). By the way, if you feel you don't want to extend credit to a client who absolutely expects it, you should not do business with that client. You must constantly check your credit system to make sure it's functioning properly (more than half your accounts should pay in full on receipt of your statement).

If you have a client who won't pay, you have to initiate collection procedures. You start with a reminder that the account has not been paid. This can simply be the sending of your invoice stamped "Past Due." Or you might use a pleasant form letter to bring the debt to the attention of the client. If this fails you should make a request to your client for an explanation. Obviously it isn't an oversight that the client has failed to pay. There may be a valid explanation for not paying. In any case, you must find out—usually by sending a letter requesting the necessary information. If the client still does not pay, you can assume that you're not going to collect without applying pressure. What kind of pressure? Whatever kind—within the bounds of the law—that you judge will get your money without your having to use an attorney or collection agency. You can escalate through all the following options:

- sending letters
- making telephone calls
- sending registered letters, mailgrams, and telegrams
- cutting off credit
- threatening to report to a credit bureau
- threatening to use an attorney or collection agency
- using an attorney or collection agency

Of course, you should never threaten people unless you intend to back up your words. You must act decisively if after threatening to take a certain action, you still are not paid. The use of attorneys, collection agencies, and small-claims courts is discussed on pages 216–221. You will bear an expense in using an attorney or collection agency to collect, but you may still be able to get part of the money owed you. And you will have a reputation as someone who won't stand for clients who don't pay what they owe.

Sales and Miscellaneous Taxes

Many states and cities have taxes that affect illustrators and graphic designers. Included here are sales taxes, unincorporated-business taxes, commercial-occupancy taxes, and inventory taxes. You should check in your own state and locality to determine whether any such taxes exist and apply to you. By far the most common tax is the sales tax, and it deserves a more extensive discussion.

The sales tax is levied on sales of tangible personal property. For example, if a book is sold by a bookstore, a sales tax must be paid. When you are finding out about the sales tax in your state, be certain to check on the following points:

- If you only sell reproduction rights—and you get back your original art without any retouching—is the sale taxable? Since reproduction rights are not tangible property, many states do not tax their sale.
- If you do sell the artwork itself as well as the reproduction rights, can you accept a resale certificate from your client instead of collecting the tax? If the client is going to resell the art, you may not have to collect the sales tax. Instead, the client collects the sales tax when it resells the art as part of its finished product.
- If you sell out of state, do you have to collect the sales tax? If an out-of-state sale is exempt from tax, you should keep shipping receipts and the like so you can prove where you delivered the art in the event of an audit.
- If you include expenses in your bill, should the tax be collected only on your fee for the sale of the art or should it be collected on your fee plus the amount of the expenses? If you are advised to collect on the total amount, find out what would happen if you billed the expenses separately from your fee for the art.
- If you sell your art to certain charitable or governmental organizations, are they exempt from having to pay the sales tax? If so, they will probably have to provide you with a certificate showing that they are exempt from paying the tax.
- Is production equipment used to create tangible property exempt from the sales tax? Some states have this exemption and consider cameras, stat machines, and even layouts to be production equipment. Thus if you were selling a layout, you might not have to collect tax on this basis.
- Finally, if you register with the sales-tax bureau, you may be entitled not to pay tax on items that you purchase for resale or production. This might cover anything to be incorporated into an artwork that will be resold or any item to be used in producing a product for sale.

These laws vary from state to state and city to city. You must check in your locality. The simplest way is by calling your local sales tax bureau. Find out how your state handles the issues listed here so that you can collect the tax—or refrain from collecting it—in a legal manner. Also, if you are relying on someone's exemption as a reason not to collect the tax—perhaps because he or she will resell the art, or the art will be used to produce tangible items for sale, or the sale was to a charity—be certain to obtain written proof of the exemption. Otherwise you may be liable to pay the tax if, in fact, it should have been collected. Your client may also be liable, but that will be small consolation if the client is no longer in business or has moved its operations to South America.

Small Business Administration

The Small Business Administration is interested in helping small businesses succeed. Its offices are located throughout the country. You can attend the many courses that SBA sponsors, such as Free Pre-Business Workshop, Preparing a Business Plan, and Small Business Tax Workshop. Many of these courses are free; others charge a modest admission fee. The SBA also makes available many publications to enhance the chances of a small business being successful, such as *Checklist for Going into Business*. A full bibliography of SBA publications is available from the nearest SBA field office or by writing to the SBA, Washington, D.C. 20416. The publications are either free or inexpensive.

In addition, you can call your local SBA office and speak to or meet with a counselor who will help you with your specific problem. While these counselors are likely to have had limited contact with designers and illustrators, you may still get some helpful advice. The Service Corps of Retired Business Executives (SCORE) has been formed under the SBA and brings the experience and wisdom of successful business people to the counseling program.

CHAPTER 8

Your Business Records

TO MAKE INTELLIGENT BUSINESS DECISIONS, you must have good business records. These records are also a necessity for completing your tax forms, keeping track of your jobs, and maintaining files so you can take advantage of reuse opportunities.

Tax Records

If you want to avoid trouble with the Internal Revenue Service, you must keep your books in order. One of the most common reasons for the disallowance of deductions is simply the lack of records to corroborate the expenses. Your records can, however, be simple. And you don't have to know a lot of technical terms. You only have to record your income and expenses accurately so that you can determine how much you owe in taxes for the year.

You will probably want to keep a simple ledger or diary in which you enter your items of income and expense as they arise. This would mean that you enter the items regularly as they occur—at least on a weekly basis—and don't wait until the end of the year to make the entries. If you're consistent this way, you will be able to take some expenses even if they're not documented by receipts or canceled checks. The ledger or diary should include a log of business travel, local automobile mileage, and the details of any entertainment or gift expenses.

It's wise to have either canceled checks or receipts for most of your expense items. You should open a business checking account so that the distinction between personal and business expenditures is clear. If an item raises a question, you will want to make a note in your records as to why it is for business and not personal.

You should also keep a permanent record of expenditures for capital assets—those assets that have a useful life of more than 1 year—such as a photocopier. This is necessary for you to justify the depreciation expense you will compute for the assets. In addition, grant letters, contracts, and especially tax returns should be retained as part of your permanent files.

Even if you use an accountant, you will have to keep your records neatly and in a regular manner. To do this you should have an Expense Ledger and an Income Ledger. The Expense Ledger could be set up in the form shown on page 125. Each time you incur an expense, you make two entries. First you put the amount under Total cash if you paid with cash or Total check if you paid by check. Then you enter the amount under the appropriate expense heading. In this way you can be certain of your addition, because the total of the entries under Total cash and Total check should equal the total of the entries under all the columns for specific expenses. If you paid $48 in cash for office supplies on January 2, 1982, the entry of $48 would appear once under Total cash and once under Office supplies. If on January 4 you then paid $150 for the use of several photographs, the entry of $150 would appear under Total check and under Photography/illustration expense. Ledger books with many columned sheets can be purchased at any good stationery store.

If you coordinate the expense categories in your Expense Ledger with those on Schedule C of your income-tax form (pages 146–147), you can save a lot of time when you have to fill out your tax forms.

How should you file receipts you get for paying your expenses? A simple method is to have a Bills Paid file in which you put these receipts in alphabetical order. An accordion-type file works fine, and you'll be able to locate the various receipts easily.

Expense Ledger

Date	Item	Total cash	Total check	Legal and accounting	Art supplies	Office supplies	Salaries	Model fees	Advertising	Props and wardrobe	Entertainment	Rent	Utilities	Commissions	Free-lance assistants	Meals and lodging	Transportation	Telephone	Printing	Equipment	Typesetting	Insurance	Photography/illustration	Miscellaneous

After you have set up your Expense Ledger, you have to set up your Income Ledger. This can be done with the following format:

Income Ledger

Date	Client or customer	Job no.	Total Received	Fee	Billable Expenses	Sales tax	Other
1/3	Acme Advertising	35	$1155	$700	$375	$80	
1/6	Johnson Publishing	43	$460	$315	$145		

We've assumed that you are using the simplest form of bookkeeping. If you were to use more complicated bookkeeping, you would probably have your books set up by an accountant and the entries made by a bookkeeper. However, if you accurately keep the records we've just described, you'll be able to support your deductions in the event of an audit.

Tracking and Billing Jobs

Especially if you are a designer, you should know the precise expense for each job. If you're working for a fee plus expenses, you usually need to show the client proof of expenses in the form of copies of receipts. If you're working on a flat-fee basis, as illustrators are more likely to do, you need to know whether you charged enough both to cover expenses and make a reasonable profit.

This problem can be handled by setting up a "job" envelope or "job file" for each job. The envelope or file (we'll refer only to envelope hereafter) creates one specific place where all the records for each job are placed—all the receipts, releases, contracts, and other documents. It should contain suppliers' receipts, labor-cost invoices, and petty cash or other vouchers indicating what you used from your own inventory, the car mileage used on your own car or a record of taxi trips, and the like. Thus, when the job has been completed, you or your accountant, secretary, or bookkeeper can go to one single file or source to secure all the information needed to prepare an invoice.

On each job envelope you should mark the client's name and delivery date. You should also establish a number for each job and write that on the envelope. All your job numbers should be in sequence. That way you will always be sure to bill for every job. Months later you can look at all your invoices. If a number is missing you will know that a job was not billed and that you need to make further inquiry.

As an additional precaution, you can set up a job ledger that contains the information you are most frequently called on to look up about particular jobs. Each job is entered into the job ledger as soon as the assignment is given. The columns in the ledger might appear in this form:

Job Ledger

Job no.	Client	Delivery date	Fee	Reimbursed expenses	Sales tax	Total	Advance	Balance Due	Billing date	Payment date

Using this kind of ledger, you can easily monitor your billing procedures and determine how quickly (or slowly) you are being paid.

Miscellaneous Files

There are a number of routine alphabetical files that you will need. You may keep separate filing-cabinet drawers with separators for your alphabetical index, or, especially when you are starting out, you may prefer the less complex accordion file. This type of file is available at any stationery store in a variety of sizes and consists of a self-contained, expandable unit with a compartment for each letter of the alphabet. The files that you will want to keep include:

- Bills payable and bills paid. The bills you must pay are usually filed alphabetically in an accordion file (as just described) and processed on a monthly or semimonthly basis. Once a bill has been paid, you should file the voucher or customer copy in your Bills Paid file. These files should be stored on an annual basis to conform to your tax records.
- Accounts receivable and accounts paid. You should make one or preferably two copies of every invoice you send out. These should be kept in a separate chronological file. You can check that file regularly to make sure you're being paid for all jobs on a reasonably timely basis. Once the bill has been paid, of course, the invoice copy should be transferred to an Accounts Paid file that, again, should be kept on an annual basis to conform to your tax records.
- Releases. Model or property releases should be filed in the job envelope for which the releases were obtained. As an added precaution, you may want to photocopy each release and maintain a separate file alphabetized by the names of the models or property owners.
- Other files. Depending upon the amount of documentation you develop, you may want to have separate drawers or accordion files for such items as credit applications, copyright applications, and contracts.

Where to Keep Your Records

You should have a part of your studio set aside for your records. It should be secure and not accessible to casual visitors. The records should be carefully organized in standard metal filing cabinets (letter or legal size, depending on your taste). The area you select for maintaining and reviewing the records should be free of clutter and unrelated activity, so that the record-keeping can be done efficiently and without mistakes.

CHAPTER 9

Taxes

IN *The Wasteland,* T.S. Eliot called April "the cruelest month." But if you work at your tax records on a regular basis, you'll be prepared for April's arrival. It is true that businesses, including freelancers, face a more difficult task in preparing their taxes than does the ordinary taxpayer who simply earns a salary. You should, however, be able to take advantage of many of the tax-saving ideas in this chapter. If you can't do it alone, you can certainly do it with the help of an accountant and a good record-keeping system such as the one described in the previous chapter.

Tax Years and Accounting Methods

Your tax year is probably the calendar year, running from January 1 through December 31. This means that your income and expenses between those dates are used to fill out Schedule C, Profit or (Loss) From Business or Profession. Schedule C is attached to your Form 1040 when you file your tax return in April.

What's the alternative to using the calendar year as your tax year? You could have what's called a fiscal year. This means a tax year starting from a date other than January 1, such as from July 1 through June 30. Most artists use the calendar year, and if you do use a fiscal year, you will almost certainly have an accountant. For these reasons we are going to assume that you are using a calendar year.

But how do you know whether income you receive or expenses you pay fall into your tax year? This depends on the accounting method that you use. Under the cash method, which most illustrators and designers use, you receive income for tax purposes when you in fact receive the income. That's just what you would expect. And you incur an expense for tax purposes when you actually pay out the money for the expense. So it's easy to know which tax year your items of income and expense should be recorded in.

What is the alternative to cash-method accounting? It's called accrual accounting. Essentially it provides that you record an item of income when you have a right to receive it and record an item of expense when you are obligated to pay it. Once again, you will probably have an accountant if you use the accrual method, so we will focus on the more typical case of the professional who uses the cash method.

One final assumption is that you are a sole proprietor and not a partnership or corporation. However, the general principles discussed in this chapter apply to all forms of doing business.

Income

Income for tax purposes includes all the money generated by your business—fees, royalties, sales of art, and so on. Prizes and awards will usually be included in income, unless they're the kind of prizes or awards that you receive without having to make any application (such as the Nobel prize). On the other hand, grants can frequently be excluded from income as long as they are not paid in return for services or primarily to benefit the grant-giving organization. Degree candidates can deduct the full amount of such grants. Professionals who are not working toward a degree can deduct grants only as follows:

- up to $300 per month
- for no more than 36 months (consecutive or otherwise) during your lifetime
- only if the grant comes from certain governmental, nonprofit, or international organizations

Expenses related to the grants are also excluded from income (and don't reduce the $300-per-month limit for people who are not seeking degrees). You can find more information about the taxation of grants in IRS Publication 17, *Your Federal Income Tax,* Chapter 7, "What Income is Taxable." All IRS publications are available free of charge from your local IRS office.

It's worth mentioning that insurance proceeds received for the loss of finished art are income. And if you barter, the value of what you receive is also income. So, for example, trading for the services of an accountant gives you income in the amount of the fair market value of the accountant's services.

Types of Income

But all income is not the same. There are the following different kinds of income:

1. Earned ordinary income, such as that from salary, fees, royalties, sales of art, and so on.
2. Unearned ordinary income, such as interest on a savings account or dividends from stock.
3. Short-term capital gains, which is profit from the sale of capital assets, such as stocks, bonds, and gold, that you have owned 1 year or less.
4. Long-term capital gains, which is profit from the sale of capital assets that you have owned for more than 1 year.

The differences among these types of income are important because they are taxed differently:

- Earned and unearned ordinary income and short-term capital gains can be taxed   as high as 50 percent.
- Earned ordinary income makes you eligible for tax benefits.
- Long-term capital gains are never taxed more than 20 percent.

The advantage of having long-term capital gains is obvious. Unfortunately, you will almost always have earned ordinary income from your business activities.

The income tax rate, by the way, is progressive. The more money you earn, the higher is the percentage you have to pay in taxes. But the higher percentages apply only to each additional amount of taxable income, not to all your taxable income. So if your taxable income increases from $2700 to $3200 and you pay a tax of 15 percent on that $500 increment, the tax on that increment will always be 15 percent—even if your highest increment is so great (perhaps $100,000 or higher) that it is taxed at 50 percent.

Expenses

Expenses reduce your income. Any ordinary and necessary business expense may be deducted from your income for tax purposes. This includes office supplies and expenses such as typing paper and postage, messenger fees, typesetting, transportation costs, business entertainment, secretarial help, legal and accounting fees, commissions paid to an agent, books or subscriptions directly related to your business, professional dues, telephone expenses, rent, and so on. On Schedule C these expenses are entered on the appropriate lines or, if not listed, under "Miscellaneous."

Because your right to deduct certain expenses can be tricky, we're going to discuss some of the potential items of expense in detail.

Home Studio

If you have your studio at a location away from your home, you can definitely deduct rent, utilities, maintenance, telephone, and other related expenses. Under today's tax laws, you would be wise to locate your studio away from home if possible, because if your studio is at home, you will have to meet a number of requirements before you can take deductions for it. To put it another way, if you're going to have your studio at home, be certain you meet the requirements and qualify to take a business deduction for rent and related expenses.

The law states that a deduction for a studio at home can be taken if "a portion of the dwelling unit is exclusively used on a regular basis (A) as the taxpayer's principal place of business, (B) as a place of business which is used by patients, clients, or customers in meeting or dealing with the taxpayer in the normal course of his trade or business, or (C) in the case of a separate structure which is not attached to the dwelling unit, in connection with the taxpayer's trade or business." Exclusivity means that the space is used only for your business activity. If the space is used for both business and personal use, the deduction will not be allowed. For example, a studio that doubles as a television room will not qualify under the exclusivity rule. The requirement of regularity means that you must use the space on a more-or-less daily basis for a minimum of several hours per day. Occasional or infrequent use certainly will not qualify.

Once the work space is used exclusively and on a regular basis, the studio expenses can qualify as deductible under one of three different tests. First, they will be deductible if the studio is your principal place of business. But what happens if you must work at other employment or run another business in order to earn the larger part of your income? In this case a dispute had developed between the Commissioner of Internal Revenue and the Tax Court as to whether the principal-place requirement refers to each business separately. Is the studio at home the principal place of the business of being an illustrator or a designer? If it is, according to the Tax Court, the fact that you also work elsewhere shouldn't matter. The commissioner has now agreed with the Tax Court, so in this situation you can take the home studio deduction. In any case, you could not deduct a studio at home under this provision if you did most of your work in another studio maintained at a different location. The second instance in which the expenses can be deductible occurs when the studio is used as a place of business for meeting with clients or customers in the normal course of a trade or business. Many illustrators and designers do open their studios at home to clients in the normal course of their business activities, so this provision might well be applicable. Finally, the expenses for a separate structure, such as a storage shed, would qualify for deduction if the structure is used in connection with your business. If you are seeking to deduct home-studio expenses as an employee rather than a freelancer, you must not only use the space exclusively on a regular basis for business and pass one of the three additional tests just described, but you must also maintain the space for the convenience of your employer. A teacher, for example, might argue that a studio at home was required by the school, especially if no studio space was available at the school and professional achievements as an illustrator or designer were expected of faculty members.

If you do use the work space exclusively on a regular basis for one of the three permitted uses just discussed, you must pass yet one more test before being able to deduct the expenses. This is a limitation on the amount of expenses that can be deducted in connection with a studio at home. Deductible expenses for business use of the home include the cost of heating, water, electricity, air conditioning, cleaning, repairs, and similar items. If you rent you can deduct the rental payments, while if you own your home you can deduct depreciation, mortgage interest, and real-estate taxes. Of course, all these expenses are divided between business and personal use, so only that portion of expenses applicable to business use is actually deductible on Schedule C.

The limitation placed on these expenses is basically that they cannot exceed the gross income from your business. For example, you rent your home and use one-quarter of it exclusively on a regular basis as your principal place of business. If the total expenses relating to the home are $8,000, the one-quarter share attributable to the business and therefore deductible is $2,000. But what happens if you show only $1,200 in gross income on Schedule C from your business? In that case the expenses relating to the studio at home are deductible only to the extent of the $1,200. The calculation if you own your home is very similar, but it is more complicated and you may need an accountant's help.

If you do own your own home, you would be wise to consult an accountant prior to taking the home-studio deduction. Taking this business deduction will limit your right as a homeowner to either be taxed at the favorable long-term capital gains rates when you sell your home or to avoid tax completely if you repurchase another home within 24 months or are 55 years of age or older. Your accountant can explain these points in greater detail and determine whether or not you as a homeowner should take the home-studio deduction.

Educational Expenses

You may want to improve your skills as a professional by taking a variety of courses. The rule is that you can deduct these educational expenses if they are for the purpose of maintaining or improving your skills in a field that you are already actively pursuing. You cannot deduct such expenses if they are to enable you to enter a new field or meet the minimal educational requirements for an occupation. For example, illustration or graphic-design students in college cannot deduct their tuition when they are learning the skills necessary to enter a new field. A professional who has been in business several years could deduct expenses incurred in learning better artistic tehcniques or even better business techniques. Both would qualify as maintaining or improving skills in your field.

Professional Equipment

If you purchase equipment that will last more than 1 year, you cannot deduct the full price of the equipment in the year that you buy it. Instead, you must deduct part of the price—price being called *basis* for tax purposes—each year until the full price has been deducted. Starting in 1981, the tax law changed to make mandatory use of the Accelerated Cost Recovery System (ACRS). This is a system that tells you what percentage of basis you are to deduct each year for different classes of equipment. Most equipment purchased by graphic artists is "5-year property." If placed in use between 1981 and the end of 1984, you would deduct 15 percent of basis for the first year of use, 22 percent for the second year, and 21 percent for each of the third, fourth, and fifth years of use. The only equipment not likely to be 5-year property would be an automobile used in the business. This would be 3-year property with 25 percent of basis deducted for the first year of use, 38 percent for the second year, and 37 percent for the third year. These percentages apply to property placed in service from the beginning of 1981 through the end of 1984, but will change for 1985 and subsequent years.

Starting in 1982 you will be able to choose to deduct the full cost of equipment in the year purchased up to a ceiling of $5,000. This ceiling will remain at $5,000 for 1983, increase to $7,500 for each of 1984 and 1985, and increase again to $10,000 after 1985.

The investment tax credit is another benefit of investing in equipment. While a deduction is subtracted from income, a credit is subtracted directly from your tax and is therefore more beneficial. The investment tax credit is taken in the year that property is acquired. It is 10 percent of basis for 5-year property and 6 percent of basis for 3-year property. Because the investment tax credit is lost for equipment that you elect to expense, you may wish to consult an accountant prior to expensing.

The Accelerated Cost Recovery System requires businesses to take more rapid deductions for equipment than used to be the case. This will save taxes, but in some cases may be disadvantageous. For example, a person challenged as a hobbyist might prefer to deduct lesser amounts each year in order to show a profit in two years out of five (refer to pages 141-144). Elections can be made to spread deductions over a longer cost recovery period. The importance of maximizing your overall tax position makes use of an accountant advisable if you have any uncertainty over the best utilization of the Accelerated Cost Recovery System.

Form 4562 is used for equipment placed in service on or after January 1, 1981, while Schedule C is used for depreciation on equipment placed in service prior to January 1, 1981.

Travel

You may be required to travel in the course of your work. Some examples of business travel include travel to do an assignment, to negotiate a deal, to seek new clients, or to attend a business or educational seminar related to your professional activities. Travel expenses (as opposed to transportation expenses, which are explained later) are incurred when you go away from your home and stay away overnight or at least have to sleep or rest while away. If you qualify you can deduct expenses for travel, meals and lodging, laundry, transportation, baggage, reasonable tips, and similar business-related expenses. This includes expenses on your day of departure and return, as well as on holidays and unavoidable layovers that come between business days.

The IRS has strict record-keeping requirements for travel expenses. These requirements also apply to business entertainment and gifts, since these are all categories that the IRS closely scrutinizes for abuses. The requirements are for records or corroboration showing:

1. the amount of the expense
2. the time and place of the travel or entertainment, or the date and description of any gift
3. the business purpose of the expense
4. the business relationship to the person being entertained or receiving a gift

If you travel solely for business purposes, all your travel expenses are deductible. If you take part in some nonbusiness activities, your travel expenses to and from the destination will be fully deductible as long as your purpose in traveling is primarily for business and you are traveling in the United States. However, you can deduct only business-related expenses, not personal expenses. If you go primarily for personal reasons, you will not be able to take the travel expenses incurred in going to and from your destination (but you can deduct legitimate business expenses at your destination).

If you are traveling outside the United States and devoting your time solely to business, you may deduct all your travel expenses just as you would for travel in the United States. If the travel outside the United States was primarily for business but included some personal activities, you may deduct the expenses as you would for travel primarily for business in the United States if you meet any of the following five tests:

1. You are an employee whose expenses are paid by an employer.
2. You had no substantial control over arranging the trip.
3. You were outside the United States a week or less.
4. You spent less than one-quarter of your time outside the United States on nonbusiness activities
5. You can show that personal vacation was not a major factor in your trip.

If you don't meet any of these tests, you must allocate your travel expenses. This is explained in IRS Publication 463, *Travel, Entertainment, and Gift Expenses.*

By the way, if your spouse goes with you on a trip, his or her expenses are not deductible unless you can prove a bona-fide business purpose and need for your spouse's presence. Incidental services, such as typing and entertaining, aren't enough.

The IRS is very likely to challenge travel expenses, especially if the auditor believes a vacation was the real purpose of the trip. To successfully meet such a challenge, you must have good records that substantiate the business purpose of the trip and the details of your expenses. For more information with respect to travel expenses, you should consult IRS Publication 463.

Transportation

Transportation expenses must be distinguished from travel expenses. First of all, commuting expenses are not deductible. Traveling from your home to your studio is considered a personal expense. If you have to go to your studio and then go on to a business appointment, or if you have a temporary job that takes you to a location remote from your home and you return home each night, you can deduct these expenses as transportation expenses. But only the transportation itself is deductible, not meals, lodging, and the other expenses that could be deducted when travel was involved.

The IRS sets out guidelines for how much you can deduct when you use your automobile for business transportation. This is a standard mileage rate, presently 20 cents for the first 15,000 miles and 11 cents for every mile over 15,000. In addition, you can deduct interest on loans to purchase your automobile, state and local taxes (other than gasoline), parking fees, tolls, and any investment credit.

However, you don't have to use the standard mileage rate. You may prefer to depreciate your automobile and keep track of gasoline, oil, repairs, licenses, insurance, and the like. By calculating both possible ways, you may find that actually keeping track of your expenses gives you a far larger deduction that the standard mileage amount.

Of course, if you use your automobile for both business and personal purposes, you must allocate a portion of the expenses to the business use to determine what amount is deductible.

Entertainment and Gifts

The IRS guidelines for documenting entertainment and gift expenses were already set out when we discussed travel.

Entertainment expenses must be directly related to your business activities. You should definitely have a receipt if you spend more than

$25 (although it's wise to have receipts or canceled checks for all your expenses in any case). Business luncheons, parties for business associates or clients, entertainment, and similar activities are all permitted if a direct business purpose can be shown. However, the expenses for entertainment must not be lavish or extravagant.

Business gifts are deductible, and you can give gifts to as many people as you want. However, the gifts are deductible only up to the amount of $25 per person each year.

For both entertainment and gift expenses, you should again consult IRS Publication 463, *Travel, Entertainment, and Gift Expenses.*

Beyond Schedule C

So far we've mainly been discussing income and expenses that would appear on Schedule C. A completed Schedule C appears on pages 146–147 so you can see how the various types of entries might be made. It's worth mentioning that some accountants for graphic designers believe that high gross receipts themselves or a high ratio of gross receipts on line 1 to net profits on line 21 may invite an audit. If you incur many expenses that are reimbursed by your clients, these accountants simply treat both expenses and reimbursement, as if they canceled each other out. This results in the same net profit, but your gross receipts are less. The expenses and reimbursements are shown on a page attached to Schedule C or in a footnote indicating the total amounts at the bottom of the front page of Schedule C. Or you could include the reimbursement as part of gross receipts and then subtract the expenses as deductions.

Schedule C is not the only schedule of importance. There are potential income tax savings—and obligations—that require using other forms.

Retirement Accounts

You, as a self-employed person, can contribute the lesser of $15,000 or 15 percent of net self-employment income to a retirement plan. This plan is called a Keogh plan, after the sponsor of the legislation that allowed such contributions. The amount that you contribute to the plan is deducted from your income on Form 1040. While you must set up the Keogh plan during the tax year for which you want to deduct your payments to the plan from your income, once you have set up the plan you are permitted to wait to make the actual payment of money until your tax return must be filed. The payments into a Keogh plan must be kept in certain special types of accounts, such as a custodial account with a bank, a trust fund, or special United States Government retirement bonds. You don't have to pay taxes on any income earned by money in your Keogh account, but you are penalized if you withdraw any money from the account prior to age 59½ (unless you are disabled or die—in which case your family could withdraw the money). The money will be taxed when you withdraw it for your retirement, but you may be in a lower tax bracket then. In any case, on withdrawal you will have the benefit of the interest earned by money that would otherwise have been spent as taxes if you hadn't created a Keogh retirement plan.

You can create a Keogh plan as long as you have net self-employment income. This is true even if you have another job and your employer also has a retirement plan for you. If you have only a small amount of self-employment income, you'll be able to make a minimum payment to a Keogh plan of the lesser of $750 or 100 percent of self-employment income.

If you are an employee, you can have an Individual Retirement Account (IRA) in addition to a Keogh plan or retirement plan from your employer. You can create such a plan anytime before your tax return for the year must be filed and pay in your money at the same time. The money you pay in—the lesser of 100 percent of salary and professional fees or $2,000—is deducted from your income for the year covered by the tax return. If you have a nonworking spouse, you may be able to contribute $2,250 to the plan as long as your spouse also benefits. In most other ways these accounts are similar to Keogh plans.

The Keogh and IRA plans will be liberalized starting in 1982 and you should obtain that updated information. Several IRS publications are also helpful, including Publication 560, *Retirement Plans for Self-Employed Individuals;* Publication 566, *Questions and Answers on Retirement Plans for the Self-Employed;* and Publication 590, *Tax Information on Individual Retirement Savings Programs.*

Child and Disabled-Dependent Care

If you have a child or disabled dependent for whom you must hire help in order to be able to work, you should be able to take a tax credit for part of the money you spend. This is more fully explained in IRS Publication 503, *Child Care and Disabled Dependent Care.*

Charitable Contributions

Illustrators and graphic designers cannot, unfortunately, take much advantage of giving charitable contributions of their artwork or copyrights. Your tax deduction is limited to the costs that you incurred in producing what you are giving away. You are penalized for being the creator of the artwork or copyright, since someone who purchased either an artwork or copyright from you could donate it and receive a tax deduction based on the fair market value of the contributed item. Groups representing creators have been working since 1969 to amend this unfair aspect of the tax laws.

Bad Debts

What happens if someone promises to pay you $500 for a job that you deliver but then never pays you? You may be able to sue him or her for the money, but you cannot take a deduction for the $500, because you never recorded the money as income since you're a cash-method taxpayer. The whole idea of a bad-debt deduction is to put you back where you started, so it applies mainly to accrual-basis taxpayers. If you lend a friend some money and don't get it back, you may be able to take a nonbusiness bad-debt deduction. This would be taken on Schedule D as a short-term capital loss, but only after you had exhausted all efforts to get back the loan.

Income Averaging

If a taxpayer's income goes up sharply in one year, a tax-saving aid may exist in the form of income averaging. What income averaging essentially does is take part of your income for 1 year and spread it back over the 4 prior years. If you were in a lower tax bracket in the prior years, you can save taxes. You don't have to recompute your taxes for all the prior years, by the way, but instead simply fill out Schedule G for the year in which you intend to average. IRS Publication 506, *Computing Your Tax Under the Income Averaging Method,* can be helpful here.

Self-Employment Tax

In order to be eligible for the benefits of the social-security system, self-employed people must pay the self-employment tax. This tax is computed on Schedule SE, *Computation of Social Security Self-*

Employment Tax. Additional information about the self-employment tax can be found in IRS Publication 533, *Information on Self-Employment Tax.* Also, the Social Security Administration publishes several helpful pamphlets, including those titled *Your Social Security* and *If You're Self-Employed . . . Reporting Your Income for Social Security.* These pamphlets can be obtained from your local Social Security office.

Estimated Tax Payments

Self-employed people should make estimated tax payments on a quarterly basis. In this way you can ensure that you won't find yourself without sufficient funds to pay your taxes in April. Also, you are legally bound to pay estimated taxes if your total income and self-employment taxes for the year will exceed taxes that are withheld by $200 or more (increasing to $300 in 1983, $400 in 1984, and $500 in 1985 and thereafter). Payments are made on Form 1040-SE, *Estimated Tax Declaration Voucher,* and sent in on or before April 15, June 15, September 15, and January 15. The details of estimated tax payments are explained in IRS Publication 505, *Tax Withholding and Declaration of Estimated Tax.*

Proving Professionalism

The IRS may challenge you on audit if they find that you've lost money for a number of years in your activities as an illustrator or graphic designer. It's demoralizing when this happens, since the auditors will call you a hobbyist and challenge your professionalism. However, you have resources and should stand up for yourself. In fact, you should probably be represented by an accountant or attorney to aid you in making the arguments to prove you're a professional (use one of the volunteer lawyers for the arts listed on page 217 if you can't afford your own attorney).

First, if you have a profit in 2 years of the 5 years ending with the year they're challenging you about, there's an automatic presumption in your favor that you intend to make a profit. That's the crucial test for professionalism—that you intend to make a profit. But if you can't show a profit in 2 years of those 5, there is no presumption saying you are a hobbyist. Instead, the auditor is supposed to look at all the ways in which you pursue your business and see whether you have a profit motive. In particular, the regulations set out nine factors for the auditor to consider. You should try to prove how each of those factors shows your profit motive. But don't be discouraged if some of the factors go against you, since no one factor is dispositive. Here we'll list the nine factors and briefly suggest how you might argue your professionalism:

1. *The manner in which the taxpayer carries on the activity.* Your record-keeping is very important. Do you have good tax records? Good records for other business purposes? Use of professional advisers, such as an accountant, is helpful. Your efforts to obtain accounts or make sales show professionalism, including seeking a representative or gallery. Membership in professional associations suggests you are not a hobbyist. Similarly, grant and contest applications show your serious intent to make a profit. The creation of a professional studio and use of professional equipment also suggest you are not a hobbyist. Maintaining your fees at a level consistent with being a professional is important, but on the other hand the fee level must not be so high as to prevent your obtaining assignments and selling your work.

2. *The expertise of the taxpayer or his or her advisers.* You would normally attach your resumé to show your expertise. You would make certain to detail your study to become a professional— whether you studied formally or as someone's assistant. Any successes are significant. Have you done assignments for clients and sold your work? Reviews or other proofs of critical success are important. Teaching can be a sign of your expertise. Obtaining statements from leading practitioners or one of the professional organizations in the field as to your professionalism aids your cause. Even the place where you work can be important, if it is known as the location of many successful design or illustration studios. You should use your imagination in seeking out all the possible factors that show your expertise.

3. *The time and effort expended by the taxpayer in carrying on the activity.* You must work on a regular basis. Of course, this includes time and effort related to marketing your work and performing all the other functions that accompany the creation of illustrations or designs.

4. *The expectation that assets used in activity may increase in value.* This factor is not especially relevant for you. You might argue, however, that the artworks and copyrights you are creating are likely to increase in value. This is most believable if you make some resales of reproduction rights or sell your artworks as originals.

5. *The success of the taxpayer in carrying on other similar or dissimilar activities.* If you have had success in another business venture, you should explain the background and show why that leads you to believe your illustration or design business will also prove successful. If the success was in a closely related field, it becomes even more important. You might expand this to include successes as an employee that encouraged you to believe you could be successful on your own.

6. *The taxpayer's history of income or losses with respect to the activity.* The regulations state, "A series of losses during the initial or start-up stage of an activity may not necessarily be an indication that the activity is not engaged in for profit." Everyone knows that businesses are likely to lose money when they start. The point is to show a succession of smaller and smaller losses that, in the best case, end up with a small profit. You might want to draw up a chart ranging from the beginning of your career to the year at issue, showing profit or loss on Schedule C, Schedule C gross receipts, the amount of business activity each year, and taxable income from Form 1040. The chart should show shrinking losses and rising gross receipts. This suggests that you may start to be profitable in the future. By the way, you can include on the chart years after the year at issue. The additional years aren't strictly relevant to your profit motive in the year at issue, but the auditor will consider them to some degree.

7. *The amount of occasional profits, if any, that are earned.* It helps to have profits. But the reason you're being challenged as a hobbyist is that you didn't have profits for a number of years. So don't be concerned if you can't show any profitable years at all. It's only one factor. Also, keep in mind that your expectation of making a profit does not have to be reasonable; it merely has to be a good-faith expectation. A wildcat-oil outfit may be drilling against unreasonable odds in the hopes of finding oil, but all that matters is that the expectation of making profit is held in good faith. Of course, you would probably want to argue that your expectation is not only in good faith but reasonable as well, in view of the circumstances of your case.

8. *The financial status of the taxpayer.* If you're not wealthy and you're not earning a lot each year, it suggests you can't afford a hobby and must be a professional. That's why showing your Form 1040 taxable income can be persuasive as to your profit

motive. If you are in a low tax bracket, you're really not saving much in taxes by taking a loss on Schedule C. And if you don't have a tax motive in pursuing your career, it follows that you must have a profit motive.

9. *Elements of personal pleasure or recreation.* Since so many people enjoy artistic pursuits, it may be hard for the auditor to understand that you are working when you create. Explain that illustration or design is a job for you as the auditor's job is one for him or her. The pleasure you get out of your work is the same pleasure that auditors get out of theirs, and so on. If you travel you're especially likely to be challenged, so have all your records in impeccable shape to show the travel is an ordinary and necessary business expense.

The objective factors in the regulations don't exclude you from adding anything else you can think of that shows your professionalism and profit motive. The factors are objective, however, so statements by you as to your subjective feelings of professionalism won't be given too much weight. An important case is *Churchman v. Commissioner,* 68 Tax Court No.59 (1977), in which an artist who hadn't made a profit in 20 years was found to have a profit motive.

Gift and Estate Taxes

The subject of gift and estate taxes is really beyond the scope of this book. It's important to plan your estate early in life, however, and the giving of gifts can be an important aspect of this planning. In addition to considering the saving of estate taxes and ensuring that your will indicates those whom you wish to benefit, you may also want to plan for the way in which your work will be treated after your death. These issues, including the giving of gifts and the choosing of executors, are discussed in detail in a new book for illustrators, graphic designers, and other creators edited by Tad Crawford and titled *Protecting Your Heirs and Creative Works* (Graphic Artists Guild, 30 East 20th Street, New York, New York 10003, $6.95).

Helpful Aids

We have mentioned that all IRS publications are available free of charge. Two publications of special interest are IRS Publication 17, *Your Federal Income Tax,* and IRS Publication 334, *Tax Guide for Small Business.* Keep in mind, however, that these books are written from the point of view of the IRS. If you're having a dispute on a specific issue, you should obtain independent advice as to whether you have a tax liability.

A good basic guide for income taxation, estate taxation, and estate planning is contained in Tad Crawford's *Legal Guide for the Visual Artist* (New York City, Hawthorn Books, $6.95). There are also two books that focus specifically on advising the creative person about taxes. These are *The Tax Reliever: A Guide for the Artist* by Richard Helleloid (Drum Books, P.O. Box 16251, Saint Paul, Minnesota 55116, $4.95 plus 50¢ postage) and *Fear of Filing* (Volunteer Lawyers for the Arts, 36 West 44th Street, New York, New York 10036, $4.00).

Finally, for preparing a current return, the most comprehensive of the guides for the general public is *J.K. Lasser's Your Income Tax* (Simon & Schuster, 1230 Avenue of the Americas, New York, New York 10020, $3.95).

SCHEDULE C
(Form 1040)
Department of the Treasury
Internal Revenue Service (3)

Profit or (Loss) From Business or Profession
(Sole Proprietorship)
Partnerships, Joint Ventures, etc., Must File Form 1065.
▶ Attach to Form 1040 or Form 1041. ▶ See Instructions for Schedule C (Form 1040).

OMB. No. 1545-0074
1981
08

Name of proprietor Jack Artist

Social security number of proprietor 000 : 00 : 0000

A Main business activity (see Instructions) ▶ service ; product ▶ design/illustration

B Business name ▶

C Employer identification number

D Business address (number and street) ▶ 133 Joyce Lane
City, State and ZIP Code ▶ Palm Beach, Florida 33480 0,0 ,0,0,0 ,0,0,0

E Accounting method: (1) ☒ Cash (2) ☐ Accrual (3) ☐ Other (specify) ▶

F Method(s) used to value closing inventory:
(1) ☐ Cost (2) ☐ Lower of cost or market (3) ☐ Other (if other, attach explanation)

G Was there any major change in determining quantities, costs, or valuations between opening and closing inventory? . . [Yes] [No: X]
If "Yes," attach explanation.

H Did you deduct expenses for an office in your home? . . . . [No: X]

Part I Income

1 a Gross receipts or sales	1a	34,385	
b Returns and allowances	1b		
c Balance (subtract line 1b from line 1a)	1c	34,385	
2 Cost of goods sold and/or operations (Schedule C–1, line 8)	2	4,448	
3 Gross profit (subtract line 2 from line 1c)	3	29,937	
4 a Windfall Profit Tax Credit or Refund received in 1981 (see Instructions)	4a		
b Other income (attach schedule)	4b		
5 Total income (add lines 3, 4a, and 4b) . . . . ▶	5	29,937	

Part II Deductions

6 Advertising	245	29 a Wages . .	2,000	
7 Amortization		b Jobs credit		
8 Bad debts from sales or services .		c WIN credit		
9 Bank service charges.	60	d Total credits		
10 Car and truck expenses	122	e Subtract line 29d from 29a .		2,000
11 Commissions	1,300	30 Windfall Profit Tax withheld in		
12 Depletion		1981		
13 Depreciation (see Instructions) .	1,680	31 Other expenses (specify):		
14 Dues and publications	175	a Miscellaneous		289
15 Employee benefit programs . .		b		
16 Freight (not included on Schedule C–1) .	340	c		
17 Insurance	650	d		
18 Interest on business indebtedness	340	e		
19 Laundry and cleaning	380	f		
20 Legal and professional services .	200	g		
21 Office supplies and postage . .	1,002	h		
22 Pension and profit-sharing plans .		i		
23 Rent on business property . . .	2,241	j		
24 Repairs	612	k		
25 Supplies (not included on Schedule C–1) .		l		
26 Taxes (do not include Windfall		m		
Profit Tax, see line 30)	588	n		
27 Travel and entertainment . . .		o		
28 Utilities and telephone	1,380	p		

32 Total deductions (add amounts in columns for lines 6 through 31p) . . . . . . ▶	32	13,604
33 Net profit or (loss) (subtract line 32 from line 5). If a profit, enter on Form 1040, line 11, and on Schedule SE, Part II, line 5a (or Form 1041, line 6). If a loss, go on to line 34	33	16,333

34 If you have a loss, do you have amounts for which you are not "at risk" in this business (see Instructions)? . . ☐ Yes ☐ No
If you checked "No," enter the loss on Form 1040, line 11, and on Schedule SE, Part II, line 5a (or Form 1041, line 6).

For Paperwork Reduction Act Notice, see Form 1040 Instructions.

Schedule C (Form 1040) 1981   Page **2**

SCHEDULE C–1.—Cost of Goods Sold and/or Operations (See Schedule C Instructions for Part I, line 2)

1 Inventory at beginning of year (if different from last year's closing inventory, attach explanation) .		**1**	
2 a Purchases	**2a**		
b Cost of items withdrawn for personal use	**2b**		
c Balance (subtract line 2b from line 2a)		**2c**	
3 Cost of labor (do not include salary paid to yourself)		**3**	1,755
4 Materials and supplies		**4**	2,693
5 Other costs (attach schedule)		**5**	
6 Add lines 1, 2c, and 3 through 5		**6**	4,448
7 Inventory at end of year . . . . :		**7**	
8 Cost of goods sold and/or operations (subtract line 7 from line 6). Enter here and on Part I, line 2. ▶		**8**	4,448

SCHEDULE C–2.—Depreciation (See Schedule C Instructions for line 13)

Complete Schedule C–2 if you claim depreciation ONLY for assets placed in service before January 1, 1981. If you need more space, use Form 4562. If you claim a deduction for any assets placed in service after December 31, 1980, use Form 4562 to figure your total deduction for all assets; do NOT complete Schedule C–2.

Description of property (a)	Date acquired (b)	Cost or other basis (c)	Depreciation allowed or allowable in prior years (d)	Method of computing depreciation (e)	Life or rate (f)	Depreciation for this year (g)
1 Depreciation (see Instructions):						
Furniture & Fixtures	1/2/80	7,200		straight line	5	1,440
Equipment	2/28/80	3,200		straight line	8	240
2 Totals		10,400			**2**	1,680
3 Depreciation claimed in Schedule C–1					**3**	
4 Balance (subtract line 3 from line 2). Enter here and on Part II, line 13 . . . . ▶					**4**	1,680

SCHEDULE C–3.—Expense Account Information (See Schedule C Instructions for Schedule C–3)

Enter information for yourself and your five highest paid employees. In determining the five highest paid employees, add expense account allowances to the salaries and wages. However, you don't have to provide the information for any employee for whom the combined amount is less than $50,000, or for yourself if your expense account allowance plus line 33, page 1, is less than $50,000.

Name (a)	Expense account (b)	Salaries and wages (c)
Owner		
1		
2		
3		
4		
5		

Did you claim a deduction for expenses connected with:	Yes	No
A Entertainment facility (boat, resort, ranch, etc.)?		X
B Living accommodations (except employees on business)?		X
C Conventions or meetings you or your employees attended outside the North American area? (see Instructions) . . .		X
D Employees' families at conventions or meetings?		X
If "Yes," were any of these conventions or meetings outside the North American area?		X
E Vacations for employees or their families not reported on Form W–2?		X

CHAPTER 10

Insurance Protection

The Problem

CONSIDER THIS SITUATION: A graphic artist was recently informed by his physician that he needed an operation and would be unable to work for 3 to 4 months. Upon returning to his studio he found a "summons and complaint" (that is, notice of a legal action against him) to the effect that he was being sued for $25,000 for invasion of privacy. The claim was by a model who asserted that the graphic artist's client had made an unauthorized use of an image that had been commissioned some 5 years ago.

Undaunted, the graphic artist went into his studio accompanied by a former associate, who tripped over a pole lying in front of the door, severely injuring his head. Hearing this commotion, the studio assistant stormed over to the doorway to announce that the person who had broken into the studio the night before had stolen most of their equipment and had also dropped a lighted cigarette into the filing cabinet where all the tax returns, business records, and client lists were located.

The graphic artist was relieved to find out that his prize portfolio was not harmed in the turmoil, since his agent had picked it up the day before to show it to a prospective ad agency client. Hours later the agent duly reported the inevitable. The agency couldn't find the portfolio, which had been left for an overnight review.

Surprisingly, insurance coverages, most of them available at reasonable cost, would afford protection in nearly all of the situations referred to above.

The amount of insurance you will need in any category depends on your personal circumstances. If you add up the cost (or replacement value, where that is what the insurance covers) for all your equipment and it comes to $5,000, then that is the amount to cover. Similarly, if you earn $10,000 per year, then the insurance to protect that income in case of sickness or an accident should provide for a benefit of about $200 per week. In each case simply ask yourself what is at risk. Then you will generally know how much coverage to secure.

When you are seeking insurance, try to deal with an agent whose clients are in business for themselves. That agent will have greater exposure than usual to your types of problems. Naturally, the best solution is to find an agent who is already dealing with a few of the other graphic artists in your area. If you are unable to locate someone on your own, consult with one of the professional societies. For example, the Graphic Artists Guild, Room 405, 30 East 20th Street, New York, New York 10003 (212) 982-9298 may be of assistance. If the national headquarters of the organization doesn't have the information, a local chapter or affiliate can probably help you. Be sure to ask the headquarters office for the organization's local contact or phone number.

Finally, when you are buying insurance, there are some crucial strategies you must employ to keep the total cost at a level you can afford. A discussion of these strategies follows.

Strategy for Buying Insurance Economically

There are a few key points to bear in mind when you are buying professional insurance:

- *Package Purchasing.* Get your insurance all at once, and all at the same place, if possible. Many business risks in this field are so unusual they might never be covered if you had to have a separate policy for each (such as invasion-of-privacy insurance). But as part of a broad business package, the coverage can probably be secured, and possibly quite inexpensively.
- *High deductibles.* Look for policies in every area with high deductibles, that is, policies where you personally cover the first few hundred dollars (or more) of losses. A major cost for insurance companies is the administrative expense of handling small claims. If you eliminate that problem for them on your policy, you may get a very substantial saving (often in the range of 20 percent to 40 percent). That approach will allow you to get more of the different coverages you need for this business.

- *High limits.* Get the highest coverage you can where the risk is open-ended. For example, on "general liability" policies that cover personal injuries you (or your staff) might cause to innocent third parties, you should be covered up to about a million dollars. Jury awards of many hundreds of thousands of dollars and more are commonplace today.
- *Focus on major risks.* Focus especially on a situation that could wipe out all your personal or business assets, or your entire income. One would be the unlimited risk associated with bodily injury to third parties, just mentioned above, that are covered by general-liability insurance. Another would be a disabling injury or illness that kept you from working for many years (your income could be replaced by disability-income insurance). Obviously, these situations are more fraught with danger than loss of a few cameras or your portfolio. As one New York insurance expert with roots in Iowa put it: "Imagine that your business operation was a farm with cows that give milk. You can afford to lose a lot of milk (your product) and even some of the cows (your tools), but you're completely wrecked without the farm."

Business Protection

On the business side the basic coverages encompass the following:

1. *Injury to third parties. General-liability insurance* covers claims of third parties for bodily-injury and property-damage incidents that occur inside or outside your studio. It can be extended to cover invasion of privacy, encompassing right of privacy and right of publicity claims, as well as plagiarism (including copyright violations), libel, and slander.
2. *Injured or sick "employees."* Those free-lance assistants you hire on a day-to-day basis may be classified as employees in many states for the purpose of claims arising from injury on the job and sickness off the job. Accordingly, you may well be required by law to have *workmen's-compensation insurance* to protect free-lance (and of course regular) staffers in case of on-the-job injury and *disability-benefits coverage* to provide income for employees who lose work time in the event of injury or sickness off the job.

In addition, with a large staff you may consider the usual

medical, retirement, and disability-income benefits programs often made available to longer-term employees.

3. *Your business property.* At stake here are your studio and fixtures, stationary equipment, typewriter, artwork, business records, and cash accounts.

- *Studio.* A *package policy* will cover studio contents against fire and theft. Special improvements such as a darkroom should be specifically indicated in the coverage. If your studio or darkroom is part of your home, your homeowner's or tenant's policy would cover these risks *if* the insurer is informed of the partial business use.

   Additions to the package policy may be of interest to established professionals: a so-called *extra-expense rider* will cover extra expenses you incur to temporarily rent another place in the event of fire or other destruction at your own studio. Similarly, you can get *business-overhead coverage* to temporarily pay for ongoing studio expenses while you are disabled from sickness or accident.

- *Movable Equipment.* The most common coverage for movable equipment is the *floater,* which can encompass worldwide coverage for loss or damage to items such as expensive cameras and lenses. If you are just starting in business, you may have a nonbusiness floater policy that you use to cover personal property. As your business becomes significant, you must convert the coverage to a commercial policy to be sure that the insurance is in effect in the event a loss occurs. Floaters cover only the specific items named in the policy. Therefore, you must update the coverage list every 6 or 12 months with your new purchases during that period. Most policies insure only against losses up to the amount of your cost (less depreciation). That will not be enough to cover the cost of replacement, given the rapidly escalating price of equipment. Accordingly, you should consider getting "stated value" floaters, which will reimburse you for the current replacement cost in the event of loss. Of course, that increases the premium.

- *Artwork and business records.* The package policy covering studio contents usually sharply limits recovery for loss of artworks or business records (often to as little as $500). To cover those items directly you need *valuable-papers coverage.* Its best use is for the time and effort that might have to be spent to replace business records that are lost or damaged (in a fire, for example). Consider the problems that would arise if you lost the card index to your picture reference file, or all your tax records. You can also use this coverage for original artwork. The problem is that there may be so many pieces that the cost will be prohibitive. You may therefore have to limit the coverage to your most select and important works.

• *Cash accounts.* An established graphic artist may be jeopardized by the acts of a dishonest employee. While it happens very rarely indeed, an employee could forge your signature on studio checks or devise other means to secure unauthorized payments from the studio. Insurance for such situations is referred to as *fidelity coverage,* which, in effect, is a bonding procedure for your employees.

Personal Protection

On the personal and family side, your insurance needs are similar to those of most other members of the public and should encompass the following:

• *Sickness and injury. Basic hospitalization* such as Blue Cross–Blue Shield (or other private plans) is essential but not enough. Extended hospitalization, intensive care, and major surgery make *major-medical coverage* almost mandatory. Interestingly, once you have the basic hospitalization, the added expense of major medical is not great.

Often overlooked, however, is what happens to your income in the event of long-term or permanent disability due to sickness or accident. Insurance coverage that provides income replacement is called *disability-income insurance* and is generally considered essential for free-lance people. If you elect a fairly long waiting period (say, 60 to 90 days of disability) before you start collecting, the cost can be quite reasonable.

• *Personal property.* The most common protection in this category is a homeowner's or tenant's policy to cover fire and theft risks associated with your house, apartment, and personal possessions. These policies often have options to cover general liability for injury to third parties who visit your residence. For expensive property that you take out of the residence, such as cameras or other valuables, you need a floater, rider, or separate policy, which is an additional premium. Remember that business uses of your residence or property almost always require a separate commercial policy.

Automobiles, of course, are covered separately for fire and theft under a comprehensive policy, and personnel injury or property damage to third persons under a general-liability auto policy.

- *Life insurance and accidental death benefits.* Life insurance is necessary only in cases where others are dependent on your income or services. That could include your family or business partner. Life insurance can be obtained either as *term insurance,* which is purely a death benefit without cash value, or as a form of savings combined with the death benefit, referred to as *whole life.* Those graphic artists who tend to travel extensively may also see value in an *accidental death and dismemberment* (AD&D) policy, which in effect is basic term life insurance, covering only the limited situation of accidental death. On an annual basis it is quite inexpensive, covering all possible accident situations, including travel. For example, it is certainly far less expensive than taking out coverage at the airport for each trip. AD&D coverage should not, however, be confused with medical coverage. AD&D pays only a death benefit and in certain cases pays for loss of sight or limbs.

PART III

Legal Guide

CHAPTER 11

Copyright

THE RIGHTS THAT YOU SELL come from your copyright. *All rights* or *world rights* is the transfer of your entire copyright; *first North American serial rights* is the transfer of a limited piece of your copyright. Your authority to sell rights stems from the federal copyright laws that protect you. These laws were first enacted in 1790 and are periodically revised, the most recent revision taking effect on January 1, 1978.

If anyone wishes to use your copyrighted illustrations or designs, he or she must get your permission. You will then be able to set a suitable fee for the use the person wants to make of them. Anyone who violates your copyright is infringing upon your legal right, and you can sue for damages and prevent him or her from continuing the infringement. Your copyright is, therefore, important in two ways: It guarantees that you will be paid when you let others make use of your work, and it gives you the power to deny use of your work if, for example, the fee is too low or you don't believe that particular person or company will use it in a way you consider esthetically satisfactory.

Rights to Copyrighted Art

If "copyrighted work" sounds ominous, it shouldn't. You have your copyright as soon as you create an artwork, whether it's a rough or a finish. This copyright is separate from the paper or other material on which the image appears. For example, you can sell a drawing but reserve the copyright to yourself. The buyer would get a physical object, but no right to reproduce your work. Or you could sell the copyright or parts of the copyright while retaining ownership of the physical object. It is common practice, especially when illustration is involved, to require the return of original artwork when selling reproduction rights.

As the copyright owner, you have the following exclusive rights:

1. The right to authorize reproductions.
2. The right to distribute copies to the public (although a purchaser can resell a purchased copy).
3. The right to prepare derivative works based on your work. Derivative works are creations derived from another work of art. Thus, an illustration or design could be the basis for a lithographic plate used to make fine prints. In such a case the fine prints would be derivative works based on the original illustration or design.
4. The right to perform your work if it is audiovisual or a motion picture.
5. The right to display the work (except that the owner of a work can display it to people who are physically present at the place where the display occurs).

The exclusive rights are yours to keep or sell as you wish. Other users of these rights must first obtain your consent.

Transferring Limited Rights

You could always transfer *all rights,* but that would be self-defeating. Whenever you sell rights, you naturally want to sell only what the user needs and is willing to pay for. The copyright law helps by requiring that transfers of exclusive rights of copyright be in writing. This requirement of a written transfer calls your attention to what rights are being given to the user. Such a transfer must be signed either by you or by your agent (if the agent has authorization from you to sign copyright transfers).

How can you tell whether the right that you are transferring is exclusive or not? Just ask the following question: If I transfer this right to two different users, will my transfer to the second user be a breach of my contract with the first user? If you transfer *first North American serial rights* to one magazine, you cannot transfer *first North American serial rights* to a second magazine. Obviously, both magazines could not be first to publish the work in North America. So *first North American serial rights* is an exclusive transfer and must be in writing and signed by you or your agent.

However, it is also possible to give a nonexclusive license to someone who wishes to use one of your images. Such a nonexclusive license does not have to be written and signed but can be given orally or in the course of dealing between the two parties. If you have not given a signed, written authorization, you know that you have sold only nonexclusive rights. This means that you can give the same license to two users without being in breach of contract with either user.

An illustrator had done an advertising assignment for a cosmetics company and delivered a number of illustrations. No written agreement was signed by the illustrator. He asked: (1) Can I sell these illustrations used by the advertiser to some other user? (2) What use can the advertiser make of the illustrations? *Answer:* The illustrator was free to resell the illustrations to other users. Since no written transfer had been made, the advertiser had gotten only nonexclusive rights. As a practical matter, however, the illustrator would almost certainly ask for the client's consent in order to keep on good terms and obtain future assignments. The question of what uses the advertiser can make of the illustrations is harder to answer. If the advertiser's purchase order or the illustrator's confirmation form or invoice specifies what uses can be made, the problem may be solved. In the absence of a complete written contract, what the parties orally agree to about usage would be considered. This can be quite difficult to prove and points to the value of having a clear written understanding before starting any assignment. Prior dealings between the parties or accepted practice in the field will also be considered by the courts if there is no written contract or the contract is ambiguous.

Since you want to sell limited rights, it's important to know how rights can be divided. Always think about the following bases on which distinctions can be made:

- exclusive or nonexclusive transfer
- duration of the use
- geographical area in which the use is permitted
- medium in which the use is permitted
- in a case involving words and images, the language in which use is permitted

If, for example, a magazine or book publisher wants to publish your work, you should make it a practice, whenever possible, not to sell *all rights* or even exclusive publishing rights. It is preferable to sell the most limited rights that the publisher needs, since it is presumably paying for only those rights that it intends to use. Your transfer might be as follows: *exclusive first-time North American magazine rights.* The shorthand for this, of course, is *first North American serial rights.* Any of your exclusive rights as copyright owner can be subdivided and sold separately. The rest of the copyright still belongs to you for further exploitation.

Copyright Assignment Form

The copyright assignment form that appears on page 161 can be used if you are getting a transfer of *all rights* back from a user. This was frequently necessary under the old law, although it should not occur very often after January 1, 1978. Also, you could use this form to transfer all rights to a user, but you would be better off working with the contract forms on pages 93–96 that provide for limited rights transfer.

Once you receive an assignment of a copyright, you should record it with the Copyright Office. This is easy to do, since you need only send $10 (there is an additional $.50 charge for each title over one) and the original or a certified copy of the assignment to the Copyright Office. The Copyright Office makes a microfilm copy of the assignment and returns the document to you along with a certificate of record. By recording the assignment within 1 month if it is made in the United States or within 2 months if made abroad, you establish your priority over others to whom the user may later, by mistake, or otherwise, transfer the same copyright.

This system of recording is useful in another way. If you are trying to find out whether a work that you want to use is copyrighted and who the copyright owner is, the Copyright Office (for $10 per hour) will search its records to help you obtain this information.

Assignment of Copyright

For valuable consideration, the receipt of which is hereby acknowledged, *[name of party assigning the copyright]*, whose offices are located at *[address]*   , does hereby transfer and assign to *[name of party receiving the copyright]*, whose offices are located at *[address]*   , his heirs, executors, administrators, and assigns, all its right, title, and interest in the copyrights in the works described as follows: *[describe work, including registration number, if work has been registered]*

, including any statutory copyright together with the right to secure renewals and extensions of such statutory copyright throughout the world, for the full term of said copyright or statutory copyright and any renewal or extension of same that is or may be granted throughout the world.

IN WITNESS WHEREOF, *[name of party assigning the copyright]* has executed this instrument by the signature of its duly authorized corporate officer on the _____ day of _____ , 198__ .

> ABC Corporation
>
> By: _____
>
> *Authorized Signature*
>
> _____
>
> *Name Printed or Typed*
>
> _____
>
> *Title*

Copyright Notice

If you have copyright simply by creating a work, you may wonder why you have to bother with copyright notice. The reason is that if your work is published without copyright notice, you are likely to lose your copyright. Publication basically means public distribution, whether by sale, lending, leasing, gifts, or offering copies to other people for further distribution. Offering or showing your work to a number of art directors is probably not a public distribution, but there is no harm in putting the copyright notice on the work before sending it out.

The copyright notice has three parts:

1. "copyright" or "Copr." or ©
2. your name or an abbreviation from which your name can be recognized, or a pseudonym by which you're known
3. the year date of first publication

An example of a proper notice would be: © Jane Artist 1981. The year date may be omitted from toys, stationery, jewelry, postcards, greeting cards, and any useful articles. So, if your design were used on greeting cards, proper copyright notice could be: © Jane Artist or even © JA.

It's a good idea to have a stamp with your copyright notice: © Jane Artist 19___. When your work is ready to leave your studio, you simply stamp on the copyright notice. Since the work is unpublished, the year date you put in the copyright notice should be the year of creation.

On publication, either in the United States or abroad, the year of first publication should appear in the notice. If the work is going to be distributed abroad, it is best to use ©, your full name, and the year date of first publication. You could also be wise to include the phrase "All Rights Reserved."

Placement of Copyright Notice

The copyright notice symbolizes your status as copyright owner. It warns the public of your rights over your creations. To fulfill these functions, the copyright notice must be placed on the work in a position and manner that will give reasonable notice of your claim of copyright.

For an unpublished work the notice could go on the border or on the back. For a work published in a book or magazine, the most obvious place would be adjacent to the image. However, there are a number of other placements that would be considered reasonable. If, for example, the magazine objected on esthetic grounds to an adjacent copyright notice, the notice could appear in any of the following locations:

1. For a work reproduced on a single page, notice can go under the title of the contribution on that page or anywhere on the same page if it's clear from the format or an explanation that the notice applies to the image.

2. For works appearing on a number of pages of a magazine, the notice can go under a title at or near the beginning of the spread, on the first page of the main body of the spread, immediately after the end of the spread, or on any of the pages comprising the spread if the spread is no more than 20 pages, the notice is prominent and set apart from other materials on the page, and it is clear from the format or an explanation that the notice applies to the entire spread.

3. For works reproduced on either one page or a number of pages, the notice can go with a separate listing of the contribution by full title and author on the page bearing copyright notice for the magazine as a whole or on a table of contents or listing of acknowledgments appearing near the front or back of the magazine.

With so many possible placements to choose from, it is difficult for the magazine to deny use of the copyright notice on esthetic grounds. A magazine, by the way, is one type of collective work—a work including contributions by a number of creators. Other types of collective works would be anthologies and encyclopedias. The placements of copyright notice shown for magazines apply to all collective works.

You may wish to place copyright notice on a photographic slide or group of slides. A single slide would have the notice on its mounting, while a group of slides intended to be shown in sequence as an audiovisual piece would have the copyright notice on the projected image with or near the title, with credits and similar information at or immediately following the beginning of the work or at or immediately before the end of the work. These placements also apply to motion pictures.

An artist sold *one-time right* for an image to a magazine. When she asked for copyright notice in her name, the magazine said that its copyright notice at the front of the magazine would protect her copyright. The artist asks: Will the magazine's copyright notice actually protect my contribution to the magazine? If it will, why should I bother to ask for notice in my own name? *Answer:* The magazine is correct up to a point. The copyright notice for a collective work *will* protect the copyrights of individual contributors such as the artist (although it will not generally protect the copyright in advertisements). However, the artist will lose two benefits that come from having copyright notice in her own name. First, if someone wants to reproduce the work, he or she will probably go to the magazine since copyright notice is in the magazine's name. If the magazine sells reuse rights to that person, the artist will have no right to sue the user for infringement. All the artist can do, if she happens to find out that such a use was made, is sue the magazine for the amount received by the magazine. Second, the copyright law allows you to make a group registration for works first published as contributions to periodicals during a 12-month period, as long as your own copyright notice appeared on each contribution. A group registration saves you money by registering a number of works for a single $10 registration fee. Registration is not required to obtain your copyright, but it does offer a number of benefits, as the section on registration explains.

The Public Domain

Artworks that are not protected by copyright are in the public domain. This means that they can be freely copied by anyone—they belong to the public at large. This includes works whose copyrights have expired and works that have lost copyright protection because of incorrect copyright notice.

However, the new copyright law gives you a number of opportunities to save your copyright if one of your works is published with an incorrect notice or without any notice at all.

First, an incorrect copyright notice will not affect the validity of your copyright in the following cases:

1. If an error is made in the name in the copyright notice.
2. If a year date in the copyright notice is earlier than the date of first publication.

If the wrong name appears in the copyright notice, a person who gets permission to use the work from the person named in the notice has a defense to your suit for infringement. You can cut off this defense by registering your work or recording with the Copyright Office a document signed by the person named in the notice that states you are the copyright owner. In any case, however, the person named in the notice will have to give you any proceeds realized from licensing your work.

In the case of a year date earlier than the date of first publication, the term of the copyright runs from the earlier date. The term of copyright is your life plus 50 years, so it really doesn't matter if the copyright term starts earlier than the year of first publication. An illustration or design created in 1981 and published in 1983 will have a valid copyright until 50 years after the creator's death, regardless of which date is used in the copyright notice.

Omitted Notice

The complete absence of the copyright notice on a published work of art raises the risk that your copyright will go into the public domain. Some types of incorrect notice are also treated as if the notice had been completely omitted:

1. the omission of your name or the date
2. the use of a year date that is more than 1 year after the year of first publication

However, even for a completely omitted notice, your copyright will remain valid in the following situations:

1. If the omission of copyright notice is from a relatively small number of copies, your copyright will remain valid without any further action on your part.
2. If the omission is from more than a relatively small number of copies, you can save the copyright from going into the public domain by registering within 5 years of the publication and making a reasonable effort to have copyright notice placed on the copies that lack notice.
3. If the copyright notice has been left off by a user in violation of an express written requirement that a condition of the use is placement of the copyright notice on the copies, your copyright will remain valid.

This last saving provision suggests that the stamp you use for copyright notice might be elaborated to make inclusion of the copyright notice a condition of any public distribution. Such a stamp could read:

COPYRIGHT © Jane Artist 19_____.
An express condition of any authorization to use this work is that copyright notice in the artist's name appear on all publicly distributed copies of the work as follows:
© Jane Artist, year of first publication.

This provision could also be placed on your confirmation form or invoice, as long as the user is aware of this condition prior to making any use of your work.

Duration of Copyright

If you protect your copyright by requiring copyright notice at the time of first publication, your copyright will normally last for your lifetime plus 50 years. A work created in 1983 by an illustrator or a designer who dies in 2004 will have a copyright that expires in 2054. Copyrights run through December 31 of the year in which they expire.

If you create a work jointly with another artist, the copyright will last until 50 years after the death of the survivor.

If you create a work anonymously or using a pseudonym, the copyright will last 75 years from the date of publication or 100 years from the date of creation, whichever term is shorter. However, you can convert the term to your life plus 50 years by advising the Copyright Office of your identity prior to the expiration of the term.

If you work for hire, as explained in the section on working for hire (pages 167–168), the copyright term will be 75 years from the date of publication or 100 years from the date of creation, whichever term is shorter. Remember, however, that when you do a work for hire, you are no longer considered the creator of the work for copyright purposes. Instead, your employer or the person commissioning the work is considered the work's creator and completely owns the copyright.

For copyrights protected under the old federal copyright law (in other words, those works registered or published with copyright notice prior to January 1, 1978), the copyright term will be 75 years. However, the old copyright law required that copyrights be renewed at the end of 28 years. Pre-1978 copyrights that are in their first 28-year term must be renewed on Form RE.

Finally, you may have illustrations and designs that you created prior to January 1, 1978, but never registered or published. These works were protected by common-law copyright (which has basically been eliminated by the new law). The law provides that such works shall now have protection for your life plus 50 years. In no event shall the copyright expire before the year 2002 and, if the works are published, the copyright will run at least until 2027.

Since copyrights remain in force after the creator's death, estate planning must take copyrights into account. You can leave your copyrights to whomever you choose in your will. If you don't do this the copyrights will pass to your heirs.

Termination of Transfers

Because copyrights last for such a long time, the new copyright law adopted special termination provisions to protect creators. It isn't possible to know how much a license or right of copyright will be worth in the distant future. So the law provides:

1. For licenses or rights of copyright given by the artist on or after January 1, 1978, the transfer can be terminated during a 5-year period starting 35 years after the date of the transfer. If the right of publication is included in the transfer, the 5-year period for

termination starts 35 years from the date of publication or 40 years from the date of the transfer, whichever is earlier.

2. For transfers made prior to January 1, 1978, by the artist or the artist's surviving heirs (as defined in the copyright law), the transfer can be terminated during a 5-year period starting 56 years from the date copyright was originally obtained, or starting on January 1, 1978, whichever is later.

The termination provisions do not apply to transfers made by will or to work made for hire. Also, a derivative work made prior to termination may continue to be exploited even after termination of the transfer in the original image on which the derivative work is based.

Termination requires that you give notice of your intention to terminate 2 to 10 years in advance of the actual date of termination. If works of yours have maintained value for such a long period that the termination provisions could benefit you, it would be wise to have an attorney assist you in handling the termination procedures.

Work for Hire

You must be aware of one hazard under the copyright law. For an employee, work for hire means that the employer owns all rights of copyright as if the employer had in fact created the illustration or design. An employee can, of course, have a contract with an employer transferring rights of copyright back to the employee.

However, a free-lance artist may also be asked to do assignments as work for hire. This treats you like an employee for copyright purposes, but doesn't give you any of the benefits employees normally receive. The Graphic Artists Guild and many other professional organizations representing creators have condemned the use of work-for-hire contracts with free-lancers.

The copyright law safeguards free-lancers by requiring that a number of conditions be met before an assignment will be considered work for hire:

1. The work must be specially ordered or commissioned.
2. The artist and the user must both sign a written contract.
3. The written contract must expressly state that the assignment is done as work for hire (but also beware of any other phrases that sound as if you're being made an employee for copyright purposes).

4. The assignment must fall into *one* of the following categories:
   - a contribution to a collective work, such as a magazine, an anthology, or an encyclopedia.
   - a supplementary work, which includes illustrations or designs done to illustrate a work by another author (but only if the illustrations or designs are of secondary importance to the overall work)
   - part of an audiovisual work or motion picture
   - an instructional text
   - a compilation (which is a work formed by the collection and assembly of many preexisting elements)
   - a test
   - answer material for a test
   - an atlas

If these four conditions are not satisfied, you cannot be doing work for hire.

If you do work for hire, you are giving the maximum in rights to the user. You can't terminate the rights that the user receives, the way you eventually could with an *all rights* transfer. Of course, the more rights you sell, the greater the payment that you should demand.

Contributions to Magazines

If you sell to a collective work such as a magazine without signing anything in writing specifying what rights you are transferring, the law presumes that you have transferred only the following nonexclusive rights:

1. the right to use your contribution in that particular collective work, such as that issue of the magazine
2. the right to use your contribution in any revision of the collective work
3. the right to use the contribution in any later collective work in the same series

If you sold work to a magazine, that same magazine could reprint it in a later issue without paying you (unless you agree or specify otherwise). But the magazine could not authorize a different magazine to reprint the work, even if the same company owned both magazines. If you sold your work to an anthology, it could be used again in a revision of that anthology (unless you agree or specify otherwise). However, it could not be used in a different anthology. Also, the owners of the collective work would have no right to change the art when reusing it.

An artist has completed an assignment for a magazine. No agreement was ever reached about what rights were being transferred to the magazine. However, the artist has now received a check with a legend on its back stating, "By signing this check, you hereby transfer all rights of copyright in your work titled _____ to this magazine." The artist asks: (1) Can this legend on a check be a valid transfer of copyright? (2) Should I cash the check or return it and demand a check without such a legend? *Answer:* There has been a disagreement among copyright authorities as to whether signing such a check creates the written instrument required for a copyright transfer. The safest course is to return the check and request one that does not have the legend. You should definitely do this if you have not used a confirmation form specifying the rights transferred or if you have not yet completed the assignment. If you have completed the assignment on the basis of a confirmation form that specifies what rights you are transferring, you could cross out the legend and deposit the check without signing it. The best practice, however, is to have a clear understanding about rights before you start and simply return any check that recites a greater rights transfer than what you have previously agreed to. The failure of the magazine to pay according to the terms agreed to would be a breach of contract for which the publication would be legally liable.

Registration of Published Art

The forms for registering your copyrights are shown on pages 178–179. To register, you send Form VA, 2 copies of your published work, and $10 to the United States Copyright Office, Library of Congress, Washington, D.C. 20559.

But if you have copyright the moment you create a work, why should you bother to register? The reason is that registration gives you the following benefits:

1. You must register to sue for a copyright violation.
2. Registration creates a presumption in your favor that your copyright is valid and the statements you made in the Certificate of Registration are true.
3. Registration in some cases limits the defense that can be asserted

by infringers who were "innocent," that is, who infringed in reliance on the absence of copyright notice in your name.

4. You must register prior to an infringement's taking place if you are to be eligible to receive attorney fees and statutory damages (except that a registration within 3 months of publication will be treated as if made on the date of publication).

If you have published contributions in magazines, the registration of the magazine will not register your contribution (unless you transferred all rights to the magazine, which you don't want to do). When you are registering your published contributions to magazines or newspapers, you need only deposit one complete copy of the magazine or of the section of the newspaper containing your contribution.

It is also possible to have a group registration for published contributions to periodicals, such as magazines and newspapers. In making such a group registration, you would use the basic Form VA and also use Form GR/CP shown on page 180. To qualify, your contributions must satisfy the following conditions:

1. Each contribution has identical copyright notice in your name.
2. All the contributions were published during one 12-month period (not necessarily a calendar year).

The group-deposit provision allows you to register many contributions for a single $10 registration fee. Additional regulations will be issued by the Copyright Office to cover registration of groups of related published works.

Registration of Unpublished Art

So far we have been discussing the registration of published illustrations or designs. However, you can also register unpublished art, including sketches and preliminary designs. In many cases the registration of unpublished art will be easier and far less expensive than the registration of published works. The regulations provide that unpublished works may be registered in a group for a single $10 fee if:

1. The deposit materials are in an orderly format.
2. The collection bears a single title, such as "Collected Works of Jane Artist, 1981."
3. The same person claims copyright in all the illustrations or designs.

There is no limit on the number of works you can register in a group registration of unpublished illustrations or designs—all for the same $10 fee.

Another advantage of an unpublished registration is that you have to deposit only one copy of each image. The copy can be a photostat, drawing, photographic print, or other two-dimensional reproduction that can be seen without the aid of a machine. Your deposit materials should all be the same size. Transparencies must be at least 35 mm and fixed in cardboard, plastic, or similar mounts to facilitate identification, handling, and storage. Prints or photocopies should be no less than 3 by 3 inches and no more than 9 by 12 inches. The preferred size is 8 by 10 inches. If the illustration or design is in color, the reproduction that you deposit must also be in color. The deposit materials must give the work's title, clearly showing its entire copyrightable content, and specify the exact measurement of at least one dimension of the work. It would be wise to place the deposit materials securely in a binder with the title and your name on the front.

Once you have registered a work as part of an unpublished group, you do not have to reregister it if it is later published.

Form VA is used for the group registration of unpublished art.

Infringement

If someone uses one of your works without permission, that person is an infringer. You can sue an infringer to stop the infringement. At the same time you have a right to be compensated for the infringement.

You're entitled to your actual damages caused by the infringement, plus any extra profits the infringer may have made that aren't covered by your actual damages. If it would be difficult to prove your damages or the infringer's profits, you can elect to receive statutory damages, which are an award of between $250 and $10,000 for each work infringed, the exact amount being determined by the court's discretion.

Lawsuits for copyright infringement are brought in the federal courts and are expensive for both parties. For this reason infringement suits are frequently settled before trial.

The test for infringement, by the way, is whether an ordinary observer believes that one work has been copied from another. You should keep in mind that a photograph can be infringed by a drawing in the same way a book can be infringed by a film—the copyright protects against infringement regardless of whether the same medium is used.

An artist is given the assignment of designing and illustrating the cover of a leading national magazine. The cover is to include an illustration of a well-known doctor. The artist does an illustration of the doctor from a photographer's copyrighted photograph that she has in her reference files. As a precaution, she shows the finished design to her attorney. She asks: (1) Is this an infringement? (2) What should I do about it? *Answer:* The illustration will be an infringement if an ordinary observer would believe it to have been copied from the photograph. Illustrators frequently work from files of photographs and other images that they keep for reference. The attorney will advise the artist to obtain permission from the photographer and pay the appropriate fee. If that isn't possible, the image will have to be changed to such an extent that the ordinary observer will no longer believe the illustration is copied from the photograph. Even in such a case the artist might seek complete safety by requesting that the magazine agree to pay any damages, legal fees, or court costs resulting from a lawsuit for infringement. Even if the magazine refuses to indemnify the artist in this way, at least the problem can be reviewed and, in all likelihood, a solution found.

Fair Use

Not every use of copyrighted art will be an infringement. Fair use allows someone to use your copyrighted works in a way that is noncompetitive with the uses that you would normally be paid for. A fair use is not an infringement. The law gives four factors to consider in deciding whether a use is a fair use or an infringement. If you're considering using someone else's art, you would weigh these factors to decide whether you should obtain permission for the use:

1. the nature of the use, including whether it's commercial or nonprofit and educational
2. the nature of the copyrighted work
3. how much of the copyrighted work is actually used
4. what effect the use will have on the potential market for or value of the copyrighted work.

Fair use is frequently invoked for purposes such as criticism, comment, news reporting, teaching (including multiple copies for classroom use), scholarship, or research. For example, if a critic wants to write about your career as an illustrator or graphic designer, the critic could use one of your works to illustrate the article without obtaining your consent. Similarly, if a news reporter wants to feature you in a news story, the reporter can include one of your illustrations or designs as an example of your work. These are fair uses.

A designer has been retained by a corporate client to do a sales brochure. One spread is to be a montage composed of other photographs already in the possession of the client—a lake in Arizona that the company has developed, a young woman in a bathing suit, scenic views of the countryside, and so on. The designer asks: (1) Can I use these copyrighted photographs as a fair use, since the montage format creates a different image? (2) If I can't simply use these photographs, what should I do? *Answer:* The use is a commercial use. Changing the size of the photographs, or even cropping them, will not change the fact that they are being reproduced without permission. The designer should contact the copyright owners of the photographs and ask for permission to use them. If a fee is required for the use, as is likely, it can be passed along to the client. At the same time the designer should obtain a model release from the woman in the bathing suit. Otherwise she may bring an invasion-of-privacy lawsuit.

How do you obtain permission to use someone else's art? The best way is to have a standard form, such as the following one:

Permission Form

I hereby grant to *[your name]* permission to use the following works:

Title	Description
_____	_____
_____	_____
_____	_____

in the following manner: *[name of publication and extent of usage]*
As an express condition of this authorization a copyright notice and credit line shall appear in my name as follows: © *(owner's name)* 198__

_____
Copyright Owner

_____
Date

You would send an explanatory covering letter along with an extra copy of the permission form that the copyright owner would sign and return to you. You can also use this permission form when requests are made to use your work. Of course, you would carefully outline the rights you are giving and specify fees that must be paid for the usage.

Compulsory Licensing

Compulsory licensing deserves a brief mention. It is a provision in the law that allows nonprofit educational television stations, such as those in the Public Broadcasting Service, to use your published art without asking your permission. However, the Copyright Royalty Tribunal in Washington, D.C., sets rates of payment that these stations are obligated to pay to you if they make use of your work. The stations are also required to make semiannual accountings, setting forth what graphic works they have used. These accountings are filed with the Copyright Royalty Tribunal, 1111 Twentieth Street, N.W., Washington, D.C. 20036.

Moral Rights

Moral rights are widely recognized abroad. Included among them are the right to receive credit when works of yours are published and the right to have the works published without distortion. Since moral rights are not part of the copyright law in the United States, a moral-rights bill has been introduced to amend the copyright law. The most important lesson here is that you must contractually protect your right to a credit line and the publication of your work without distortions. It might be possible to argue that a strong trade custom requires a credit line—for example, in the editorial field—or that a distorted piece of art libels you since it is not in fact your work. But these can be difficult arguments to make in court, especially when a contractual provision would leave no doubt about your rights.

What Isn't Copyrightable

Illustrations and graphic designs will almost always be copyrightable. The requirements for copyrightability are *originality* and *creativity*. Originality means that the work is not plagiarized from someone else (although even an infringing work is copyrightable insofar as it may have noninfringing parts). Creativity means that there is at least a modicum of artistic skill exhibited in the work, but this is not a difficult test to meet—even a child's drawing is protected by copyright.

What is not copyrightable? Ideas are not, although the creative expression of an idea is. For example, the idea of illustrating a particular landscape is not copyrightable, but the illustration of the landscape definitely is copyrightable. Typeface designs are not copyrightable, although many designers feel that they should be. Calligraphic alphabets are not copyrightable, although calligraphic letters with artistic decorations are copyrightable. Book designs are now in a gray area with respect to copyrightability. The Copyright Office has traditionally not accepted book designs for copyright, but the Graphic Artists Guild has urged that this position be reconsidered. The issue of copyright for book design has not yet been tested in the courts. Book jackets, of course, are usually copyrightable. On the other hand, titles, names, and short phrases that may accompany your work are usually not copyrightable, because they lack enough creative expression. Works of a useful nature will not be copyrightable, unless they also have an artistic element. A lamp base would not be copyrightable, but an artwork on the lamp base certainly would be.

Patents and Trademarks

Patents and trademarks are often confused with copyrights. Protection for illustration and graphic design comes from the copyright law.

A utility patent can be obtained for inventions of machines or processes that are useful, original, and not obvious to people with skill in that field. A utility patent is far more expensive to obtain than a copyright, since the services of a patent attorney are almost always a necessity. These services can cost $1,000 or more, depending on the complexity of the patent. A design patent is somewhat less expensive to obtain, and it protects manufactured items that have ornamental, original, and unobvious designs. If a designer created an innovative design for a chair or other product, a design patent might be appropriate.

Trademarks are distinctive names, emblems, or mottos that manufacturers use to identify their products to the public. Using someone else's trademark is forbidden because the public would then become confused as to whose product it was buying. It's wise to consult an attorney before selecting a trademark, since you wouldn't want your trademark to be an infringement of someone else's. Trademarks gain protection simply by being used, although they can also be registered for federal and state protection. If a designer creates a corporate-identity package for a client, including a logo, the client will usually take whatever steps are necessary to protect its new identity symbols.

The Old Copyright Law

The new copyright law—effective January 1, 1978—has required an explanation that is lengthy even without going over what the law used to be before January 1, 1978. However, illustrations or designs created before that date were governed by the old copyright law. If, for example, you published a work without copyright notice under the old law, it immediately went into public domain. The new law doesn't revive these lost copyrights. Sales to magazines and rights in commissioned works were also governed by different presumptions. The details of the old copyright law are discussed in *Legal Guide for the Visual Artist,* by Tad Crawford (Hawthorn Books, New York City, $6.95). If your works created before January 1, 1978 had copyright protection, after January 1, 1978 they are governed by the new copyright law.

An illustrator made sketches of an automobile show in 1975 but never published them. In 1982 he is able to place some of the illustrations with a magazine. His question: Since the sketches were drawn before January 1, 1978, will the old copyright law govern the sale to the magazine? *Answer:* The new copyright law will govern the sale, because it takes place after January 1, 1978. If the illustrator had sold the illustrations to the magazine in 1976, the old copyright law would have governed. This would be true even if a dispute arose as to the 1976 sale after January 1, 1978.

More Copyright Information

One of the best sources for copyright information is the Copyright Office. The *Copyright Information Kit* is available free by writing to the Copyright Office, Library of Congress, Washington, D.C. 20559. It contains all the registration forms as well as circulars describing the activities of the Copyright Office. The office will also provide you with as many free copies of the registration forms as you may want. The Copyright Office will not, however, give you legal advice about copyright. A booklet focusing on the new copyright law as it applies to illustrators, graphic designers, and other artists is *The Visual Artist's Guide to the New Copyright Law,* by Tad Crawford

(Graphic Artists Guild, 30 East 20th Street, New York, New York 10003, $5.95 per copy).

The Copyright Forms

No discussion of copyright would be complete without an explanation of the copyright forms. Form VA is the basic form used for the visual arts—to register either published or unpublished works. Form GR/CP would be used in addition to Form VA if you wanted to register works published as contributions to periodicals that qualify for group treatment. Form VA has helpful instructions, but the following step-by-step approach cuts through any verbiage. We have not included the Copyright Office instructions for either Form VA or Form GR/CP, since you will automatically receive those instructions when you request the forms from the Copyright Office.

Looking at Form VA on pages 178–179, let's assume first that you want to register a single unpublished artwork. In space 1 you would give the title of the work and indicate "illustration" or "graphic design" as the nature of the work. In space 2 you would give your name as author and indicate that the work is not work made for hire. You would also give your birth date, state your nationality, and indicate that your contribution to the work was neither anonymous nor pseudonymous. Where it says "Author of," you would again state "illustration" or "graphic design" or explain in more detail if other artists' work is also used. In space 3 you would give only the year in which the work was completed. Space 4 would have your name and address as those of the copyright claimant. In space 5 you would indicate that no earlier registration had been made for the work. Space 6 you would leave blank unless the art incorporates preexisting work, in which case you would describe the preexisting material and the additions that you made. In space 7 you would give your name and address for correspondence. In space 8 you would check the box for author, sign your name, print or type your name, and give the date. Finally, in space 9 you would show your name and address so that the Certificate of Registration could be mailed to you. Of course, if your situation doesn't fit the facts in these answers, you would make the necessary changes as you go through the form.

Taking the next typical case, you want to make a group registration of unpublished works. You follow the directions just given for registering a single unpublished work with a few changes. In space 1 the title of the work is the collection's title, such as "Collected Works of Jane Artist 1980." It is helpful to state the number of

FORM VA

UNITED STATES COPYRIGHT OFFICE

REGISTRATION NUMBER
VA   VAU
EFFECTIVE DATE OF REGISTRATION
Month   Day   Year

DO NOT WRITE ABOVE THIS LINE. IF YOU NEED ADDITIONAL SPACE, USE CONTINUATION SHEET (FORM VA/CON)

(1) Title

TITLE OF THIS WORK:

NATURE OF THIS WORK: (See instructions)

Previous or Alternative Titles

PUBLICATION AS A CONTRIBUTION: (If this work was published as a contribution to a periodical, serial, or collection, give information about the collective work in which the contribution appeared.)

Title of Collective Work   Vol.   No.   Date   Pages

(2) Author(s)

IMPORTANT: Under the law, the "author" of a "work made for hire" is generally the employer, not the employee (see instructions). If any part of this work was "made for hire" check "Yes" in the space provided, give the employer (or other person for whom the work was prepared) as "Author" of that part, and leave the space for dates blank.

1

NAME OF AUTHOR:

Was this author's contribution to the work a "work made for hire"?   Yes   No

DATES OF BIRTH AND DEATH:
Born   Died
(Year)   (Year)

AUTHOR'S NATIONALITY OR DOMICILE:
Citizen of { (Name of Country) } or { Domiciled in (Name of Country) }

AUTHOR OF: (Briefly describe nature of this author's contribution)

WAS THIS AUTHOR'S CONTRIBUTION TO THE WORK:
Anonymous?   Yes   No
Pseudonymous?   Yes   No
If the answer to either of these questions is Yes, see detailed instructions attached

2

NAME OF AUTHOR:

Was this author's contribution to the work a "work made for hire"?   Yes   No

DATES OF BIRTH AND DEATH:
Born   Died
(Year)   (Year)

AUTHOR'S NATIONALITY OR DOMICILE:
Citizen of { (Name of Country) } or { Domiciled in (Name of Country) }

AUTHOR OF: (Briefly describe nature of this author's contribution)

WAS THIS AUTHOR'S CONTRIBUTION TO THE WORK:
Anonymous?   Yes   No
Pseudonymous?   Yes   No
If the answer to either of these questions is Yes, see detailed instructions attached

3

NAME OF AUTHOR:

Was this author's contribution to the work a "work made for hire"?   Yes   No

DATES OF BIRTH AND DEATH:
Born   Died
(Year)   (Year)

AUTHOR'S NATIONALITY OR DOMICILE:
Citizen of { (Name of Country) } or { Domiciled in (Name of Country) }

AUTHOR OF: (Briefly describe nature of this author's contribution)

WAS THIS AUTHOR'S CONTRIBUTION TO THE WORK:
Anonymous?   Yes   No
Pseudonymous?   Yes   No
If the answer to either of these questions is Yes, see detailed instructions attached

(3) Creation and Publication

YEAR IN WHICH CREATION OF THIS WORK WAS COMPLETED:
Year
(This information must be given in all cases.)

DATE AND NATION OF FIRST PUBLICATION:
Date   (Month)   (Day)   (Year)
Nation   (Name of Country)
(Complete this block ONLY if this work has been published.)

(4) Claimant(s)

NAME(S) AND ADDRESS(ES) OF COPYRIGHT CLAIMANT(S):

TRANSFER: (If the copyright claimant(s) named here in space 4 are different from the author(s) named in space 2, give a brief statement of how the claimant(s) obtained ownership of the copyright.)

- Complete all applicable spaces (numbers 5-9) on the reverse side of this page
- Follow detailed instructions attached
- Sign the form at line 8

DO NOT WRITE HERE

Page 1 of . . . . pages

Copyright/179

DO NOT WRITE ABOVE THIS LINE. IF YOU NEED ADDITIONAL SPACE, USE CONTINUATION SHEET (FORM VA/CON)

PREVIOUS REGISTRATION: **⑤** Previous Registration

- Has registration for this work, or for an earlier version of this work, already been made in the Copyright Office? Yes........ No........

- If your answer is "Yes," why is another registration being sought? (Check appropriate box)
  - ☐ This is the first published edition of a work previously registered in unpublished form.
  - ☐ This is the first application submitted by this author as copyright claimant.
  - ☐ This is a changed version of the work, as shown by line 6 of the application.

- If your answer is "Yes," give: Previous Registration Number............................ Year of Registration.....................

COMPILATION OR DERIVATIVE WORK: (See instructions)   **⑥** Compilation or Derivative Work

PREEXISTING MATERIAL: (Identify any preexisting work or works that this work is based on or incorporates.)
....
....
....
....

MATERIAL ADDED TO THIS WORK: (Give a brief, general statement of the material that has been added to this work and in which copyright is claimed.)
....
....
....

DEPOSIT ACCOUNT: (If the registration fee is to be charged to a Deposit Account established in the Copyright Office, give name and number of Account.)   **CORRESPONDENCE:** (Give name and address to which correspondence about this application should be sent.)   **⑦** Fee and Correspondence

Name   Name

                                        Address

Account Number   (Apt.)

                                        (City)   (State)   (ZIP)

CERTIFICATION: ✱ I, the undersigned, hereby certify that I am the: (Check one)   **⑧** Certification (Application must be signed)

☐ author ☐ other copyright claimant ☐ owner of exclusive right(s) ☐ authorized agent of _____
(Name of author or other copyright claimant or owner of exclusive right(s))

of the work identified in this application and that the statements made by me in this application are correct to the best of my knowledge.

☞ Handwritten signature: (X)

Typed or printed name   Date

MAIL CERTIFICATE TO   **⑨** Address For Return of Certificate

....
(Name)

....
(Number, Street and Apartment Number)

....
(City)   (State)   (ZIP code)

(Certificate will be mailed in window envelope)

ADJUNCT APPLICATION
for
Copyright Registration for a
Group of Contributions to Periodicals

FORM GR/CP

UNITED STATES COPYRIGHT OFFICE

- Use this adjunct form only if you are making a single registration for a group of contributions to periodicals, and you are also filing a basic application on Form TX, Form PA, or Form VA. Follow the instructions, attached.
- Number each line in Part B consecutively. Use additional Forms GR/CP if you need more space.
- Submit this adjunct form with the basic application form. Clip (do not tape or staple) and fold all sheets together before submitting them.

REGISTRATION NUMBER
TX   PA   VA

EFFECTIVE DATE OF REGISTRATION
(Month)   (Day)   (Year)

FORM GR/CP RECEIVED
Page _____ of _____ pages

DO NOT WRITE ABOVE THIS LINE. FOR COPYRIGHT OFFICE USE ONLY

(A) **Identification of Application**

IDENTIFICATION OF BASIC APPLICATION:
- This application for copyright registration for a group of contributions to periodicals is submitted as an adjunct to an application filed on: (Check which)

☐ Form TX   ☐ Form PA   ☐ Form VA

IDENTIFICATION OF AUTHOR AND CLAIMANT: (Give the name of the author and the name of the copyright claimant in all of the contributions listed in Part B of this form. The names should be the same as the names given in spaces 2 and 4 of the basic application.)

Name of Author: ....

Name of Copyright Claimant: ....

(B) **Registration For Group of Contributions**

COPYRIGHT REGISTRATION FOR A GROUP OF CONTRIBUTIONS TO PERIODICALS: (To make a single registration for a group of works by the same individual author, all first published as contributions to periodicals within a 12-month period (see instructions), give full information about each contribution. If more space is needed, use additional Forms GR/CP.)

☐ Title of Contribution: ....
Title of Periodical: .... Vol ..... No ..... Issue Date .... Pages ....
Date of First Publication: .... Nation of First Publication .... (Country)
(Month) (Day) (Year)

☐ Title of Contribution: ....
Title of Periodical: .... Vol ..... No ..... Issue Date .... Pages ....
Date of First Publication: .... Nation of First Publication .... (Country)
(Month) (Day) (Year)

☐ Title of Contribution: ....
Title of Periodical: .... Vol ..... No ..... Issue Date .... Pages ....
Date of First Publication: .... Nation of First Publication .... (Country)
(Month) (Day) (Year)

☐ Title of Contribution: ....
Title of Periodical: .... Vol ..... No ..... Issue Date .... Pages ....
Date of First Publication: .... Nation of First Publication .... (Country)
(Month) (Day) (Year)

☐ Title of Contribution: ....
Title of Periodical: .... Vol ..... No ..... Issue Date .... Pages ....
Date of First Publication: .... Nation of First Publication .... (Country)
(Month) (Day) (Year)

☐ Title of Contribution: ....
Title of Periodical: .... Vol ..... No ..... Issue Date .... Pages ....
Date of First Publication: .... Nation of First Publication .... (Country)
(Month) (Day) (Year)

☐ Title of Contribution: ....
Title of Periodical: .... Vol ..... No ..... Issue Date .... Pages ....
Date of First Publication: .... Nation of First Publication .... (Country)
(Month) (Day) (Year)

artworks in the collection. And in space 3 the year of completion is the year in which the most recently completed work in the collection was finished.

Now let's assume that you want to register a published work. Again the steps are basically the same as for the registration of a single unpublished illustration or design, with the following changes. In space 1 you would so indicate if the work had been published as a contribution to a collective work such as a magazine, an anthology, or an encyclopedia, and give the required information with respect to the collective work. In space 3 you would give not only the year of creation but also the date and nation in which the first publication took place. In space 5 you would indicate whether the work had previously been registered and, if it had been, check the box indicating the reason for the new registration and give the year and number of the previous registration. Space 6 you would fill out only if the illustration or design had been derived in some way from another work. Everything else would be the same as for the registration of a single unpublished illustration or design.

Finally, you might seek to register a group of published contributions to periodicals, if you qualify as explained under the section on registration of published works. To do this you would use not only Form VA but also Form GR/CP shown on page 180. Form VA is filled out as for a published work, but with a few changes. Space 1 is left blank, except for the title where you write "See Form GR/CP, attached." In space 3 you give the year of creation, but leave blank the information with respect to publication. Next you go to Form GR/CP. Here in space A you indicate that Form VA is the basic application. In space B you fill in the required information with respect to each contribution and the periodical in which it appears. And that's all.

Once you send off your registration form, deposit materials, and fee, you'll have to wait while your application is processed by the Copyright Office. But your registration takes effect the moment that the proper forms, deposit materials, and fee are received by the Copyright Office, no matter how long it is before you actually receive the Certificate of Registration.

CHAPTER 12

Invasion of Privacy and Releases

The laws guaranteeing privacy are an important area for you to understand. Both illustrators and designers use images of people taken from every conceivable situation. Illustrators frequently work from life or photographic references. Designers may use both illustrations and photographs that incorporate people's images. It will often be necessary to obtain a release from the person whose image is being used in an artwork. This is because of that person's right of privacy, a right that can be invaded in the following ways:

1. by using a person's photograph, likeness, or name for purposes of advertising or trade
2. by disclosing embarrassing private facts to the public
3. by using an illustration, photograph, or other likeness in a way that suggests something fictional or untrue
4. by physically intruding into a person's privacy, for example, by trespassing to take a photograph

The law of privacy abounds with subtle interpretations. The best advice is to obtain a release if you have any doubt about whether the way you're obtaining an image or the use you intend to make of it could be an invasion of privacy. However, there are many situations when you clearly will not need a release. This chapter will give examples of many common situations so you'll know whether a release is needed.

In order to be thorough, this chapter includes situations that have arisen involving photographers and photographic images. It is the use of the image, not the nature of the medium, that is important with respect to privacy. The graphic artist must be familiar with the cases involving photography in order to discern potential invasions of privacy when using any image of a person. The artist must keep in mind that he or she is not protected from liability for an invasion of privacy simply by using an image taken by a photographer. Everyone who participates in causing an invasion of privacy runs the risk of being sued. This includes the illustrator working from reference materials or the designer incorporating a photograph into a design. For this reason you must be concerned with whether an appropriate release has been obtained and, if the release was obtained by a photographer or some other party, whether the release adequately protects you. If you are working directly from a subject or have taken the reference photograph yourself, then you should obtain a release such as those shown on pages 201–203.

As a practical matter, most invasion-of-privacy lawsuits are brought against publishers, advertising agencies, or corporations—those parties with the money to pay a judgment. However, you should not rely on this fact. If you suspect that a privacy problem may arise, discuss this with your client at the earliest opportunity to avoid taking any unnecessary risks. If you are concerned about the possibility of a privacy lawsuit and your client is not worried (and therefore refuses to obtain a release that protects you), you should insist that the client agree to pay your damages, legal fees, and other expenses that may result if there is an invasion-of-privacy lawsuit. You should obtain such an indemnification agreement in writing before starting work.

Privacy

The creation of privacy as a legal right came about in 1903 by a statute enacted in New York State. Since that time almost every state—with a few exceptions as of this writing—has either enacted a similar statute or recognized the right of privacy in court decisions. The law with respect to privacy can differ from state to state, but New York has been the leader in the privacy area and most law with respect to privacy is the same in all jurisdictions. If you're wondering about a situation in which the law appears unclear, you should use a release or consult a local attorney.

Privacy is the right to peace of mind and protection from intrusions or publicity that would offend the sensibilities of a normal person living in the community. It is an individual right granted to living people. If a person's privacy is invaded, that person must bring suit—not the spouse, children, or anyone else. The right to sue for an invasion of privacy ends upon the death of an individual whose privacy was invaded. If the lawsuit for the invasion was started prior to death, some states allow the legal representative to continue the lawsuit; while other states dismiss the suit. Very few states, however, permit a lawsuit to be started after a person's death for an invasion of the deceased person's privacy. Also, because the right belongs to individuals, the names of partnerships or corporations are not protected by the privacy laws.

Advertising or Trade Purposes

The New York statute provides, "Any person whose name, portrait or picture is used within this state for advertising purposes or for the purposes of trade without . . . written consent . . . may maintain an equitable action in the supreme court of this state . . . to prevent and restrain the use thereof; and may also sue and recover damages for any injuries sustained by reason of such use."

What are advertising or trade purposes? For advertising we naturally think of advertisements for products or services. For trade the immediate association is with an image of a product that is being sold to the public. For example, when photographer Ronald Galella sent out a Christmas card with a photograph he had taken of Jacqueline Onassis on the card, a court found this to be an advertising use and an invasion of her privacy. Even an instructional use can, in certain cases, be for advertising purposes. A woman was photographed for a railroad company and appeared in a poster instructing passengers how to enter and leave the railcars safely. The court, in a 3–2 vote, decided that the unselfish purpose of the poster could not change its nature as advertising. The woman's privacy had been invaded.

An example of a trade use would be placing a person's image on postcards for public sale. Such use is intended to create a desirable product that the public will purchase.

The problem is that advertising and, especially, trade purposes become more difficult to identify when the images are used in media protected by the Fifth Amendment. Freedom of speech and press narrow the right of privacy.

The Public Interest

Public interest is the other side of the coin. The public interest is served by the dissemination of newsworthy and educational information. It is not limited to matters of current news but extends to whatever the public is legitimately interested in. Using a photograph or illustration to accompany a news story about a person who has won a prize for public service in no way requires a release. An illustration of a scientist could be used with an article in a book commenting on the scientist's discoveries, even if these discoveries are not current news.

Unfortunately it isn't always so easy to know whether a purpose is for advertising or trade as opposed to being for the public interest. The best way to get a feeling of what is permitted and what isn't is by examining situations that are likely to come up.

Specific Situations: Places, Subjects, and Uses

PHOTOGRAPHING IN PUBLIC PLACES

Photographs can usually be taken in public places without any restrictions. Of course, making a movie or photographing in such a way as to disrupt the community's normal flow of activity may require a permit from the local authorities. The main problem is not taking the pictures but using them. Even though someone's photograph was taken in a public place, you cannot use it for advertising or trade purposes without the person's consent. On the other hand, you are free to use the same image in the public interest, such as for newsworthy purposes, without worrying about releases.

BYSTANDERS AT PUBLIC EVENTS—REQUIREMENT OF RELATEDNESS

Let's say you're going to incorporate some photographs of a parade into a design. The photographs of the parade naturally include a lot of shots of bystanders. Can you include bystanders in the design when the article is published? Yes, you can and you don't need a release. This is because the parade is newsworthy. When someone joins in a public event, he or she gives up some of the right to privacy.

But what if the magazine wants you to use a photograph of a bystander on its cover—not just as one face among others, but singled out? Is this focusing on that bystander to such a degree that you'll need a release? This happened at *New York* magazine when its cover was designed to feature the photograph of a bystander beneath the caption "The Last of the Irish Immigrants." The bystander had, in fact, been photographed at the St. Patrick's Day Parade in New York City, but he was not Irish. And, while his name did not appear on the cover or in the article, he sued for the use of the photograph. Essentially he argued that the use would have been in the public interest if it had just been to illustrate an article, but placing the photograph on the cover made the primary purpose to sell the magazine—a trade use.

New York's highest court didn't agree. Even though the photograph was on the cover, it was illustrating an article about an event of genuine public interest. And the cover was related to the contents of the article. This is a crucial requirement: that the image in fact be appropriate to illustrate the article. Since the bystander participated in the parade by being there, the use of his image on the cover was not an invasion of privacy. This would have been equally true, by the way, if an illustrator had drawn the bystander for the cover using the photograph as a reference.

This same challenge comes up frequently with book jackets. Not long ago the well-known football quarterback Johnny Unitas sued for invasion of privacy when his photograph was used in the jacket design of a book about football. The court held for the publisher, saying that the jacket design was related to the contents of the book and therefore was not for purposes of trade.

Going a step further, what about a cover design for a company's annual report that includes a photograph of a customer purchasing an item in one of the company's retail stores? The customer turned out to be a lawyer who sued for the invasion of his privacy. The court stated that no case had ever held the annual report—required by the Securities Exchange Commission—to be for purposes of advertising or trade. The court indicated that, if pressed, it would have decided that this use of a customer in a retail store was related to the presentation of a matter in the public interest.

USES THAT ARE NOT RELATED

An Illinois case provides a good example of the possibility of an invasion of privacy by an unrelated use. An imprisoned criminal was slipped a pistol by his girl friend, escaped from jail and fatally shot a detective who was trying to recapture him. A magazine retold the story three months later in an article titled, "If You Love Me, Slip Me a Gun." A photograph of the deceased detective's wife was used to illustrate the story, showing her grief-stricken over her husband's death. An appeals court concluded that this use could be found to be unrelated to the thrust of the story and shocking to basic notions of decency. The issue was whether use of the image served the public interest by providing newsworthy or educational information or merely served the publisher's private interest in selling more copies of the magazine. There is no doubt, by the way, that the use of the image of the widow would have been in the public interest to illustrate a factual article about the death of her husband in the line of duty. But use in a sensationalized way that was not related to the article could make it for purposes of trade—to sell copies of the magazine by capitalizing on the widow's grief.

A classic case of unrelated use involved an article about street gangs in the Bronx in New York City. The photograph illustrating the article showed a number of people in a street scene in that area. The people who sued, and won, were in no way connected with street gangs, so the use of their images was for trade purposes.

FICTIONAL USE

If an illustration or photograph is used in a false way, it can't be legitimately related to an article in the public interest. The illustration can be perfectly innocent—for example, a young woman looking across a bay on a moonlit night. Now suppose a writer exercises all his or her ingenuity and comes up with a wild, entirely fictional story. Using the illustration of a real person to accompany the story raises the risk of an invasion-of-privacy lawsuit. The use of the illustration is not related to a story or article in the public interest. Legally speaking, it is merely to entertain by highlighting an imaginative yarn. In fact, the general rule is that media used solely for entertainment are far more likely to invade someone's privacy than media used in the public interest. A novel, a fictional film, or a television serial are held to be solely for entertainment value. The risk of invasion of privacy is greater in those cases than in a biography, a documentary, or a television news program. A fictional use of an illustration or a photograph is for trade purposes, since its only goal is considered to be the enhancement of sales.

It would definitely be an invasion of privacy to use an illustration of a real businessman carrying a briefcase as a visual for an article about the escape of a desperate and violent bank robber with the loot. But what if that same photograph—of an ordinary businessman on his way home from the office—is used to accompany an article praising him for accomplishments he has not attained? It might say that he has just come from an international convention of scientists and is carrying in his briefcase the remarkable invention for which his peers have so justly applauded him. But the man isn't a scientist and has no invention. This fiction could be extremely embarrassing. It all adds up to an invasion of privacy. Famous baseball pitcher Warren Spahn successfully prevented publication of a biography of him because it contained so many mistakes. Not surprising, except for the fact that the mistakes were all laudatory—all designed to make him even more of a hero than he already was. Praise will not avoid an invasion of privacy unless the praise has a basis in fact.

INCIDENTAL ADVERTISING USES

You've drawn a famous baseball player for the pages of a sports magazine. The illustrations properly accompany an article about the performance of the player's team. But then the magazine surprises you. They take those same illustrations and use them to advertise the magazine. You feel uneasy when you see the advertisement, because you never got a release. You knew it was for editorial use, and you didn't see why you needed one.

This type of case has come before the courts a number of times—with an athlete, an actress, a well-known author, and others. The courts have uniformly held that no invasion of privacy takes place in these situations if the purpose of the advertisement is to show that the magazine carries newsworthy articles. The illustrations or photographs for the original article were not an invasion of privacy because they were in the public interest. If the advertisement is to inform the public about the types of newsworthy and educational articles that the magazine runs, the advertisement is protected in the same way as the original article. This is true even if the advertisement is not advertising the specific issue in which the article appeared, but rather advertising the magazine generally.

But you have to be very careful here. If the illustrations are not used in the same way they were when they accompanied the original article, you may end up with an invasion of privacy. Obviously it would be an invasion of privacy to take the same illustrations and say that the person endorsed the value of the magazine. Or to use the illustrations on posters that are sold to the public. Advertising incidental to a protected editorial use—to show that the publication serves the public interest because of the nature of its contents—is a narrow exception to the general rule banning the use of illustrations or photographs for advertising or trade purposes without the consent of the person portrayed.

A related case occurred when a newspaper photographed a paid model to illustrate a new bathing suit for a fashion item. The photograph included in the background several 10-year-old boys who happened to be at the swimming pool. The text accompanying the photograph ended by describing the bathing suit as "a bikini, very brief pants plus sawed-off tank top. Colored poor-looking brown, the suit is by Elon, $20, Lord & Taylor." Lord & Taylor did not pay to have the item appear. Rather, the newspaper published it as a newsworthy piece of information. The court agreed that the item was in the public interest and that the use of the boys in the photograph was not for advertising or trade purposes. So the boys lost their invasion-of-privacy suit. If Lord & Taylor had paid for the fashion "news" item to be run, the results would presumably have been different. Even though the item would seem to have been published for its current interest, it in fact would be an advertisement in disguise if paid for. This would have violated the boys' rights.

PUBLIC DISCLOSURE OF EMBARRASSING PRIVATE FACTS

The public disclosure of embarrassing private facts can be an invasion of privacy. Peculiar habits, physical abnormalities, and so on can easily be captured by visual images. There is no benefit to the public interest, however, in making public such information about a private citizen. On the other hand, if the information is newsworthy, no invasion of privacy will occur. The examples discussed here show how disclosures that normally would invade privacy are protected when they are newsworthy.

One case involved a husband and wife photographed in the ice-cream concession they owned. The man had his arm around his wife and their cheeks were pressed together—a romantic pose. This image was then used to illustrate a magazine article about love. The court decided that the image was not embarrassing or offensive. In fact, the couple had voluntarily assumed the pose in a public place. And, in any case, it did relate to an article serving the public interest. So the couple lost their invasion-of-privacy suit.

In another case a body surfer well known for his daring style gave an interview in which he told of his peculiar behavior—eating insects, putting out cigarettes in his mouth, pretending to fall down flights of stairs, and fighting in gangs as a youngster. When he found out that these odd traits would be included in the magazine article, he sued on invasion-of-privacy grounds. The court decided that these facts could be included in the article because they were relevant in explaining his character. And his character was of public interest since it related directly to his exploits as a body surfer. But if his body surfing had not been legitimately newsworthy, the disclosure of facts of that kind could certainly have been an invasion of privacy.

CRIMINALS AND VICTIMS

The commission of a crime and the prosecution of criminals are certainly newsworthy, since they are of legitimate concern to the public. Photographs and illustrations of alleged or convicted adult criminals can thus be used in the course of reporting news to the public. However, many states protect the identity of juvenile defendants and victims of certain crimes, such as rape. You have to check your own state's laws to determine what restrictions you may face. It's worth noting that the United States Supreme Court decided recently that the disclosure of the identity of a deceased rape victim did not give grounds for an invasion-of-privacy action. The court pointed out that the victim's identity was a matter of public record. The embarrassment caused to the victim's father, who initiated the lawsuit, could not outweigh the value of communicating newsworthy information to the public. And a recent state court decision has denied a 14-year-old rape victim recovery in an invasion-of-privacy suit based on the disclosure of her identity as a victim of rape. The reasoning is again that the identity is newsworthy and, therefore, cannot be an invasion of privacy.

PUBLIC FIGURES

Public figures must sacrifice a great deal of their right of privacy. This follows from the fact that public figures are, by definition, newsworthy. The public wants to know all about them. The media are merely serving this public interest by making the fullest disclosure of the activities of public figures. So the disclosure of a private fact—which would be an invasion of privacy if a private citizen is involved—may very well be newsworthy and permissible if a public figure is being discussed. For example, a braless tennis professional competing in a national tournament momentarily became bare-chested while serving. A photographer captured this embarrassing moment and the image appeared nationwide. The event was newsworthy. But in a similar case—a private citizen's skirts being blown up in the funhouse at a county fair—the event was not newsworthy and publication of the image was an invasion of privacy.

Who is a public figure? Anyone who has a major role in society or voluntarily joins in a public controversy with the hope of influencing the outcome is a public figure. This includes politicians, famous entertainers, well-known athletes, and others who capture the public imagination because of who they are or what they've done—whether good or bad. Beyond this, however, it also encompasses private citizens who take a stand on a controversy of public interest, such as a housewife publicly campaigning to defeat the budget of a local school board. However, the United States Supreme Court has decided in one case that "public figure" does not include a woman who is in the process of getting divorced from a well-known businessman. When the grounds for her divorce decree were incorrectly reported in a national magazine, the court found she was a private citizen who had not voluntarily become involved in activities of public interest—despite her social status and the fact she had voluntarily given several press conferences to provide information about her divorce to the press.

The more famous the public figure, the greater the right of privacy that the public figure sacrifices. The president of the United States has almost no right of privacy, since practically everything about the life of the president is of interest. A housewife speaking out about a matter of public interest, however, would sacrifice far less of her right of privacy than the president.

One of the leading invasion-of-privacy cases arose from photographer Ron Galella's pursuit of Jacqueline Onassis. Faithful to the creed of the *paparazzi,* he jumped and postured about her while taking his photographs, bribed doormen to keep track of her, once rode dangerously close to her in a motorboat while she was swimming, invaded her children's private schools, leapt in front of her son's bicycle to photograph him, interrupted her daughter on the tennis courts, and romanced a family servant to keep himself current on the location of the members of her family. Could she prevent Galella from harassing her in this way? Or did her status as a public figure make her fair game for whatever tactics a *paparazzi* might choose to employ?

The court's decision struck a compromise between Onassis's right of privacy and the legitimate public interest in knowing of her life. It prohibited Galella from approaching within 25 feet of her. It prohibited him from blocking her movements in public places or from doing anything that might reasonably be foreseen to endanger, harass, or frighten her. But it did not stop him from taking and publishing his photographs, because that served the public interest.

The right of the public to know the appearance of public figures is simply an extension of the rules relating to what is newsworthy and informational. It's important to realize, however, that public figures keep their right of privacy with respect to commercial uses. If you use a public figure's image to advertise a new aftershave lotion, you have definitely committed an invasion of privacy. In fact, the right of publicity discussed in the next chapter shows that public figures can actually have a property right in their names, portraits, or pictures (see pages 204–205).

If an invasion of privacy is found to have occurred, the intention behind the invasion won't matter in the ordinary case involving a private person who is not involved in a matter of public interest. But the courts have determined that a higher standard should apply to false reports of matters in the public interest, including reports involving public figures. To recover for invasion of privacy in cases involving public figures, the public figure must show that the false report was published with knowledge of its falsity or a reckless disregard as to whether or not it was true. This can be a difficult standard to meet, but it reflects the concern of the United States Supreme Court to protect the First Amendment rights of the news media.

STALE NEWS

At some point news becomes stale and the use of someone's image is no longer newsworthy. For example, motion pictures of a championship boxing match were not longer newsworthy when, 15 or 20 years after the bout, they were used as part of a television program titled "Greatest Fights of the Century." The boxer's claim, based on invasion of privacy, could not be defeated on the ground that the program disseminated news. Similarly, the story of a sailor who saved his ship by sending a wireless message was newsworthy when it happened. But to use the sailor's name and portray him by an actor in a commercial film released one month later was a trade use and an invasion of the sailor's right of privacy. Its dissemination was no longer protected as newsworthy.

On the other hand, a child prodigy remained newsworthy 25 years later, despite having vanished completely from public sight. In fact, the prodigy hated his early fame and had sought obscurity, but the court concluded that the public interest would be served by knowing whether his early promise had ever been realized. The magazine article about him, although it embarrassed him and brought him into the public view in a way he dreaded, was not an invasion of his privacy.

RECOGNIZABLE PERSON

One way graphic artists avoid invasion-of-privacy problems is by retouching images so the people aren't identifiable. If you can't identify someone, no invasion of privacy can occur.

A novel case involved a photograph of the well-known actress Pola Negri, which was used to advertise a pharmaceutical product. The advertiser argued that the photograph of the actress had been made 40 years before. Today her appearance was quite different, so no invasion of privacy could take place. Needless to say, the court rejected this argument. Whether the likeness was made last year or 40 years ago doesn't matter if it is put to an advertising use and the person pictured is still alive.

A recognizable likeness, even if it is somewhat altered, can constitute an invasion of privacy. For example, *Playgirl* magazine ran a picture showing a nude black man sitting in the corner of a boxing ring with his hands taped. Although the picture was captioned "Mystery Man," it clearly was a likeness of boxer Muhammed Ali. In fact, an accompanying verse referred to the figure as "the Greatest." The picture was fictional and offensive. It certainly was not newsworthy or instructive since it didn't even accompany an article. The court decided that an invasion of Ali's privacy had occurred. The nude picture was for purposes of trade—to attract the public's attention and sell the magazine.

PARTS OF THE BODY

If a person must be recognizable for an invasion of privacy to occur, it follows that you can use unidentifiable parts of the body for advertising and trade use without fear of causing an invasion of privacy. Arms, legs, the backs of heads, and so on are all right as long as the person is not identified.

But why do most agencies still insist on a release from models in these cases? Simply because the release can serve as the contract with the model. It gives written proof that the model agreed to render services for a specified fee that you (or the agency) agreed to pay. While you may not have to be concerned about an invasion-of-privacy suit, it also saves you from having to worry about a breach-of-contract suit.

DOGS, HORSES, CARS, AND HOUSES

What about using images of property belonging to someone else, such as a German shepherd or the interior of a house? This shouldn't be an invasion of privacy, especially if the owner isn't identified in any way with the image. For example, you could use the image of a horse running in a field for an advertisement. The owner would have no right to object, since the right of privacy protects people, not animals. By the same token you should be able to use a car, the interior of a house, or other private property in an advertisement as long as the owner cannot be identified. But if you promised to pay for the right to create these images of the person's property, or if you used the images in violation of an understanding that you reached with the owner, you may very well face a breach-of-contract lawsuit. As a practical matter, you should seriously consider obtaining a release if you plan to use the image for advertising or trade, since it could also serve as your contract with the owner and would eliminate any risk of a lawsuit, however frivolous.

TRESPASSING

Photographers sometimes trespass to take photographs. This is unlawful regardless of whether the photographs are newsworthy, and you should seek legal counsel before using such images. A trespass—an unlawful entry on a person's property—can serve as the basis for an invasion-of-privacy lawsuit. It doesn't even matter whether the photographs are published, since the invasion can be based solely on the trespass.

A Florida case involving a police raid on a controversial private school stated this prohibition colorfully. The police had television-news cameramen accompany the raiding party that rousted students and faculty from bed. The cameramen took embarrassing footage that was televised. The court said that to permit such conduct

> could well bring to the citizenry of this state the hobnail boots of a nazi stormtrooper equipped with glaring lights invading a couple's bedroom at midnight with the wife hovering in her nightgown in an attempt to shield herself from the scanning TV camera. In this jurisdiction, a law enforcement officer is not as a matter of law endowed with the right or authority to invite people of his choosing to invade private property and participate in a midnight raid of the premises.

But in a similar case a newspaper photographer, at the request of police, took photographs of the silhouette of the body of a girl who had died tragically in a fire. Her mother learned of the death by seeing the published photographs taken inside the mother's burned-out home. She sued for an invasion of her own privacy. The court concluded that the photographs were newsworthy and, under the circumstances, the photographer had not committed a trespass in coming on the mother's premises without her permission.

Nor can trespass be justified when a public figure is involved. Breaking into a senator's office to obtain newsworthy information is an invasion of privacy. The First Amendment does not protect against illegal acts committed in the course of obtaining newsworthy or informative images.

INTRUSION INTO PRIVATE PLACES

Similarly, the graphic artist must exercise caution in using photographs that have been taken in a context which implies privacy. Photographing a private citizen without consent in the seclusion of his or her home may of itself be an invasion of privacy. Certainly there are public places that can become as private as the home. A person using a public restroom or going into a hospital does so with the understanding that he or she will have the same privacy as at home. Because of this, images obtained in these places can be an invasion of privacy.

One case involved employees of *Life* magazine seeking to expose a quack doctor. Pretending to be patients, they gained access to the doctor's home and took photographs with hidden cameras. Subsequently *Life* used the photographs in an exposé about the doctor. While the story was newsworthy, the intrusion was an invasion of privacy. And the court said that the later publication of the photographs could be used as a factor in increasing the damages flowing from the invasion.

Images of patients also present problems. For example, the publication of a patient's likeness to accompany an article written by the doctor could be regarded as for the purposes of advertising the doctor's skills. Or the exhibition of a film showing a birth by Cesarian section could be a trade use if admission is charged. However, if the use is in the public interest, such as an article about a new medical development or an instructive film (especially if no admission fee is charged), you are on safer ground. To avoid uncertainty, you will usually want a release from the patient. In addition to the releases shown on pages 201–203, the American Medical Association has release forms designed for doctors who wish to photograph patients or bring outsiders into the operating room.

BUSINESS PREMISES

The right of privacy does not protect corporate or other business names. The taking and use of photographs or other images of business premises cannot, therefore, be an invasion of the privacy of the corporation or other business. It could be a trespass, unfair competition, or breach of contract, however, as discussed in the next chapter.

Two cases illustrate this. In one case a satiric magazine used a photograph of a real bar to illustrate a fictitious story titled "The Case of the Loquacious Rapist." The actual name of the bar—Busy Bee—appeared in the photograph, although the fictional bar in the accompanying satire was called The Stop and Frisk. There simply was no invasion of privacy here. Nor did an invasion of privacy occur when a photograph of the business name Jollie Donuts and the premises of the donut shop appeared in a nationally televised broadcast. This was not the name, portrait, or picture of a person.

What about a patron who is photographed on the business premises? Can he sue for the use of his image? After a bomb threat a government building was evacuated and a number of the employees went to a nearby hotel bar. A television camera crew photographed a government employee in the bar and broadcast the film on the evening news. The employee lost his invasion-of-privacy suit, since he had become, however involuntarily, an actor in an event of public interest.

EXHIBITION

As more graphic artists exhibit in galleries, the question is often asked whether an exhibition can be an invasion of privacy.

The courts have found that the sale of postcards, portraits, or posters using someone's likeness is a trade use. A unique image or limited edition exhibited for sale in a gallery might also be a trade use. It could be argued, however, that the exhibition and sale of such a work is in the public interest, much like the sale of an illustration or design in a book collecting examples of a graphic artist's work. Looking at it from this point of view, the courts might consider the media used, the nature of the subject matter, and the extent of the invasion. Presumably a person striking a voluntary pose in a public place would have a much harder time recovering than someone who was pictured in an embarrassing pose in a private place. That doubt exists in this area, however, suggests the wisdom of obtaining a release.

If the work of art were exhibited in a museum for educational purposes and not for sale, it would not appear to be a trade use. No case has held this with respect to an illustration or design, but several cases state that the exhibition of a film without an admission charge is not a trade use. So it is less likely that an invasion of privacy would occur if an exhibition was for educational purposes and the work was not offered for sale. However, an embarrassing image, especially if obtained in a place that normally is private, might still cause an invasion of privacy.

What about a poster of a political figure campaigning? While the poster was offered for sale, the court decided that it served the public interest by disseminating knowledge about political candidates. The candidate, by the way, was comedian Pat Paulsen, who had licensed the right to make posters to a competitive company. If Paulsen had not been running for public office in 1968 when the distribution occurred, he might have found protection under the right of publicity discussed in the next chapter.

Not only is the area of exhibition likely to see more lawsuits in the future, but also the laws may differ from state to state. Again, the safest course is to obtain a release.

Damages

It can be difficult to measure what damages should be payable to someone who wins an invasion-of-privacy suit. After all, the injury is to peace of mind and the right to seclusion. Yet a person suing for invasion of privacy has a right to recover substantial damages, even if the only damage suffered is his or her mental anguish. The fact that the damages are difficult to ascertain or can't be precisely determined in terms of money is not a reason to deny recovery for the invasion. Nor are the damages limited to compensation for the mental anguish that a person of ordinary sensibilities would suffer in the situation. The damages can extend beyond this to cover any actual financial losses. The exact amount of damages is decided on a case-by-case basis, depending on the facts involved.

If someone commits an invasion of privacy, it really doesn't matter what the motives were. It's the acts constituting the invasion that create a right to sue. The New York statute does state that anyone who "knowingly" invades another's privacy may be subject to punitive damages. These are extra damages awarded not to compensate the person who has been injured, but rather to punish the offender and prevent similar acts in the future. As to false reports about public figures, see page 192.

Releases

New York's statute requires that a release be in writing, but in most other states an oral release will be valid. The release gives you the right to use someone's image without invading his or her right of privacy. However, you would be wise always to have written releases, such as those that appear on pages 201–203. This is because the releases must be appropriate for the use you intend to make of the image. Also, the details of oral understandings tend to fade from memory and can be difficult to prove in court. If a photographer or someone else has obtained the release, ask for a copy and make certain that it protects you and the use you intend to make of the image.

The release must be signed by the proper person—normally the person whose image is used. But if that person is a minor, the parent or guardian must sign. Most states have now adopted 18, rather than 21, as the age of reaching majority, but you should check the law in your own state.

The release should specify what use will be made of the likeness. For example, the model might consent to the use of the image "for advertising dress designs in trade magazines." Use of the image in other situations, such as advertising cigarettes on a billboard, would at the least be a breach of contract. So you might want to broaden the release by use of a phrase such as "any and all purposes, including advertising in all forms."

The release should give permission to the party that will actually use the image. If an illustrator or designer is using a photograph and relying on a release obtained by a photographer, this point becomes especially important. The release should not only give consent to the photographer but also to agents, assigns, and legal representatives. You, in turn, must be able to show your client, such as an advertising agency, that they too are protected under the terms of the release.

If you are dealing directly with the model, it is wise to have your own release form signed—even if an advertising agency or a new client gives you its form that you also have the model sign. If, for some reason, you are relying on the client's form and not getting your own form signed, you should check very closely to see that the client's form protects you. If you feel it doesn't, you should request that the client indemnify you—that is, agree to pay your losses and expenses that may result if the release is, in fact, inadequate to protect you.

The payment of money to the model isn't necessary for a valid release, but it may be a wise step to take. In this way a release differs from a contract, since you must give something of value if you want to make a contract binding. Normally for a release you would give a fee and, if you do, you naturally should state that in the release. One revealing case involved a woman who received no fee for consenting to use of her likeness in advertising for a perfume. Twenty years later she was able to revoke her consent, despite the money spent by the manufacturer to obtain a trademark and develop the market for the product. In fact, you might want not only to pay to prevent the revocation but also to specify in the release how long the subject's consent is to be effective. When a man agreed at the age of 24 to the advertising use by a health spa of before-and-after photographs of himself, the advertising use of such photographs 10 years later was an invasion of privacy. Nor did the man even revoke his consent in this case. But he hadn't received a fee, and the court felt his consent lasted only for a reasonable time after the making of the photographs.

Tough cases develop when images are altered. Does the release permit such changes? Or are they perhaps allowed by trade custom?

A model agreed to an advertisement for a bookstore. The release gave an irrevocable consent to the bookstore and its assigns to use her image "for advertising purposes or purposes of trade, and I waive the right to inspect or approve such . . . pictures, or advertising matter used in connection therewith." The bookstore's advertisement showed the model reading in bed and was captioned "For People Who Take Their Reading Seriously." The bookstore then violated its contract with the photographer by assigning rights of use to a bedsheet manufacturer known for its offensive advertisements. The manufacturer altered the advertisement so the model in bed was in the company of an elderly man reading a book titled *Clothes Make the Man* (described by the court as a "vulgar" book). The implication was that the model had agreed to portray a call girl for the bedsheet advertisement. These changes in the content made a different image in the view of the court and gave the model a right to sue for invasion of privacy. So while the image could be assigned for other advertising uses, it could not be altered in such an objectionable manner. To protect yourself from liability, it's wise to limit in your confirmation or invoice forms the uses that can be made of a likeness to those permitted in the release.

On the other hand, a basketball player signing a release allowing the advertising use of his likeness in "composite or distorted" form could not complain when a glass of beer was added to make an advertisement for beer. Nor could an actress complain when the photographs taken for a movie poster were retouched to emphasize the sexuality of the woman portrayed. Since the actress had consented to the use of her "likeness" in advertising for the movie, the court felt trade usage permitted the sexual emphasis. But in a very similar case involving a movie actor shown in a composite design notifying his admirers by telegraph where to see his new film, the court said the actor's release for publicity extended only to a true image—not a composite portraying something that never occurred. This shows how dangerous it can be to rely on trade custom. If trade custom conflicts with a clear written contract, it won't even be admissible in court. So a carefully drafted release is a far safer approach.

When using a release, always fill in the blanks—the date, the model's name, your name, any addresses, any fees, and so on. It's important that you keep records enabling you to relate the release to the image for which it was given. This can be done by use of a numbering system matching the releases to the images.

If you deal directly with the models, you should make a practice of getting the release signed at the session. Don't put it off, even if you're not exactly certain what the final use of the image will be. Also, while you don't have to have a witness for the release, it can help in proving proper execution of the release.

The releases shown here follow the principles that we've discussed. The form can, of course, be modified to meet special needs that you may have. These releases can also serve as a reference, so that you can compare releases provided to you in order to be certain that you are sufficiently protected.

Release—Short Form

In consideration of $_____ , receipt of which is acknowledged, I, _____ , do hereby give _____ , his (her) assigns, licensees, and legal representatives the irrevocable right to use my name (or any fictional name), picture, portrait, or photograph in all forms and media and in all manners, including composite or distorted representations, for advertising, trade, or any other lawful purposes, and I waive any right to inspect or approve the finished product, including written copy, that may be created in connection therewith. I am of full age.* I have read this release and am fully familiar with its contents.

Witness: _____   Signed: _____

Address: _____   Address: _____

Date: _____ , 19 _____

Consent (if applicable)

I am the parent and guardian of the minor named above and have the legal authority to execute the above release. I approve the foregoing and waive any rights in the premises.

Witness: _____   Signed: _____

Address: _____   Address: _____

Date _____ , 19__

*Delete this sentence if the subject is a minor. The parent or guardian must then sign the consent paragraph.

Model Release—Long Form

In consideration of _____ Dollars ($_____), receipt of which is acknowledged, I do hereby irrevocably authorize _____, of _____(address), City of _____, County of _____, State of_____ , his (her) legal representatives, assigns, and those acting under his (her) permission and on his (her) authority, to copyright, publish, and use in all forms and media and all manners for advertising, trade, promotion, exhibition, or any other lawful purpose whatsoever, pictures, portraits, or photographs of me in which I may be included in whole or in part, or composite or distorted in character, or form, in conjunction with my own or a fictitious name, or reproductions thereof in color or otherwise or other derivative works made through any medium.

I do hereby waive any right that I may have to inspect or approve the finished product or the advertising or other copy that may be used in connection therewith or the use to which it may be applied.

I hereby release and agree to hold harmless _____, his (her) legal representatives, assigns, and all persons acting under his (her) permission or authority, from any liability by virtue of any blurring, distortion, alteration, optical illusion, or use in composite form whether intentional or otherwise, that may occur or be produced in the creation of the pictures, or in any processing tending toward the completion of the finished product, unless it can be shown that they and the publication thereof were maliciously caused, produced, and published solely for the purpose of subjecting me to conspicuous ridicule, scandal, reproach, scorn, and indignity.

I do hereby warrant that I am of full age and have every right to contract in my own name in the above regard.* Further, I have read the above authorization and release, prior to its execution, and I am fully familiar with the contents thereof.

Witness: _____   Signed: _____

Address: _____   Date: ____ , 19____

Consent (if applicable)

I am the parent and guardian of the minor named above and have the legal authority to execute the above release. I approve the foregoing and waive any rights in the premises.

Witness: _____   Signed: _____

Address: _____   Address: _____

Date _____ , 19__

*Delete this sentence if the subject is a minor. The parent or guardian must then sign the consent paragraph.

Release—By Owner of Property

In consideration of the sum of _____ Dollars (_____), receipt of which is acknowledged, I do hereby irrevocably authorize _____, of _____(address), City of _____ , County of _____, State of _____, his (her) legal representatives, assigns, and those acting under his (her) permission and on his (her) authority, to copyright, publish and use in all forms and media and in all manners for advertising, trade, promotion, exhibition, or any other lawful purpose whatsoever, pictures, portraits, or photographs of the following property that I own and have sole authority over to license for the creation of such images: _____

_____

regardless of whether said use is composite or distorted in character or form, in conjunction with my own or a fictitious name, or reproduction thereof is made in color or otherwise or other derivative works are made through any medium.

I do hereby waive any right that I may have to inspect or approve the finished product or the advertising or other copy that may be used in connection therewith or the use to which it may be applied.

I hereby release, discharge and agree to hold harmless _____ _____, his (her) legal representatives, assigns, and all persons acting under his (her) permission or authority, from any liability by virtue of any blurring, distortion, alteration, optical illusion, or use in composite form whether intentional or otherwise, that may occur or be produced in the creation of the pictures, or in any processing tending toward the completion of the finished product, unless it can be shown that they and the publication thereof were maliciously caused, produced, and published solely for the purpose of subjecting me to conspicuous ridicule, scandal, reproach, scorn, and indignity.

I do hereby warrant that I am of full age and have every right to contract in my own name in the above regard. Further, I have read the above authorization and release, prior to its execution, and I am fully familiar with the contents thereof.

Witness: _____   Signed: _____

Address: _____   Date: _____, 19____

CHAPTER 13

Beyond Privacy

INVASION OF PRIVACY is not the only risk you and your clients face when bringing images before the public. Both private individuals and the public are protected by other laws drawn from a variety of sources. This chapter will elaborate on what you must know about in addition to privacy so you can pursue your professional activities without violating any laws or legal rights.

Right of Publicity

The right of publicity is possessed by athletes, entertainers, and other people who seek to create a value in their name or likeness by achieving celebrity status. It is different from the right of privacy, which protects peace of mind and the right to live free of unwanted intrusions. The right of publicity is a property right based on the value inherent in a celebrity's name or likeness. The right of privacy protects everyone. The right of publicity protects only those who have succeeded in becoming celebrities. The right of privacy cannot be assigned. The right of publicity, like other property rights, can be assigned. The right of privacy ends when the person whose privacy was invaded dies. The right of publicity can survive the celebrity's death and benefit his or her heirs or assignees.

If you use an image of a baseball player for a company that manufactures baseball cards, the company is going to need a license from the player in order to use that likeness on its baseball cards. Or if a company wants to use the likeness of a football player in a game for children, a license from the player will be needed to avoid having the game violate his or her right of publicity. In one interesting case a baseball player gave a license to a sporting-goods company and its assignees to use his name, facsimile signature, initials, portrait, or nickname in the sale of its gloves, baseballs, and so on. The sporting-goods company sold baseballs to a meat company for use in a promotion with meats. They also gave the meat company the right to use the player's name and likeness in connection with the promotion. The player sued to prevent the meat company from using his name and likeness in this way, but he lost because he had assigned his right of publicity without limiting what types of companies it could be assigned to.

The right of publicity protects against commercial exploitation. It cannot prevent the reporting of events that are newsworthy or in the public interest. For a guide to what is newsworthy or in the public interest, you can refer back to the many examples given in the chapter on privacy.

The courts have said that the right of publicity will survive a celebrity only if that person exploits the right while alive. This means that celebrities must take steps to exercise these rights—for example, by means of contracts to use their name or likeness for endorsements or on products—if assignees or heirs are to be able to assert the right after the celebrity's death. If a celebrity's right of publicity would be violated by the commercial use of a likeness, a license should be obtained from the celebrity.

Libel

Libel is communicating to the public a false statement about someone that damages the person's reputation. Altered images can create a false impression and damage someone's reputation. So can errors in production.

But the most common area of libel with respect to visuals is the association of an innocent image with a text that is libelous. There is, by the way, no reason the graphic artist would be responsible in such a case if he or she had nothing to do with the offending text. For example, an illustration might show a man and woman riding in a carriage. It can't possibly say anything false. But suppose the illustration is printed in a newspaper and the caption says that the man and woman are convicted embezzlers, and this isn't true. Despite the innocence of the image, the combination with the caption creates a libel.

The First Amendment cuts into the individual's protection against libel. In a libel suit brought by a public official or public figure over a report that is newsworthy, the person suing must show that the false statement was made with reckless disregard for whether it was true or false or with actual knowledge that it was false. This is a very difficult standard to meet. The question of who is a public figure, already discussed under invasion of privacy, becomes important in libel because of the higher standard of proof required. For private individuals who become involved in matters of public interest, the states may set a lower standard. For example, the private individual might have to show only negligence in the publication of the false material in order to recover. For private individuals suing for libel over a matter not in the public interest, proof that the defendant knew the statement was false would be necessary only to get the extra damages called punitive damages.

Libel is in general of less concern to graphic artists than to writers. However, if you fear that use of an image may libel someone, you should consult an attorney and consider obtaining a release from the person who might bring the libel suit.

Private Property

In the last chapter we discussed whether using images of dogs, horses, automobiles, interiors of houses, and other private property could cause an invasion of privacy. As long as the owner was not identified, it did not appear that his or her privacy could be invaded. Two cases, however, illustrate some risks other than invasion of privacy that you should keep in mind.

A photographer was commissioned to photograph a woman's dog. The woman purchased several prints, and, as far as she was concerned, the transaction was finished. The photographer, however, sold the dog's photographs to an advertising agency that used them for dog-biscuit advertisements in local and national newspapers. The woman sued the photographer, his agent, the advertising agency, the dog-biscuit company, and the newspapers based on the use of the photographs of the dog. The court decided that the photographer and his agent had breached the original contract with the woman, since the customer is the owner of all proprietary rights in works done on commission. Because of this the photographer and his agent would have to pay damages for their breach of contract, while the other defendants would merely be barred from running the advertisement again. The illustrator and designer must exercise caution to avoid being placed in this photographer's predicament due to an unauthorized use.

If the dog had been wandering the streets and the artist had created the picture on his or her own initiative, the owner would presumably not have had any right to object to a subsequent advertising use, since the artist would have owned all the proprietary rights. An intriguing point here, however, is that the copyright law has changed since this case was decided. After January 1, 1978, the artist owns the copyright of the images of the dog, whether the owner commissions the pictures or the dog is photographed running free in the streets. Could this change the result of the case if it were to come up again? We don't think so, because the courts would probably conclude that an implied provision of the contract to create an image of the dog is that the image will be only for the owner's use. Despite the artist's owning the copyright, the contract would implicitly forbid reuse for purposes other than those intended by the owner. But we will have to await future litigation before we know with certainty the effect of the new law.

The other case may be unique, but it's certainly worth taking into account. It arose out of the New York World's Fair of 1964. A postcard company took photographs of the buildings, exhibits, and other activities going on inside the fairgrounds. These were then sold on postcards, albums, and related items. Admission was charged for entrance to the World's Fair, and, in fact, the World's Fair Corporation had entered into a contract with another company to exploit similar pictures of the buildings, exhibits, and so on. In addition to this, the postcard company had bid for the right to make the postcards and sell the commercial items both inside and outside the fairgrounds. On considering these special facts, the court decided that an injunction should be granted to prevent the postcard company from continuing its commercial exploitation. The court likened the buildings and exhibits to a show in which the World's Fair Corporation had a property interest. Two of the five judges dissented, however, and said they didn't think anything could prevent selling items incorporating photographs of the exteriors of the buildings. This case is probably limited to its unique facts—an unsuccessful bidder commercially using images of unusually attractive buildings on private grounds to which admission is charged. It could hardly prevent you from making postcards of the Empire State Building or the New York City skyline. But the cautious graphic artist will take the case into account before launching a similar enterprise.

Unfair Competition

The protection of businesses against unfair competition is primarily to prevent confusion among members of the public as to the source of goods or services. It is a protection that is highly flexible. For example, titles are not copyrightable. Yet this protection against unfair competition could be used to prevent one title from too closely imitating another. If the public came to identify a work by one title—such as *The Fifth Column,* by Ernest Hemingway—no one could use a similar title for a competing work. An obvious application would be to prevent one graphic artist from using the name of another in order to pass off his or her own work. So if Jane Artist is well known, another artist adopting her name would be unfairly competing. Nor could one graphic artist imitate the style of another and try to pass off the work. In a case involving cartoon strips, the court stated that using the title of a cartoon strip and imitating the cartoonist's style was unfair competition.

There is another aspect to the doctrine of unfair competition. In some cases artists have tried to use the claim of unfair competition to prevent distorted versions of their work from being presented to the public by licensees. The reasoning is that the distorted version is not truly created by the artist. Presenting it to the public injures the artist's reputation and unfairly competes with his or her work. Such an attempt to create moral rights (discussed on page 174) from American legal doctrines is difficult at best.

Obscenity

Censorship has a long history. Few people realize today that the censors' fascination with pornography is relatively recent, dating from the era of Queen Victoria. Prior to that censors focused on supressing sedition against the Crown and heresy against the Church. In the United States censorship conflicts with the First Amendment guarantees for free speech and free press. The result is an uncomfortable and rather arbitrary compromise as to what sexually oriented materials can be banned. Works of serious artistic intention are protected from censorship under guidelines set forth by the United States Supreme Court. Specifically, the factors in determining obscenity are:

(a) whether 'the average person, applying contemporary community standards, would find that the work, taken as a whole, appeals to the prurient interest . . . ; (b) whether the work depicts or describes, in a patently offensive way, sexual conduct specifically defined by the applicable state law; and (c) whether the work, taken as a whole, lacks serious literary, artistic, political, or scientific value.

This definition applies to conduct that takes place after June 21, 1973.

The laws affecting obscene materials prohibit such uses as possession for sale or exhibition, sale, distribution, exhibition, importation through customs, and mailing. Distributors are usually the defendants, although in some jurisdictions eager prosecutors have now started going after actors in films on a conspiracy theory. Especially regarding the contemporary community standard as applied by the average person, it is difficult to know what the result of an obscenity prosecution may be from one locality to the next. The court has clarified that the average person in the community does not include children, since a much lower "average" would be reached for judging what is obscene if children were included.

A number of statutes outlaw the use of children in the portrayal of sexually explicit acts, whether or not the acts are obscene. Whether these laws would apply to images of minors used in an educational context would appear to raise substantial First Amendment questions. Beyond this, however, the courts have ruled that pornographic materials intended for an audience of minors can be subjected to higher standards than those of the average citizen applying contemporary community standards.

The First Amendment does provide procedural safeguards in cases raising issues of obscenity. Essentially, before materials may be seized as obscene, an adversary hearing must be held at which both sides are able to present their views with respect to whether the items are obscene. Only after this review can law-enforcement officials confiscate materials that have been determined to be obscene.

Flag Desecration

State and federal flags are protected from desecration by both state and federal statutes. Desecration includes mutilation, defacement, burning, or trampling on such a flag. It also covers the use of any representation of a flag for advertising or commercial uses, such as product packaging or business stationery. Each statute has special exceptions, so that the New York statute does not apply to the use of the flag on an "ornamental picture, article of jewelry, stationery for use in private correspondence, or newspaper or periodical, on any of which shall be printed, painted or placed, said flag, standard, color, shield or ensign disconnected or apart from any advertisement."

The police power to prevent desecration of the flag is not absolute but must be weighed against the right of the individual to have freedom of expression. When the use of a flag is a form of speech, the First Amendment may protect conduct that would otherwise be criminally punishable as a desecration. In one case an artist made artworks using the United States flag in conjunction with a Vietcong flag, a Russian flag, a Nazi swastika, and a gas mask. The United States flags were wrapped around the shapes of a gun caisson and an erect penis. Antiwar music played in the background to accompany the exhibit. After losing several times in the courts, the gallery owner finally won vindication from a criminal conviction for flag desecration. His First Amendment rights outweighed the danger to the community posed by these uses of the flag.

If you are considering the use of flags, especially for advertising or commercial purposes, you should definitely seek advice from an attorney to be certain that you aren't committing a criminal offense.

Other Protected Symbols

Both state and federal statutes protect a variety of official or well-known names and insignia from unauthorized use, especially if the use is commercial. For example, special federal regulations govern the use of all the following emblems, insignia, and names:

- "Smokey Bear" character or name
- "Woodsy Owl" character, name, or slogan
- Use of likeness of the great seal of the United States, or the seals of the president or vice-president
- "Johnny Horizon" character or name
- "The Golden Eagle Insignia"
- Swiss Confederation coat of arms
- 4-H Club emblem fraudulently used
- Red Cross emblems
- Badges or medals of veterans' organizations
- Military medals or decorations
- Official badges, identification cards, or other insignia
- Misuse of names, words, emblems, or insignia in such a way as to mislead the public to believe that one is acting on official business

Violations vary from item to item on this list but include advertising, product packaging, and uses designed to mislead the public. The safest course is to consult with the secretary of the appropriate agency if you are planning to use its emblem, insignia, or name. For example, you would consult the secretary of the interior if you wanted to use the "Johnny Horizon" character or name or "The Golden Eagle Insignia." If this doesn't seem practical or problems arise, you should get help from your own attorney.

State statutes also protect many badges, names, or insignia of governmental agencies and various orders and societies (such as the United States Spanish War Veterans, Veterans of Foreign Wars of the United States, the American Legion, and so on). As a general rule, if you are going to make use of any insignia belonging to a private group or governmental body, you should check in advance to be certain you are not violating the law. Contacting the group is a good way to start, but ultimately you may again want advice from your attorney.

Coins, Bills, and Stamps

Counterfeiting statutes limit the freedom with which you can reproduce currency and stamps. The purpose of the counterfeiting statutes, of course, is to prevent people from passing off fake currency or stamps. Because of this, you can probably make copies as long as you are certain there is no chance of the copies being mistaken for real currency or stamps. For example, an illustration that distorts the image of paper money is far less likely to create a problem than an exact photograph which is to be incorporated in a design. Although the following discussion focuses on photographic reproductions, it applies equally to illustrations—especially if the illustration is highly realistic.

However, to be completely safe, you would be wise to follow the restrictive guidelines that have been set out in the law. Printed photographs of paper money, checks, bonds, and other obligations and securities of the United States and foreign governments are permissible for numismatic, educational, historical, and newsworthy purposes, and for numismatic advertising (but not for general advertising purposes). In the permissible cases, the printed photographs must be in black and white and either less than three-quarters or more than one and a half times the size of the photographed currency. The photograph should directly relate to the permissible purpose and not simply be used because it is decorative or eye-catching.

Films, microfilms, and slides of paper money, checks, bonds, and so on can be made in color or black and white for projection on a screen or broadcasting. They cannot be used in advertising, however, except for numismatic advertising. Nor can any prints or reproductions be made from the film or slide without the permission of the secretary of the treasury.

Photographs of canceled or uncanceled United States postage stamps are permissible for philatelic, educational, historical, and newsworthy purposes in articles, book, journals, newspapers, or albums. Black-and-white photographs may be of any size, as may color photographs of canceled stamps. However, color photographs of uncanceled stamps must be either less than three-quarters or more than one and a half times the size of the actual stamp. For uncanceled foreign stamps the same restrictions apply as to permissible uses. Black-and-white photographs of uncanceled foreign stamps may be of any size, but color photographs must meet the same size limitations as photographs of uncanceled United States stamps. Also, while philatelic advertising is permitted, the size limitations must be met for color photographs of either United States or foreign stamps that have not been canceled. "Cancellation," by the way, means an official cancellation—the stamp must actually have been used for postage.

Films, microfilms, and slides of both United States and foreign stamps may be in either black and white or color for projection or broadcasting. However, advertising in such cases is still limited to philatelic purposes.

Once the photograph of currency or a stamp has been used, the plate and negatives, including glossy prints, should be destroyed.

You may notice that coins aren't mentioned at all. This is because photographs, films, or slides of the United States or foreign coins may be used for any purposes including advertising. Such photographs of coins don't present the type of risk that the counterfeiting statutes are designed to guard against.

The United States Secret Service has responsibility for enforcing the laws relating to counterfeiting. Its representatives will give you an opinion as to whether the particular use you intend to make is legal, but their opinion would not prevent a later prosecution by either the department of justice or any United States attorney. The address for obtaining such an opinion is Office of the Director, United States Secret Service, Department of the Treasury, Washington, D.C. 20223.

Deceptive Advertising

The Federal Trade Commission Act, passed in 1914, stipulates that "unfair methods of competition are hereby declared unlawful." One of the important areas in which the Federal Trade Commission has acted is misleading or false advertising. If you produce work for advertising agencies, the total impression of the advertisement must not be false or misleading. While some puffery of or bragging about products is permitted, the advertisement must not confuse even an unsophisticated person as to the true nature of the product. It isn't difficult to imagine how visuals can be used to mislead. One example would be the use of props that don't fairly represent the product, such as a bowl of vegetable soup with marbles in the bottom of the bowl to make the vegetables appear thicker. This isn't permissible. On the other hand, the advertising agency doesn't want to create trouble for its client. So in most cases the agency's legal staff will take the necessary steps to ensure that the advertising is not misleading or deceptive.

Aside from the activities of the Federal Trade Commission, there are a number of ways that advertising is controlled. Other federal laws govern the advertising and labeling of a number of specific products. State laws form a patchwork of regulations over different products. The Council of Better Business Bureaus has adopted its own *Code of Advertising* to ensure that fair standards are followed. Many individual industries have set standards to govern the advertising of their products, although the application of these standards to local distributors or dealers can be difficult. Often the media that sell advertising will refuse to accept advertisements that are not considered in good taste. And self-regulation by individual advertising agencies has recently been followed by the creation of the National Advertising Review Council.

The council's purpose is "to develop a structure which would effectively apply the persuasive capacities of peers to seek the voluntary elimination of national advertising which professionals would consider deceptive." The council is composed of the Council of Better Business Bureaus and three groups representing the advertising industry—the American Advertising Federation, the American Association of Advertising Agencies, and the Association of National Advertisers. The council has an investigative division (the National Advertising Division of the Council of Better Business Bureaus) and an appeals division (the National Advertising Review Board). However, it cannot force an advertiser to stop making deceptive claims; it can only bring peer pressure to bear.

A typical case involved an advertisement for dog food that photographically depicted "tender juicy chunks" that appeared to be meat but in actuality were made from soybeans. The investigative division demanded that the deceptive advertising be corrected. After sufficient time for a response had passed without the division's hearing from the dog-food company, officials referred the matter to the appeals division. After the referral, however, the dog-food company did respond and stated that the advertising in question had been changed to eliminate the elements found to be deceptive. Because of this the appeals division dismissed the complaint. This is a good illustration of the disposition of a typical complaint.

Most advertising agencies want to avoid problems as much as you do. You should be able to rely on their expert attorneys for guidance in any area that raises questions. And if you truthfully present the product, you certainly shouldn't have anything to worry about.

CHAPTER 14

Choosing a Lawyer

WHAT DO YOU DO when you need a lawyer? You've been handed a contract and don't want to try to navigate through the legalese without some expert advice. Or you opened your favorite magazine and saw a piece of your art, which was very nice except that you never got paid by the magazine or by anybody else. Or somebody smacked into your car and the insurance company doesn't want to settle. Or you've just had your first child and are wondering whether you need a will.

Of course, you may already have a lawyer and feel pleased with his or her performance. But what if you don't; where do you turn? That depends on the nature of your legal problem. This is a time of greater and greater specialization in the field of law. You have to evaluate whether your problem needs a specialist or can be handled by a lawyer with a general practice. For example, suppose you haven't been paid for an assignment you successfully completed. Any lawyer with a general practice should be able to handle this for you. What if you've been offered a book contract for a collection of your work? Here you'd be wise to find a lawyer with a special understanding of copyright law and the publishing field. Or you think that you should draft your will. Do you have a lot of assets, including special property in the form of copyrights and original art, or do you have a very modest estate? If your estate is complex you'll want to use an estate-planning specialist, particularly if you're concerned about who will own your works and how they will be treated after your death. But if your estate is modest and you're not especially concerned about what happens to your art, a general practitioner should be able to meet your needs.

One implication of legal specialization, by the way, is that you may not use the same lawyer for each legal problem you have to solve. On the other hand, if you have a good relationship with your regular lawyer, he or she should direct you to specialists when you need them. This is probably the best way of making sure you have access to the expertise that is called for.

Lawyer's Fees

Before discussing ways of contacting the lawyer you need, it's worthwhile to stop a moment and discuss the cost of legal services. You *can* afford these services. In the long run, using lawyers at appropriate times will save you money and, quite possibly, a lot of anguish.

How do you find out what a lawyer charges? Ask! If you're worried about paying for that first conference, ask on the phone when you call. If you're worried about what the whole legal bill will run, get an estimate the first time you sit down with the lawyer. Keep in mind that some lawyers will work on a contingency arrangement if you can't afford to pay them. This means that they will take a percentage of the recovery if they win but not charge you for their services if they lose. Or they may combine a flat fee with a contingency or require you to pay the expenses but not pay for their time. Some will even barter legal services for art. In other words, it isn't all cut and dried.

And you don't necessarily need a law firm with five names in the title—maybe a legal clinic can do the trick or one of the volunteer lawyers for the arts groups. So let's move ahead to the problem of contacting the right lawyer for you.

Informal Referrals

Ask a friend, another artist, or your uncle who won that lawsuit the summer before last. People usually know when they've received good legal service. If your problem is similar to theirs, their lawyer may be right for you. You certainly know other professionals in your own business. If you start asking them, you'll probably come up with a good lead.

This may not sound scientific, but it's the way most people do find lawyers and it's not a bad way. It gives you a chance to find out about the lawyer's skills, personality, and fees. It gives you confidence because the recommendation comes from someone you know and trust. Of course, when you talk to the lawyer, make sure that he or she is the right person for your special problem. If he or she hasn't handled a case like yours before, you may want to keep looking. Or if a particular lawyer doesn't feel your problem is what he or she handles best, you should request a referral to another lawyer.

Volunteer Lawyers for the Arts

All across the country lawyers are volunteering to aid needy artists, writers, composers, and other creative people. There's no charge for these legal services, but you have to meet certain income guidelines and, perhaps, pay the court costs and any other expenses. If you qualify, that's great, but even if you don't qualify for free help, you may get a good referral to someone who can help you.

Rather than listing all the volunteer-lawyers groups, we're giving you the names of three of the most active. You can call the group nearest you to find out whether there are any volunteer lawyers for the arts in your own area.

Bay Area Lawyers for the Arts
Fort Mason Center Building 310
San Francisco, California 94123
(415) 775-7200

Lawyers for the Creative Arts
111 North Wabash Avenue
Chicago, Illinois 60602
(312) 263-6989

Volunteer Lawyers for the Arts
36 West 44th Street
New York, New York 10036
(212) 575-1150

Professional Associations

We can't emphasize enough the value of belonging to an appropriate professional organization, such as the Graphic Artists Guild. But even if you don't belong, you might still try contacting such an organization in your area to ask for a lawyer who understands the legal problems of illustrators and designers. The society's members have probably had problems similar to yours at one time or another. The executive director or office manager should know which lawyer helped in such a case and how the matter turned out. If the society's officers can't give you a name immediately, they can usually come up with one after asking around among the members. Needless to say, you're going to feel more comfortable asking if you belong to the organization. Professional organizations are listed on pages 222–24.

A different type of organization that can aid you is exemplified by the Joint Ethics Committee in New York City. The Joint Ethics Committee will mediate or arbitrate a dispute if the parties are willing to do this. It is described more fully on pages 222–24.

Legal Clinics

Legal clinics are easy to find, since they advertise their services and fee schedules in media such as newspapers and the Yellow Pages, where they are listed under "Attorneys" or "Lawyers." Another good way to find a clinic is through your network of friends and acquaintances, some of whom have probably either used a clinic or know of one to recommend. In many ways a clinic is just like any other law firm. The good clinic, however, will have refined its operation so it can handle routine matters efficiently and in large volume. This allows the institution of many economies, such as using younger lawyers and paralegals (who are assistants with the training necessary to carry out routine tasks in a law office), having forms and word-processing equipment, and giving out pamphlets to explain the basic legal procedures relevant to your case. Not all clinics, by the way, call themselves clinics. They may simply use a traditional type of law-firm name but advertise low-cost services based on efficient management.

What types of matters can the legal clinic handle for you? Divorce, bankruptcy, buying or selling real estate, wills, and other simple, everyday legal problems. What types of problems should you not take to a clinic? The complicated or unusual ones, such as book contracts, invasion-of-privacy suits, questions about copyright, and so on. The clinic can be efficient only when it handles many cases like yours. The special problems faced by the illustrator or graphic designer will not be the problems the clinic can handle best. And if you're wondering whether there are legal clinics specially designed for creators of artistic works, the answer is not yet. But it's not a bad idea, especially for an urban area where many graphic artists earn their livelihood.

Lawyer Referral Services

A lawyer referral service is usually set up by the local bar association. It can be found in the Yellow Pages under "Lawyer Referral Service." If it's not listed there, check the headings for

"Attorneys" and "Lawyers." If you still can't find a listing, call your local or state bar association to find out whether such a lawyer referral service is being run for your area.

Unfortunately the 300 local referral services are not of uniform quality. Two criticisms are usually levied against them: first, their not listing lawyers by area of specialty, and, second, their listing lawyers who need business rather than the best legal talent available. Even referral services that do list lawyers by specialty may not have a category that covers the unique needs of illustrators and graphic artists.

But the advantages of a good referral service shouldn't be overlooked. A good service puts you in touch with a lawyer with whom you can have a conference for a small fee—$10 or $15. If you don't like that lawyer, you can always go back to the service again. Some services do assign lawyers on the basis of specialty and, in fact, send out follow-up questionnaires to check on how the lawyers perform. This tends to improve the quality of the legal services. And a number of services require the lawyer to have malpractice insurance so you can recover if the lawyer is negligent in representing you. Such services are certainly another possible avenue for you to take in searching for a good lawyer.

Collection Agencies

While we're on the subject of lawyers, it's certainly worth briefly mentioning a few alternatives. If, for example, you are having trouble collecting some of your accounts receivable, you might consider using a collection agency. Such agencies are easy to find, since they're listed in the Yellow Pages. They will go after your uncollected accounts and dun them with letters, phone calls, and so on until payment is made. Payment for the agency is either a flat fee per collection (such as $8 for a debt under $75, $22 for a debt between $75 and $200, and so on) or a percentage of the amount recovered. These percentages vary from as little as 20 percent to as much as 45 percent. If the agency can't collect for you, you're right back where you started and you need a lawyer.

What are the pros and cons of using collection agencies? On the plus side is the fact that you have a chance at recovering part of the money owed to you without the expense of hiring a lawyer. The negative side is the agency's fee and the fact that some agencies resort to unsavory practices. Needless to say, this may lose you clients in the long run. But a reputable collection agency may be able to aid you by recovering the money owed to you so there is no need to go to court. Of course, if you have the stamina and determination to act as your own collection agency (phoning, sending letters, and so on), that may be the best solution of all.

Small Claims Court

When small sums of money are involved and your claim is a simple one, using a lawyer may be too expensive to justify. Most localities have courts that take jurisdiction over small claims, those ranging from a few hundred dollars in some areas to a few thousand dollars in other areas, and you can represent yourself in these small claims courts. To find the appropriate small claims court in your area, look in the phone book under local, county, or state governments. If a small claims court is not listed there, a call to the clerk of one of the other courts is a quick way of finding out whether there is such a court and where it's located.

The procedure for using a small claims court is simple and inexpensive. Your filing fee will vary from about $3 to $15 depending on the locality. You fill out short forms for a summons and complaint. These include the defendant's accurate name and address, the nature of your claim stated in everyday language, and the amount of your claim. If you aren't sure of the defendant's exact business name and it isn't posted on the premises, the clerk of the county in which the defendant does business should be able to help you. The clerk will set a date for the hearing and send the summons requiring an appearance on that date to the defendant. If you have witnesses, you bring them along to testify. If the witnesses don't want to testify or if you need papers that are in the possession of the party you're suing, ask the court to issue a subpoena to force the witnesses to come or the papers to be produced. Of course, you bring along all the relevant papers that you have, such as confirmation forms, invoices, and so on.

The date for your hearing will probably be no more than a month or two away. Many small claims courts hold sessions in the evening, so don't worry if you can't come during the day. The judge or referee will ask you for your side of the story. After both sides have had their say, the judge will often encourage a settlement. If that's not possible, a decision will either be given immediately or be sent to you within a few weeks. The decision can be in favor of you or the other party or it can be a compromise. After winning, you may need the help of a marshall or sheriff to collect from a reluctant defendant, although most losers will simply put a check in the mail. Of course, the laws governing small claims courts vary from jurisdiction to jurisdiction, so it's helpful if you can find a guide specially written for your own court. Asking the clerk of the court is one way to find out whether such a guide exists. Or you might give a call to your Better Business Bureau or Chamber of Commerce.

APPENDIX

Professional Organizations and Associations

American Institute of Graphic Arts

> 1059 Third Avenue, New York, New York 10021, (212) PL2-0813. Leading organization for display, publication, and preservation of general graphic and design works in printed media.

Art Directors Club (of New York)

> 488 Madison Avenue, New York, New York 10022, (212) 838-8140. Sponsor of major national advertising and corporate art directing award show; exhibits and publishes work of excellence in that field. Art Directors Clubs of Boston, Connecticut, New Jersey, Philadelphia, and many other areas perform similar functions on a local level.

Artists Equity Association

> 3726 Albermarle Street N.W., Washington, D.C. 20016, (202) 244-0209. Deals with issues affecting rights of artists generally, with primary emphasis on the fine arts.

Artists Equity Assocation of New York

> 225 West 34th Street, New York, New York 10001, (212) 736-6480. Concerned with issues affecting artists' (primarily fine artists') rights.

Association of Medical Illustrators

> 6650 N.W. Highway, Suite 112, Chicago, Illinois 60631, (312) 763-7350. Concerned with standards in teaching and practice of medical illustration.

Association of American Editorial Cartoonists

> c/o Jim Lange, Oklahoma City *Oklahoman*, Oklahoma City, Oklahoma 73125, (405) 232-3311. Concerned with economic welfare, standards, and professional ethics for all editorial cartoonists.

Cartoonists Guild

> 156 West 72nd Street, New York, New York 10023, (212) 873-4023. Concerned with the professional standards of free-lance cartoonists and their economic welfare, with some emphasis on magazine cartooning.

Creative Arts Public Service Program (CAPS)
  250 West 57th Street, New York, New York 10019, (212) 247-6303. One of the leaders among the numerous state funds throughout the country that provide grants to individuals of that state, for artistic achievement. The names and addresses of other states' agencies that provide such funding can be obtained from *American Council for the Arts* (ACA), 570 Seventh Avenue, New York, New York 10018; (212) 354-6655.

College Art Association
  16 East 52nd Street, New York, New York 10022, (212) 755-3532. National organization that concerns itself with standards in teaching of art; its annual meeting is also an important meeting ground for those interested in the job market for faculty positions.

Foundation for the Community of Artists
  280 Broadway, Room 412, New York, New York 10007, (212) 227-3770. Concerned with programs, actions, and legislation pertaining to artists' (primarily fine artists') rights; publisher of outstanding newspaper in this field titled *Artworkers News.*

John Simon Guggenheim Memorial Foundation
  90 Park Avenue, New York, New York 10020, (212) 687-4470. One of the leading foundations making individual grants to artists; others can be found by examining *The Foundation Grants Index,* published annually by The Foundation Center, 888 Seventh Avenue, New York, New York 10019; (212) 975-1120 ($27).

Graphic Artists Guild
30 East 20th Street, Room 405, New York, New York 10003, (212) 982-9298. The leading national organization in the field of activities to promote and protect graphic designers and illustrators in all areas with legislation, publications, information, and group insurance programs. Chapters are active in Atlanta, Boston, Dallas, Greensboro (NC), Honolulu, Long Island, Los Angeles, Miami, Nashville, New York City, Orange County (Calif.), St. Louis, Salt Lake City, San Francisco, and Seattle. Contact the national headquarters for details.
  Publications include such landmark volumes as: *Pricing and Ethical Guidelines; Protecting Your Heirs and Creative Works; The Visual Artist's Guide to the New Copyright Law.*
  In addition, the Guild sponsors a wide array of seminars and works that are of vital importance to graphic artists.
  Contact the national headquarters for details.

Joint Ethics Committee
  Post Office Box 179, Grand Central Station, New York, New York 10017. Mediates or arbitrates disputes between graphic artists and clients. Has done so successfully for some 35 years. Sponsored jointly by the Art Directors Club of New York, the American Society of Magazine Photographers, the Graphic Artists Guild, the Society of Illustrators, and the Society of Photographers and Artists Representatives.

National Cartoonists Society (NCS)
  9 Ebony Court, Brooklyn, New York 11229, (212) 743-6510. Concerned primarily with the art of cartooning and standards in the profession, and acts as a fraternal organization among cartoonists in all disciplines.

National Endowment for the Arts (NEA)
Visual Arts Program, 2401 E Street, N.W., Washington, D.C. 20506, (202) 634-6369. Provides grants to individuals and organizations in the arts.

Society of American Graphic Artists
1083 Fifth Avenue, New York, New York 10028, (212) 289-1507. Concerned with standards and practices of printmakers.

Society of Illustrators
128 East 63rd Street, New York, New York 10021, (212) 838-2560. Leading cultural force in the preservation of works of past illustrators and in the exhibition, publication, and preservation of works of living illustrators; active social and educational programs for illustrators, other members of the public interested in the art form, and students of art and illustration; sponsors the leading show of current work in the field and the basic visual reference book for the industry, both titled *Illustrators Annual*. Societies of Illustrators in other cities such as Los Angeles are important in their area but are not directly affiliated.

Society of Publication Designers
3 West 51st Street, New York, New York 10019, (212) 582-4077. Sponsors educational meetings and the leading national annual exhibition and publication in the field of publication design.

Society of Photographers and Artists Representatives (SPAR)
P. O. Box 845, FDR Station, New York, New York 10150, (212) 628-9148. Primarily New York-based representatives of artists, photographers, and some designers; sponsors educational programs for members and representatives just entering the field, and supplies members with a current list of advertising art directors in New York City.

Type Directors Club
12 East 41st Street, Room 401, New York, New York 10017, (212) 683-6492. Concerned with professional standards and artistic achievements in the field of type design and utilization; sponsors the major national show and new annual publication on these subjects.

Visual Artists and Galleries Association (VAGA)
1 World Trade Center, Suite 1535, New York, New York 10048, (212) 466-1390. Concerned with marketing and preserving rights for reproduction of both fine and commercial art works.

Volunteer Lawyers for the Arts (VLA)
36 West 44th Street, New York, New York 10036, (212) 575-1150. Provides free legal services to individuals and organizations satisfying its income requirements; can direct you to similar services in a number of other cities including Chicago, San Francisco, and Houston (see page 217).

West Reps
1258 North Highland Avenue, Suite 102, Los Angeles, California 90048, (213) 469-2254. West Coast based artists' and photographers' representatives.

BIBLIOGRAPHY A

Books

The page number at the end of an entry refers to the discussion of the work in the text. Additional publishing information such as the date of publication, price, and address of the publisher is included in that text discussion.

Marketing

American Art Directory, R. R. Bowker, New York, New York (pages 34 and 35).

American Showcase, American Showcase, New York, New York (pages 14, 23, 38, 45 and 47).

American Universities and Colleges, American Council on Education, Washington, D.C. (page 10).

Art Directors' Annual, Art Directors Club, New York, New York (pages 48 and 52).

Art Directors' Index to Illustration, Graphics and Design, John Butsch and Associates, Chicago, Illinois (pages 45 and 47).

Audio-Visual Market Place, R. R. Bowker, New York, New York (page 7).

Business Publications, Standard Rate and Data Service, Skokie, Illinois (page 17).

Consumer Magazine and Farm Publications, Standard Rate and Data Service, Skokie, Illinois (page 17).

Contact Book, Celebrity Service, New York, New York (page 12).

Contract—Directory of Sources, Gralla Publications, New York, New York (page 22).

Decor "Sources" Annual, Commerce Publishing Company, St. Louis, Missouri (page 21).

Education Directory; Colleges and Universities, National Center for Education Statistics, Washington, D.C. (page 10).

Gebbie Press All-In-One Directory, Gebbie Press, New Paltz, New York (page 16).

Gift and Decorative Accessories Magazine, Geyer McAllister Publications, New York, New York (page 20).

Gift and Decorative Accessory Buyers Directory, Geyer McAllister Publications, New York, New York (page 20).

Illustrators' Annual, Society of Illustrators, New York, New York (pages 38, 49 and 54).

Interior Design Buyers Guide, Interior Design Publications, New York, New York (page 22).

Kelly's Manufacturers & Merchants Directory, Kelly's Directories, Kingston-Upon-Thames, Surrey, England (page 21).

L.A. Workbook, Alexis Scott, Los Angeles, California (pages 14, 23, 49 and 57).

Literary Market Place, R. R. Bowker, New York, New York (page 8).

Madison Avenue Handbook, Peter Glenn Publications, New York, New York (pages 7 and 47).

Magazine Industry Market Place R. R. Bowker, New York, New York (page 19).

Mail Order Business Directory, B. Klein Publications, Coral Springs, Florida (page 24).

Membership Directory, American Institute of Graphic Arts, New York, New York (page 13).

Membership Directory, American Society of Interior Designers, New York, New York (page 22).

New York Publicity Outlets, Public Relations Plus, Washington Depot, Connecticut (page 19).

O'Dwyer's Directory of Corporate Communications, J. R. O'Dwyer Co., New York, New York (page 11).

O'Dwyer's Directory of Public Relations Firms, J. R. O'Dwyer Co., New York, New York (page 22).

Photography Market Place, second edition, Fred W. McDarrah, R. R. Bowker, New York, New York (pages 12 and 13).

Publication Design Annual, Hastings House, New York, New York (page 54).

RSVP, Richard Lebenson and Kathleen Creighton, Brooklyn, New York (pages 49 and 57).

Sources, Commerce Publishing, St. Louis, Missouri (page 21).

Standard Directory of Advertisers, National Register Publishing Company, Skokie, Illinois (page 11).

Standard Directory of Advertising Agencies, National Register Publishing Company, Skokie, Illinois (page 5).

The Best Ever, Mead Corporation, Dayton, Ohio (page 13).

The Creative Black Book, Friendly Publications, New York, New York (pages 38, 45, 47 and 57).

The International Buyer's Guide of the Music-Tape Industry, Billboard Publications, New York, New York, and Los Angeles, California (page 13).

The Thomas Register, (page 23).

Typography Annual, Watson-Guptill, New York, New York (page 55).

Ulrich's International Periodicals Directory, R. R. Bowker, New York, New York (page 18).

Working Press of the Nation, vol. 5, National Research Bureau, Burlington, Iowa (page 14).

World Travel Directory, Ziff-Davis Publishing Company, New York, New York (page 24).

Business

IN GENERAL

Legal Guide for the Visual Artist, Tad Crawford, Hawthorn Books, New York, New York (page 100).

Pricing and Ethical Guidelines, The Graphic Artists Guild, New York, New York (page 73).

The Writer's Legal Guide, Hawthorn Books, New York, New York (page 100).

TAXES

Child Care and Disabled Dependent Care, Internal Revenue Service, Washington, D.C. (page 139).

Computing Your Tax Under the Income Averaging Method, Internal Revenue Service, Washington, D.C. (page 140).

Protecting Your Heirs and Creative Works, Tad Crawford, editor, The Graphic Artists Guild, New York, New York (page 144).

If You're Self-Employed . . . Reporting Your Income for Social Security, Social Security Administration, Washington, D.C. (page 141).

Fear of Filing, Volunteer Lawyers for the Arts, New York, New York (page 145).

Information on Self-Employment Tax, Internal Revenue Service, Washington, D.C. (page 141).

J. K. Lasser's Your Income Tax, Simon & Schuster, New York, New York (page 145).

Legal Guide for the Visual Artist, Tad Crawford, Hawthorn Books, New York, New York (page 145).

Questions and Answers on Retirement Plans for the Self-Employed, Internal Revenue Service, Washington, D.C. (page 139).

Retirement Plans for Self-Employed Individuals, Internal Revenue Service, Washington, D.C.(page 139).

Tax Guide for Small Business, Internal Revenue Service, Washington, D.C. (page 144).

Tax Information on Depreciation, Internal Revenue Service, Washington, D.C. (page 135).

Tax Information on Individual Retirement Savings Programs, Internal Revenue Service, Washington, D.C. (page 139).

Tax Withholding and Declaration of Estimated Tax, Internal Revenue Service, Washington, D.C.(page 141).

The Tax Reliever: A Guide for the Artist, Richard Helleloid, Drum Books, St. Paul, Minnesota (page 145).

Travel, Entertainment and Gift Expenses, Internal Revenue Service, Washington, D.C. (pages 136 and 138).

Your Federal Income Tax, Internal Revenue Service, Washington, D.C. (pages 130 and 144).

Your Social Security, Social Security Administration, Washington, D.C. (page 141).

LEGAL

Copyright Information Kit, United States Copyright Office, Library of Congress, Washington, D.C. (page 176).

Legal Guide for the Visual Artist, Tad Crawford, Hawthorn Books, New York, New York (page 176).

The Visual Artist's Guide to the New Copyright Law, Tad Crawford, Graphic Artists Guild, New York, New York (pages 100 and 176).

The Writer's Legal Guide, Tad Crawford, Hawthorn Books, New York, New York (page 100).

BIBLIOGRAPHY B

Periodicals

The magazines that reproduce exceptional examples of work done for clients have certain areas of emphasis. For *CA—Communication Arts* it is often corporate media; for *Art Direction,* usually advertising; for *Print,* editorial illustration. Nonetheless, all these publications review a wide spectrum of commercial work in most of the related areas.

In addition, *U & lc* covers the creative use of typography (occasionally in conjunction with illustration and photography); *Push Pin Graphic* focuses on conceptual issues in illustration, design, and, more recently, photography; and *Graphics Design U.S.A.* provides short notes on the professional activities of art directors and designers, including some job and account changes.

American Artist Business Letter, 1515 Broadway, New York, New York 10036, (212) 764-7300. Marketing, business, and legal tips for artists, craftspeople, and those getting started in the commercial arts.

Art Direction, Room 802, 19 West 44th Street, New York, New York 10036, (212) 345-0450.

Art Workers News, Foundation for the Community of Artists, 280 Broadway, Room 412, New York, New York 10007, (212) 227-3770. Business, legal, and other information of interest primarily to fine artists.

CA—Communication Arts, P.O. Box 10300, Palo Alto, California 94303, (415) 326-6040.

Free-lance Art Monthly, Suite 14, 310 Melvin Drive, Northbrook, Illinois 60062, (312) 272-4434. Marketing and business tips for commercial artists; reproduces some portfolio work.

Graphics Design U.S.A., 120 East 56th Street, New York, New York 10022, (212) 759-8813.

Print, 335 Lexington Avenue, New York, New York 10016, (212) 682-0830.

Today's Art and Graphics, 6 East 43rd Street, New York, New York 10017, (212) 949-0800. Mixture of business and visual information for both fine and commercial artists.

U & lc, 2 Dag Hammarskjold Plaza, New York, New York 10017, (212) 371-0699.

INDEX

ABOUT THE AUTHORS

TAD CRAWFORD, General Counsel for the Graphic Artists Guild, is the author of *Legal Guide for the Visual Artist* and *The Writer's Legal Guide*. In addition to teaching art law at the School of Visual Arts in New York City, he lectures nationwide on the legal and business issues of importance to visual artists.

ARIE KOPELMAN is a business and legal advisor for graphic designers and illustrators. He is also the General Counsel to the Society of Illustrators and serves as principal consultant to the Graphic Artists Guild in the compilation of their book *Pricing and Ethical Guidelines*.

Both authors have been instrumental in creating courses and seminars on the subject of business guidance for graphic designers and illustrators under the sponsorship of the Graphic Artists Guild. They are also the authors of the highly acclaimed book *Selling Your Photography: The Complete Marketing, Business and Legal Guide* (published by St. Martins Press).